International Political Economy Series

General Editor: **Timothy M. Shaw**, Professor and Director, Institute of International Relations, The University of the West Indies, Trinidad & Tobago

Titles include:

Pradeep Agrawal, Subir V. Gokarn, Veena Mishra, Kirit S. Parikh and Kunal Sen
POLICY REGIMES AND INDUSTRIAL COMPETITIVENESS
A Comparative Study of East Asia and India

Roderic Alley
THE UNITED NATIONS IN SOUTHEAST ASIA AND THE SOUTH PACIFIC

Dick Beason and Jason James
THE POLITICAL ECONOMY OF JAPANESE FINANCIAL MARKETS
Myths versus Reality

Mark Beeson
COMPETING CAPITALISMS
Australia, Japan and Economic Competition in Asia-Pacific

Deborah Bräutigam
CHINESE AID AND AFRICAN DEVELOPMENT
Exporting Green Revolution

Shaun Breslin
CHINA AND THE GLOBAL POLITICAL ECONOMY

Kenneth D. Bush
THE INTRA-GROUP DIMENSIONS OF ETHNIC CONFLICT IN SRI LANKA
Learning to Read between the Lines

Kevin G. Cai
THE POLITICAL ECONOMY OF EAST ASIA
Regional and National Dimensions
THE POLITICS OF ECONOMIC REGIONALISM
Explaining Regional Economic Integration in East Asia

Steve Chan, Cal Clark and Danny Lam (*editors*)
BEYOND THE DEVELOPMENTAL STATE
East Asia's Political Economies Reconsidered

Gregory T. Chin
CHINA'S AUTOMOTIVE MODERNIZATION
The Party-State and Multinational Corporations

Yin-wah Chu (*editor*)
CHINESE CAPITALISMS
Historical Emergence and Political Implications

Abdul Rahman Embong
STATE-LED MODERNIZATION AND THE NEW MIDDLE CLASS IN MALAYSIA

Dong-Sook Shin Gills
RURAL WOMEN AND TRIPLE EXPLOITATION IN KOREAN DEVELOPMENT

Jeffrey Henderson (*editor*)
INDUSTRIAL TRANSFORMATION IN EASTERN EUROPE IN
THE LIGHT OF THE EAST ASIAN EXPERIENCE

Takashi Inoguchi
GLOBAL CHANGE
A Japanese Perspective

Dominic Kelly
JAPAN AND THE RECONSTRUCTION OF EAST ASIA

L. H. M. Ling
POSTCOLONIAL INTERNATIONAL RELATIONS
Conquest and Desire between Asia and the West

Pierre P. Lizée
PEACE, POWER AND RESISTANCE IN CAMBODIA
Global Governance and the Failure of International Conflict Resolution

S. Javed Maswood
JAPAN IN CRISIS

Ananya Mukherjee Reed
PERSPECTIVES ON THE INDIAN CORPORATE ECONOMY
Exploring the Paradox of Profits
CORPORATE CAPITALISM IN CONTEMPORARY SOUTH ASIA (editor)
Conventional Wisdoms and South Asian Realities

Cecilia Ng
POSITIONING WOMEN IN MALAYSIA
Class and Gender in an Industrializing State

Fahimul Quadir and Jayant Lele (editors)
DEMOCRACY AND CIVIL SOCIETY IN ASIA: VOLUME 1
Globalization, Democracy and Civil Society in Asia
DEMOCRACY AND CIVIL SOCIETY IN ASIA: VOLUME 2
Democratic Transitions and Social Movements in Asia

Ian Scott (editor)
INSTITUTIONAL CHANGE AND THE POLITICAL TRANSITION IN HONG KONG

Mark Turner (editor)
CENTRAL–LOCAL RELATIONS IN ASIA–PACIFIC
Convergence or Divergence?

Ritu Vij
JAPANESE MODERNITY AND WELFARE
State, Civil Society and Self in Contemporary Japan

Fei-Ling Wang
INSTITUTIONS AND INSTITUTIONAL CHANGE IN CHINA
Premodernity and Modernization

Fulong Wu and Chris Webster (editors)
MARGINALIZATION IN URBAN CHINA
Comparative Perspectives

Xiaoke Zhang
THE POLITICAL ECONOMY OF CAPITAL MARKET REFORMS IN SOUTHEAST ASIA

International Political Economy Series
Series Standing Order ISBN 978-0-333-71708-0 hardcover
Series Standing Order ISBN 978-0-333-71110-1 paperback
(*outside North America only*)

You can receive future titles in this series as they are published by placing a standing order. Please contact your bookseller or, in case of difficulty, write to us at the address below with your name and address, the title of the series and one of the ISBNs quoted above.

Customer Services Department, Macmillan Distribution Ltd, Houndmills, Basingstoke, Hampshire RG21 6XS, England

The Political Economy of Capital Market Reforms in Southeast Asia

Xiaoke Zhang

Associate Professor in Political Economy and Asian Studies, University of Nottingham, UK

First published 2011 by
PALGRAVE MACMILLAN

Palgrave Macmillan in the UK is an imprint of Macmillan Publishers Limited, registered in England, company number 785998, of Houndmills, Basingstoke, Hampshire RG21 6XS.

Palgrave Macmillan in the US is a division of St Martin's Press LLC, 175 Fifth Avenue, New York, NY 10010.

Palgrave Macmillan is the global academic imprint of the above companies and has companies and representatives throughout the world.

Palgrave® and Macmillan® are registered trademarks in the United States, the United Kingdom, Europe and other countries.

ISBN 978–0–230–25282–0

This book is printed on paper suitable for recycling and made from fully managed and sustained forest sources. Logging, pulping and manufacturing processes are expected to conform to the environmental regulations of the country of origin.

A catalogue record for this book is available from the British Library.

Library of Congress Cataloging-in-Publication Data
Zhang, Xiaoke.
  The political economy of capital market reforms in South East
  Asia / Xiaoke Zhang.
    p.   cm.
  Includes bibliographical references and index.
  ISBN 978–0–230–25282–0
  1. Capital market—Government policy—Asia, Southeastern.   2. Asia, Southeastern—Economic conditions.   3. Asia, Southeastern—Economic policy.   I. Title.
  HG5740.8.A3Z43 2011
  332′.0415095—dc23   2011021395

10   9   8   7   6   5   4   3   2   1
20   19   18   17   16   15   14   13   12   11

Printed and bound in the United States of America

For Meng-Jie and his generation

Contents

List of Tables

Acknowledgements

In the research and preparation of this book, I accumulated debts to various individuals and institutions. I benefited from the assistance of the Research Department of the *New Straits Times*, the Central Library of the University of Malaya, the Institute of Southeast Asian Studies and the Thailand Information Centre of Chulalongkorn University. I extend my appreciation to the many interviewees in Malaysia, Singapore and Thailand who consented to take the time to discuss their views with me and to generously share their knowledge. I thank the following people for helping me to improve the central argument of this book in one way or another: Andrew Baker, Phil Cerny, Phil Cowley, Edmund Terence Gomez, Eric Helleiner, Duncan McCargo, Pasuk Phongpaichit, Thitinan Pongsudhirak, Geoffrey Underhill and Andrew Walter. Thanks are also due to the anonymous reviewer who provided extensive and constructive comments on the book. While carrying out field research for this study, I received financial support from the British Academy and the Asia Research Fund of the University of Nottingham. Finally, Timothy Shaw, the series editor, and Renée Takken and Alexandra Webster at Palgrave Macmillan provided a generous mixture of advice and guidance at crucial points. Needless to say, the responsibility for all errors and omissions remains solely with me.

Xiaoke Zhang

List of Acronyms and Abbreviations

ADB	Asian Development Bank
ADBI	Asian Development Bank Institute
AF	*Asian Finance*
AMF	*Asian Money and Finance*
AMSET	Association of Members of the Stock Exchange of Thailand
BBMR	*Bangkok Bank Monthly Review*
BOT	Bank of Thailand
BN	Barisan Nasional (National Front)
BNM	Bank Negara Malaysia
BP	*Bangkok Post*
BPER	*Bangkok Post Economic Review*
BT	*Business Times*
CCM	Companies Commission of Malaysia
CDRAC	Corporate Debt Restructuring Advisory Committee
CEC	Central Executive Committee
CIC	Capital Issues Committee
CMMP	Capital Market Master Plan
CPF	Central Provident Fund
EAAU	East Asia Analytical Unit
EIUCR	*Economist Intelligence Unit Country Report*
ENP	Effective number of parties
EPF	Employees Provident Fund
EPU	Economic Planning Unit
FEER	*Far Eastern Economic Review*
FDI	Foreign direct investment
FIC	Foreign Investments Committee
FT	*Financial Times*
GDP	Gross domestic product
GLCs	Government-linked companies
GRC	Group Representation Constituencies
HLFC	High Level Finance Committee
IMF	International Monetary Fund
ID	*Investors Digest*
KLSE	Kuala Lumpur Stock Exchange
MAS	Monetary Authority of Singapore

MB	*Malaysian Business*
MCA	Malaysian Chinese Association
MIC	Malaysian Indian Congress
MSBA	Malaysian Stock Brokers Association
MSC	Malaysian Securities Commission
NEP	New Economic Policy
NESDB	National Economic and Social Development Board
NP	Number of parties
NPL	Non-performing loans
NST	*New Straits Times*
OECD	Organisation for Economic Co-operation and Development
PAP	People's Action Party
PAS	Parti Islam Se Malaysia (Islamic Party)
PPP	People Power Party
PSDC	Public Sector Divestment Committee
ROC	Registrar of Companies
SCI	Singapore Confederation of Industries
SEC	Securities and Exchange Commission
SES	Stock Exchange of Singapore
SET	Stock Exchange of Thailand
SGX	Singapore Exchange
SOEs	State-owned enterprises
ST	*Straits Times*
TFSA	Thai Finance and Securities Association
TRT	Thai Rak Thai (Thais Love Thais)
UMNO	United Malays National Organisation
WSJ	*Wall Street Journal*

1
Politics and Capital Market Reforms

Examining the impact of political institutions on economic policy and development has been all the rage for the past decades. It has become a virtual truism among both political scientists and economists that political institutions or rules that shape the behaviour of political actors and the exercise of policy authority weigh heavily on the design and implementation of economic policy. Extensive research on the policy impact of institutions has given rise to novel theoretical approaches and generated important empirical insights. The historical-institutionalist, cultural-organisational and rational-choice models have now permeated the explanations of the consequences of various political institutions.[1] Equally importantly, empirical analyses have highlighted the role of domestic institutional variations in shaping the incentives of policy-makers to promote economic policies conducive to social welfare, and their ability to implement these policies in a consistent, coherent and efficient manner.[2]

While political institutions impinge strongly upon the making of economic policies in all countries, their impact on the policy processes of developing countries are expected to be particularly salient. Developing countries have typically displayed greater varieties than advanced industrial societies in the basic institutional structures of national politics (Geddes 2003; Przeworski et al. 2000). These structures have often experienced frequent and dramatic changes, as evidenced in the ongoing process of democratic transitions, constitutional changes and electoral reforms in the past decades. Concomitant with these variations and changes in political institutions have been significant differences in the national orientation and pattern of economic policy-making across developing countries.[3]

In developing countries, causal relations between political institutions and economic policies have varied along more dimensions than can be captured easily in a book. While situated firmly within the influential body of scholarship on the policy consequences of institutions, this book has a modest but specific analytical objective. For reasons that will become clear below, it seeks to explore the impact of political parties on financial policy changes in relation to the development of capital markets in emerging market countries. The fundamental question that motivates this book concerns what differences political parties make in terms of policy choices and market outcomes. The book focuses on illustrating the ways in which party system structures interact with internal party organisation to shape the incentives of politicians to provide capital market reforms and their capabilities to both enact reform policies and commit to maintaining them. The central claim is that valuable inferences can be made about market reform approaches and outcomes based on the internal and external organisational characteristics of political parties. And, in so doing, this book extends the theoretical debate about the effects of political institutions and seeks to make three contributions.

First, this book advances its central propositions on the basis of three country cases from Southeast Asia—Malaysia, Singapore and Thailand. Research on the policy impact of political institutions in general and political parties in particular has been conducted overwhelmingly within the context of advanced industrial societies. To the extent that attention has been paid to developing and emerging market countries, it has been largely concentrated on East Central Europe and Latin America.[4] Systematic studies on the role of various political structures and rules in the evolution of economic policy and market institutions in Southeast Asia are rare; scholarly efforts to examine the effects of political parties on financial policy processes are even rarer. Until recently, Southeast Asian political studies have not been situated squarely within major theoretical debates on national institutional variations and their consequences, despite a wealth of differences in political structures and outcomes in the region. As a result, scholars (Kuhonta et al. 2008) have lamented that the study of Southeast Asian politics has fallen mostly into oblivion in the mainstream of political science. Emerging comparative analyses (Hicken 2002; Kuhonta 2004; MacIntyre 2003) of the institutional sources of socio-economic policy patterns in Southeast Asia have begun to fill this considerable void. This builds on these analyses and illustrates the causal linkage between political parties and capital market reforms in Malaysia, Singapore and Thailand.

Second, this book develops a theoretical model that captures the integrated impact of party systems and party organisation. In the recent political economy literature, two broad strands of theorising are salient for understanding the connection between political parties and policy patterns. The first strand examines inter-party configurations (Haggard and Kaufman 1995; Hallerberg and Basinger 1998; Horowitz and Browne 2008; MacIntyre 2003) while the second strand deals with intra-party organisation (Eaton 2002; Garman et al. 2001; Grossman and Helpman 2006; Hankla 2006; McGillivray 2004). While both strands have provided remarkable insights into the importance of political parties in shaping policy processes, little systematic effort has been made to assess the effects of inter-party structures in close and explicit interaction with those of intra-party attributes.[5] While neither of these two strands of studies has claimed that inter-party or intra-party variables alone can explain policy outcomes fully, they have failed to theorise the interaction between the external and internal dimensions of political parties. Such failure has not only given rise to analytical ambiguities, as will be shown below, but also precluded a holistic understanding of the policy impact of parties.

The theoretical account to be provided in this book seeks to remedy the problem, arguing that a tight focus on both inter-party and intra-party variables yields a considerable degree of explanatory purchase in illustrating the incentives structures that shape the propensity of politicians to provide capital market reforms and enact reform programmes. The basic premise underpinning the argument is that the external and internal organisational structures of political parties, despite their analytical distinctions, are never found apart empirically and act symbiotically in the policy-making process. They constitute an institutional ensemble within which policy interests are defined, political resources structured and market outcomes determined. Specifically, this book considers party system concentration and party organisational strength in an integrated theoretical framework and underscores the varied ways in which these two variables combine to produce different policy patterns both across countries and over time.

Third, this book deliberately refrains from addressing the policy effects of political institutions at the macro level and adopts an approach that explicitly emphasises political parties as meso-institutions by which the interests and actions of political actors are aggregated into policy outcomes. Extant analyses often employ broad dimensions along which policy processes in different countries are compared: territorial structures (federal versus unitary), government systems (presidential versus parliamentary) and political regimes (democratic versus authoritarian). While shedding important light on systemic causal relationships, these dimensions are sometimes too homogenising to capture cross-country variations in policy patterns. Some studies (Inman and Rubinfeld 1997; Weingast 1995) show federalism to facilitate market-promoting governance whereas others (Gerring et al. 2005; Sylla 1999) demonstrate the opposite. Empirical analyses of the effects of different government systems on policy efficiency are equally inconclusive.[6] Nowhere have the limitations of the macro-analytical approach been illustrated more clearly than in the effects of political regimes on economic growth: no consistent causal patterns have emerged from extensive, decades-long empirical studies (see de Haan and Siermann 1995; Helliwell 1994; Mulligan et al. 2004; Przeworski and Limongi 1993).[7]

That multiple and even opposing lines of arguments have been advanced on both sides reveals the perils of focusing exclusively on the macro-level attributes of political institutions. There are theoretical and methodological reasons for believing that it would be difficult to extrapolate the contents and patterns of public policies from these attributes. Theory-building on the impact of political institutions, especially as it relates to substantive outcomes like capital market reforms, may be best advanced by focusing on less aggregate factors such as political parties. Two federal or parliamentary systems, while formally similar, can differ in the external and internal organisation of parties and so generate different policy outcomes. By the same token, some autocracies may be able to enact market reforms more successfully than many democracies, mainly because the former have stronger parties. This book intends to bring the policy effects of political parties to the foreground by examining their independent causal weight in isolation of macro-political institutions. It thus gains the possibility of developing a single analytical approach that can be applied across different territorial structures, government systems and political regimes.

Capital market reforms

As an important element of modern financial systems, capital markets refer to stock exchanges and bond markets where securities, which are negotiable and fungible instruments representing financial value, are traded. The securities concerned are divided into equity securities, such as shares in companies, and debt securities, which mainly include bonds and debentures. Capital markets both enable individuals and firms to lend their savings to those who need them and allow companies and governments to raise long-term funds. Another vital and, arguably more important component of financial systems, particularly in developing countries, are commercial banks that function as an acceptor of deposits and a grantor of largely short-term credit.[8] While enjoying comparative advantages in providing different financial services, capital markets and banks co-exist and constitute the most crucial sources of external financing for individuals, firms and governments. They provide a means of not only transferring and distributing risks across the economy but also mobilising savings from numerous sources and channelling them to various uses and investors.[9]

For much of the post-war period, financial systems in developing countries were predominantly bank-based. Banks functioned as the central institutions not only for allocating financial resources but also for managing macro-economic and development policies. In those developing countries where capital markets existed, they tended to be small in size and low in trading activity. Capital markets, which played a marginal role in financial intermediation and resource allocation, remained on the periphery of national financial systems. The economic literature (Fry 1995; Wellons et al. 1986) has identified several policy and institutional impediments to capital market growth in developing countries. These converge on high entry barriers in the securities industry and the lack of competition, restricted foreign access to domestic equity markets, government controls over the operations of securities companies, and weak regulatory frameworks and inadequate supervisory mechanisms.

Many developing country governments moved towards reducing these impediments in the 1980s and 1990s when they were under growing pressures to reform capital markets as part of broader financial liberalisation programmes. These pressures derived directly from the ongoing process of financial globalisation that prompted developing countries to promote capital market growth as an important strategy for improving the efficiency of domestic financial sectors and for attracting foreign capital. Equally significantly, key international financial institutions, noticeably the International Monetary Fund (IMF) and the World Bank, insistently urged developing countries to embrace the market-oriented, neo-liberal norms and practices that played a crucial role in promoting capital market reforms. Particularly in the aftermath of financial crises, such as those that affected Latin America, East Asia and East Central Europe in the 1990s and early 2000s, there were political pressures from these institutions for the removal of entry barriers in the securities industry, the opening up of stock markets to foreign investors and the improvement of securities market governance.

Instituting capital market reforms is a complex process that encompasses a variety of different yet interlinked measures. For the sake of analytical clarity, these measures can be broadly categorised into two seemingly contradictory sets: deregulatory and regulatory. Deregulatory measures have centred on the decision of governments to open up domestic equity markets to foreign investors and allow them to purchase shares. Restrictions on foreign investments have been removed in conjunction with government efforts to permit stock-broking companies to set their commission rates in line with market conditions and to remove barriers to entry in the securities industry by encouraging new entrants, both domestic and foreign, to undertake securities businesses. These deregulatory reforms have been designed to create competition by offering advantages to competitors and imposing disadvantages on incumbent firms in capital markets where government controls have long fostered oligopolistic market structures. They have also aimed to reduce the cost of capital and increase the pool of financial resources available to local industrial firms, broaden the investor base and make the domestic financial sector more efficient.

The liberalisation of capital markets has been accompanied by the privatisation of state-owned enterprises (SOEs). In many developing and emerging market countries, privatisation programmes have been enacted to stimulate the development of equity markets as well as to increase government revenues and promote economic efficiency. The programmes help expand the size of stock markets and enliven trading activity, as state assets are sold through share offerings and large privatised firms get listed. They have also increased opportunities for investors to diversify their portfolios and reduced investment risks and enhanced the depth of equity markets (Bortolotti et al. 2007; Megginson and Netter 2001).[10] In those countries where privatisation has been implemented in a consistent manner, governments have signalled a commitment to market-oriented policies and private property rights. This has in turn reduced political uncertainties, rendered equity investments attractive and fostered stock market growth (Jones et al. 1999; Perotti and van Oijen 2001).

Capital market reforms do not merely involve deregulatory measures. As noted earlier, poorly developed capital markets in many developing countries have been due not only to policy and institutional restrictions but also to weak market governance. Both ex-ante and ex-post analyses (see Bekaert et al. 2003; Fuchs-Schündeln and Funke 2004; Levine and Zervos 1998; Martell and Stulz 2003) of financial and stock market liberalisation have reached the conclusion that liberalisation is very unlikely to achieve its desired goals and can have devastating costs in the absence of effective regulation. A growing body of work on privatisation (Guriev and Megginson 2007; Megginson 2005; Roland 2008) has also underlined how state asset divestment has generated suboptimal and even disastrous outcomes under the conditions of weak legal rules. Successful market reforms have thus been predicated upon the ability of governments to strengthen the overall framework regulating accounting standards, information disclosure and investment protection, all of which have been crucial to the functioning of an open and liberalised capital market. Similarly, privatisation can only contribute towards capital market growth if it is coupled with sustained efforts to establish and improve legal and institutional rules designed to prevent oligopolistic or monopolistic practices in privatised sectors, minimise regressive redistribution effects and check rent-seeking on the part of new private owners.

The focus on capital market reforms as the dependent variable in this book is useful and interesting for several reasons. In the first place, the past two decades have witnessed increasingly intensified efforts at reforming capital markets across developing countries. Recurrent financial crises and resultant socio-economic instabilities notwithstanding, many developing country governments have continued with capital market reforms and, in fact, expanded their reform programmes (de la Torre et al. 2007; Litan et al. 2003). Continued reforms have transformed national financial architectures, reshaped the role of capital markets in the process of financial development and altered the ways in which governments orchestrate resource allocation. Some of the most fiercely fought political battles in developing countries have been about the welfare and distributional impact of capital market reforms. Despite the significant economic and political implications of capital market reforms, the large and growing literature on the policy effects of political parties has been dedicated to the study of fiscal adjustments, trade liberalisation and exchange rate policies.[11] This book uses capital market reforms to interrogate the literature and, more importantly, to explore the extent to which political parties influence financial policy processes and outcomes.

Furthermore, while capital market reforms do not meet the strict definition of public goods, they do produce the kinds of externalities that are often associated with public or collective goods. These positive externalities are twofold. First and directly, capital market reforms in general and stock market liberalisation in particular have generated a robust effect on economic growth by reducing the cost of capital and encouraging physical investment (Bekaert et al. 2003; Henry 2000; Henry and Lorentzen 2003; Patro 2005), increasing stock market liquidity and easing long-run investment in profitable projects (Levine 2001; Levine and Zervos 1996), and improving corporate governance and enhancing industrial efficiency (Bae et al. 2006; Gupta and Yuan 2009; Mitton 2006). These strong growth and efficiency effects have not been offset by macro-economic instabilities stemming from upward pressures on inflation; if anything inflation has stabilised and even fallen in many developing and emerging market countries that have enacted capital market reforms (Kim and Singal 2000).

Second and indirectly, market reforms are shown to have strongly spurred capital market growth (de la Torre et al. 2007; Fuchs-Schündeln and Funke 2004; Levine and Zervos 1998) and capital market growth has in turn contributed towards long-term economic development (Adjasi and Biekpe 2008; Beck and Levine 2004; Levine and Zervos 1996, 1998; Rousseau and Wachtel 2000). The argument here is not that market-oriented financial systems are likely to generate more positive growth effects. Indeed, financial market structures—bank-based or market-oriented—do not account for differences in economic performance: the robust growth of *both* banks and capital markets is conducive to financial development (Beck and Levine 2002; Demirgüç-Kunt and Maksimovic 2002; Levine 2002). Countries with higher levels of financial development have experienced more rapid growth (Arestis et al. 2001; Beck and Levine 2001; Blackburn et al. 2005; Carlin and Mayer 2003; Fisman and Love 2004) and lower poverty (Beck et al. 2007; Honohan 2004; Jalilian and Kirkpatrick 2005).[12] Given that most developing countries have traditionally had bank-based systems and poorly developed capital markets, the development of more balanced financial systems that promises to improve the collective welfare of society requires policy reforms that support the growth of capital markets.

It is clear that the positive association of capital market reforms and growth with key public policy objectives has been confirmed in extensive economic literatures. The focus on capital market reforms as public goods is thus interesting, given that one of the central analytical objectives of this book is to examine how political parties shape the incentives of politicians to provide financial policy changes that are public-regarding and conducive to social welfare. However, equating capital market reforms with collective goods would certainly raise an eyebrow. Some scholars and political commentators may assert that capital market reforms have functioned as a rhetorical mask for an ideological agenda propounded by the IMF, the World Bank and Western governments. Indeed, the increasing importance of the major elements of capital market reforms—stock market liberalisation and privatisation—coincided with the rise of the neo-liberal policy model endorsed in the Washington consensus in the 1980s and 1990s. This model has now been heavily criticised and often blamed for growing inequalities, social deprivations and even economic crises in many developing and emerging market countries.

This book contends that capital market reforms per se should not be held culpable for these socio-economic problems. To the extent that capital market reforms have generated mixed or even negative outcomes, this has been primarily attributable to the institutionally and politically flawed ways in which reforms have been designed and enacted. As amply demonstrated in important empirical studies (Haggard 2000a; Horowitz and Heo 2001; Lewis and Stein 1997; Zhang and Underhill 2003), well-intentioned market reforms may not be growth-enhancing if they are undertaken without adequate and effective regulatory rules to constrain malfeasant and fraudulent behaviours in the reform process. By the same token, reforms can be and have been captured by politicians as an important source of patronage and as a means of allocating rents to strategic constituents and have, as a result, generated serious policy failures and even market volatilities. Of course, there is no lack of examples in which developing countries' governments have been able to achieve public-regarding policy objectives through financial liberalisation. But an important question is: Under what circumstances are politicians more likely to have strong incentives to do so? The focus on capital market reforms helps answer the question.

The final and most important reason that capital market reforms are used as the dependent variable is that there are systematic differences both across the three country cases—Malaysia, Singapore and Thailand—and within Thailand over time. While they all started to reform capital markets in the 1980s and introduced similar reform measures over the subsequent two decades, the three countries displayed significant variations in terms of the extent to which these measures were oriented towards public policy goals, decisively initiated and resolutely implemented, as summarised in Table 1.1. Singapore was able to formulate constantly effective and coherent strategies across all the reform areas and follow them through in a consistent and sustained manner. Thailand fell at the other extreme, at least prior to the late 1990s. In general, Thai politicians were not strongly motivated to align

Table 1.1 Variations in market reform orientations and patterns

	Malaysia	Singapore	Thailand	
	Late 1980s—mid-2000s	Late 1980s—mid-2000s	Late 1980s—late 1990s	Early and mid-2000s
Orientation	Mixed incentives to pursue both public and private-regarding reform policies	Strong incentives to align market reforms with public policy interests	Weak incentives to seek public goods market reforms	Increased proclivity to provide public-regarding reform measures
Initiation	Relatively strong abilities to initiate reforms decisively	Strong abilities to introduce quick and effective reforms	Weak abilities to enact decisive and effective policies	Increased abilities to initiate more decisive market reforms
Implementation	Relatively weak abilities to sustain given reform policies over time	Strong abilities to carry market reforms through to the end	Weak abilities to commit to maintaining reform programmes	Relatively weak abilities to follow through with market reforms

capital market reforms with public-regarding objectives and often captured reforms as a vehicle for rent-seeking activities. Indecisive action typically plagued the reform process; even when external market and political pressures thrust market reforms onto the official agenda, many of these reforms were considerably diluted or abandoned in midstream. In the early 2000s, the Thai government began to adopt reform measures that focused more closely on the public interest, and became more perseverant with reform implementation. Malaysia was in the middle, with reform policies vacillating between politicians' efforts to promote market growth and economic development and their desire to orient market reforms towards particularistic interests. It was more decisive and resolute than Thailand, particularly with regard to stock market liberalisation and privatisation, but less so than Singapore in the overall process of market reforms.

Plausible causal variables

The central proposition to be advanced in this book posits that differences in the approaches and outcomes of capital market reforms in Malaysia, Singapore and Thailand are an important function of cross-country variations in party system structures and internal party strength. However, this proposition may be challenged, as the literature on the politics of economic policy-making and reforms in developing countries in general and in East Asia in particular contains important insights that point to several rival causal variables. These variables include policy resources, political regimes, technocratic capabilities and systemic forces. The many differences between Malaysia, Singapore and Thailand in terms of these variables may lead to an accusation that these three cases are not strictly comparable, weakening the explanatory power of the party-based approach. The alternative explanations thus need to be carefully assessed to test their causal logics against the empirical record of capital market reforms in the three countries before the central argument of this book can be advanced in a theoretically sound and empirically relevant manner.

Political economists have looked to financial resources at the disposal of government policy-makers for an explanation of cross-country differences in policy reform processes. While market reforms may raise aggregate output, they are very likely to produce a new distribution of political losers as well as winners. As currently theorised, governments would be able to diffuse political opposition and facilitate the organisation of support for market reforms if they devised appropriate schemes for compensating losers (Haggard and Webb 1994). However, the ability of governments to deploy compensatory schemes is a direct function of national wealth levels. Rich countries with abundant resources are better able to use such schemes to soften the resistance of those social groups adversely affected by market reforms and enact given reform policies consistently and effectively. Even if reforms deliver long-term growth in poor countries and thereby increase the resources of their governments, they would face short-term difficulties in making reforms politically feasible.

The arguments in these works would suggest that Singapore, which is much richer than Malaysia and Thailand in per capita terms, would have more policy resources to smooth the way for politically painful capital market reforms. While the Singapore government has indeed used its public housing programme to boost its popularity and maintain the loyalty of supporters, there is no evidence that policy-makers made any concessions to private market agents who stood to lose out from various reform measures, as will be shown below. Actually, it is in Malaysia and Thailand where the governments tried to persuade powerful social groups to fall in with their reform plans by providing them with various material incentives and inducements. However, the two countries differed not only from Singapore but also from each other in the ability of policy-makers to initiate reforms and maintain them over time. More crucially, there are no prior reasons to believe that financial resources can orient governments to public goods provision. Nor is there any guarantee that compensatory schemes will be used for policy purposes related to market development. In Thailand and, to a lesser extent, in Malaysia, policy resources were so frequently misused to pay off the politically powerful that they contributed towards rent-seeking in the process of capital market reforms.

Differences in political regimes between the three countries may also confound the comparative analysis of the politics of capital market reforms. The study of regime differences in Southeast Asia has been conceptually messy and even elusive. Malaysia and Singapore have been called 'semi-democracies' (Case 1996a), 'illiberal democracies' (Bell et al. 1995), 'semi-authoritarian polities' (Brooker 2000: 245–252), 'soft authoritarian regimes' (Means 1998) or 'one-party states' (Morley 1993; Rodan 1993, 1996a) while Thailand fell into the category of 'quasi-democracy' (Muscat 1994: 170–221) or 'semi-democracy' (Neher 1988) during 1980–1988 and has since been dubbed 'an unconsolidated democracy' (Case 2002) or a 'democratic authoritarian' regime (Thitinan 2003). These labels suggest political systems perched ambiguously between full democracy and closed authoritarianism or 'hybrid regimes' (Karl 1995). By dividing national political systems into many ambiguously defined subtypes of regimes, extant studies have generated growing scholarly confusion and fragmentation. These are also common weaknesses that characterise academic efforts to capture the diverse forms of hybrid regimes that have emerged in developing countries in the past decades (Collier and Levitsky 1997; Levitsky and Way 2002).

Recent attempts (Diamond 2002; Schedler 2002, 2006) to overcome these problems have emphasised the distinction between electoral authoritarianism and electoral democracy among hybrid regimes. They have prioritised 'the freedom, fairness, inclusiveness, and meaningfulness of elections' (Diamond 2002: 28) in an integrated approach to differentiating these two subtypes. This approach constitutes seven key conditions that are interactive upon each other and that must be fulfilled *simultaneously* if elections are to be called democratic. Referring to these conditions as the integral links of a 'chain of democratic choice', Schedler (2002: 41) contends that 'gross violation of any one condition invalidates the fulfilment of all the others' and 'elections become not less democratic but undemocratic'. Table 1.2 compares how the three countries have fared since the late 1980s, against the seven conditions. Elections in Malaysia and Singapore can hardly be considered democratic and the two countries may fall into the category of electoral authoritarianism. While elections in Thailand may be more democratic, their fairness and inclusiveness are invariably undermined by partial disenfranchisement, widespread electoral frauds and, most important of all, rampant vote-buying. As Stokes (2007) convincingly argues, vote-buying allows politicians to ignore the interests of voters and undermine their autonomy so seriously that it is undemocratic. If Thailand qualifies as an electoral democracy (Diamond 2002), this is a regime that has clearly demonstrated significant undemocratic attributes, at least in its electoral system.

Recent literature (Diamond 2002; Levitsky and Way 2002; Schedler 2002, 2004) has further divided electoral authoritarian regimes into the competitive authoritarian and the hegemonic, with the former having more contested and meaningful elections. Most analyses regard Malaysia as a competitive authoritarian regime, but some (Diamond 2002; Levitsky and Way 2002) call Singapore a hegemonic authoritarian polity and others (Hadenius and Teorell 2007; Howard and Roessler 2006) consider the country or at least its elections in the 1990s to be competitive authoritarian. Within electoral authoritarian regimes, elections in which the winning party or candidate receives less than 70 per

Table 1.2 Electoral democracy or electoral authoritarianism

Dimensions of elections	Malaysia	Singapore	Thailand
1 *Empowerment:* rights of citizens to wield and delegate power	Influence of unelected officials in policy processes	Crucial roles of unelected officials in state apparatuses	Military dominance of the senate prior to late 1990s
2 *Free supply:* freedom of citizens to join different parties and support candidates	Various ways to suppress opposition forces and harass opposition campaigners	Severe institutional obstacles to the development of a strong opposition	Penetration and polarisation of the opposition by the military in 1980s
3 *Free demand:* free formation of voter preferences and unrestricted access to alternative sources of information	Sundry controls over political and civil liberties; state-controlled media and subtle ways to suppress independent media outlets	Formal and informal ways to restrict political and civil liberties; media subject to state controls and suppression	No serious repression in 1990s but increased infringements on civil liberties and media repression under Thaksin
4 *Inclusion:* universal suffrage	Manipulation of the electoral rolls	No formal and informal disenfranchisement	Manipulation of residence-based electoral rolls
5 *Insulation:* freedom of citizens to express their electoral preferences	'Development grants' targeting rural voters; various ways to monitor and harass voters	No vote-buying; subtle mechanisms of monitoring and even intimidating voters	Rampant and institutionalised vote-buying; no clear evidence of voter intimidation
6 *Integrity:* honest counting of votes	Regular phantom and transfer voting	No ballot rigging or false vote counting	Multiple voting, ballot box stuffing and false counting
7 *Irreversibility:* binding and decisive results	Decisive and irreversible	Decisive and irreversible	Decisive and irreversible

Sources: Anusorn (1998), Case (2002, 2006, 2007), Gomez (1998), Lim (2002), Ooi (1998), Orathai (2002) and Yeo (2002).

cent of the popular vote qualify as competitive.[13] Using this criterion, Table 1.3 shows that with the exception of the 2001 election, all the other elections held in Singapore between 1984 and 2006 were competitive. Actually, many country specialists have concurred with the argument that elections in Singapore have been more than just democratic façades and have become genuinely contested since the early 1980s when the opposition made a forceful comeback.[14]

It is also interesting to note that the Thai general election that swept Thaksin Shinawatra's Thai Rak Thai (TRT, or Thais Love Thais) Party into office in 2001 and the one that returned the TRT to power in 2005 were much less competitive than all previous elections in Thailand since the early 1980s, as illustrated in Table 1.3. In these two landmark elections,

Table 1.3 Competitiveness of legislative elections

	Years of parliamentary elections	Per cent of popular vote won by the winning party
Malaysia	1982	60.5*
	1986	57.3
	1990	53.4
	1995	65.2
	1999	56.6
	2004	64.0
Singapore	1984	64.8
	1988	63.2
	1991	61.0
	1997	65.0
	2001	75.3
	2006	66.6
Thailand	1983	26.8§
	1986	22.5
	1988	19.3
	September 1992	21.0
	1995	22.8
	1996	29.1
	2001	40.7
	2005	60.7

Sources: Albritton (2006), *EIUCR*-Malaysia (various issues), *EIUCR*-Singapore (various issues), Nelson (2001), Rieger (2001) and Tan (2001).

* The winning party refers to the ruling multi-ethnic coalition (National Front) dominated by the United Malay National Organisation.

§ Figures for the elections held between 1983 and 1996 pertain to the shares of the popular vote won by the largest party in the coalition government, while those for the 2001 and 2005 elections refer to the shares of party-list votes secured by the Thai Rak Thai Party.

the TRT secured such an unprecedentedly large share of the popular vote and parliamentary seats, primarily as a result of the constitutional reforms of the late 1990s, that the party system and, indeed, the whole political structure became increasingly centralised under the Thaksin regime.[15] While the regime had strong mandates and was responsive to the interests of the electorate, it limited the political space for social organisations, infringed upon civil liberties, repressed critical media outlets, and undermined the power of democratic institutions, particularly the parliament and such watchdog agencies as the Elections Commission and the Constitutional Court (Case 2007; Kasian 2006: 27–31; Surin 2008). Authoritarian tendencies crept back into the Thai political scene so strongly that some scholars (Pasuk 2004) began to liken the Thaksin regime to the Malaysian and Singapore polities, and one prominent analyst (Thitinan 2008a) even called it a 'competitive authoritarian' system.

Debates over the effects of regime types on economic policies need not be rehearsed in detail here except to highlight key assumptions in two opposing clusters of literature. Earlier literature on market-oriented economic reforms emphasise political pressures from societal groups hurt by reforms and policy influences from particularistic interests as major stumbling blocks to successful reform efforts.[16] They posit political autonomy to account for the ability of state actors to fend off social demands and restrain the play of private interests in the economic policy process. Authoritarian regimes, which can repress societal and political discontents, are better able to provide state autonomy and thereby ensure the success of reforms. Challenging this pro-authoritarian proposition, more recent studies (Lake and Baum 2001; Maravall 1997; Rodrik 2000) have contended that political participation not only limits the influence of special interest groups on market reforms but also encourages social groups to be co-operative in the initiation and enactment of reform policies. Equally importantly, power dispersion inherent in democratic polities helps inhibit opportunistic and private-regarding behaviour on the part of politicians, reduce extreme results in policy processes and enhance the stability and credibility of reforms.

The above analysis of political regimes in Malaysia, Singapore and Thailand, while drawn in broad strokes, clearly indicates that the boundaries between their regime types tend to be blurry and disputable. While it may be safe to argue that Thailand has been more democratic or less authoritarian than Malaysia and Singapore for much of the past two decades, any attempt to categorise the three countries into the unambiguously defined types or subtypes of political regimes would require controversial judgements. This raises a serious question about whether the two opposing approaches to exploring the relationship between regime types and economic policies can be applied unequivocally to the three cases without stretching the concepts of democracy and authoritarianism.[17] Even if the problem of conceptual stretching can be avoided, the impact of the alternative variables suggested in the two approaches is indeterminate. One the one hand, both Malaysia and Singapore have been semi-democratic, semi-authoritarian or electoral authoritarian, but they have displayed important differences in the orientation, approaches and outcomes of capital market reforms. On the other hand, capital market reforms failed to generate public-regarding, consistent and efficient policy outcomes in more democratic Thailand as in more authoritarian Malaysia.

Cross-country variations in the patterns of capital market reforms might have derived from differences in the policy-making capacity and regulatory power of financial officials in Malaysia, Singapore and Thailand. With regard to the impact of policy and regulatory capacity, two different issues need to be distinguished. The first issue is that market reforms may not achieve their desired goals and may even result in policy failures if financial officials do not have adequate legal and administrative capacity to formulate coherent reform policies and are not invested with strong regulatory power to check private ineptitude or fraud. Technocratic competences and policy authority have varied from the higher levels of Singapore to the lower levels of Malaysia and Thailand; these differences have often been emphasised as a major determinant of the different abilities of economic officials to manage market reforms and govern the financial sector in the three countries (Hamilton-Hart 2002; Kim 2002). While policy capacity and regulatory power are important, their impact and differences should not be overemphasised. During the 1980s and 1990s, the regulatory capacity and authority of financial officials in Malaysia and Thailand as well as in Singapore were progressively and significantly strengthened in the aftermath of major financial crises. As a result, the capacity and authority of financial officials to make regulatory rules became largely comparative across the three countries in the 1990s (La Porta et al. 2006: 15).

The second and more important issue is that differences in capital market reforms have stemmed from variations in the actual abilities of financial officials to strengthen their policy capacity and enforce existing regulatory rules in the reform process. This has in turn depended upon the willingness of politicians to provide financial technocrats with increased policy capacity and enforcement powers and, more importantly, to allow them to make full use of their capacity and powers. Studies that have given independent causal weight to the policy capacity and authority of technocrats have paid little attention to the fact that their role is politically endogenous. While technocrats may possess policy expertise and informational capacity, they lack power. To the extent that they are powerful in reform processes, they are rendered so by their political patrons, who can structure the distribution of political resources and authority among different policy-makers and state agencies in line with their policy preferences. As will be illustrated below, political incentives mediated through domestic institutions determine whether politicians choose to give full play to the policy capacity of technocrats and empower their agencies in Malaysia, Singapore and Thailand.

Systemic forces are a final rival causal variable of cross-country differences in capital market reforms. As mentioned in the preceding section, political pressures from international financial institutions have provided general stimuli to market-oriented reforms across developing countries. Two specific variables, which predicate capital market reforms on different national responses to global market integration, are directly relevant to the three cases under consideration here. First, economic openness has revealed the various inefficiencies of bank-based systems and prompted policy-makers to promote securities markets as an important way to improve economic efficiencies (Hanson et al. 2003; Häusler et al. 2003). Second, increased trade and capital flows have also undercut resistance from those political actors who stand to lose out from market-oriented changes and enervated the regulatory legacies that have hampered the growth of capital markets (Braun and Raddatz 2008; Rajan and Zingales 2003). The logic of market-driven explanations is that countries that are more integrated with the global economy are likely to have stronger incentives to reform capital markets and promote their growth.

Exposures to external market pressures are undeniably important and have certainly been at play in the process of capital market reforms in Malaysia, Singapore and Thailand. They have accounted for the simultaneity of their efforts to launch important reform initiatives in the 1980s and for the similarity of major reform measures in the three countries. Despite the fact that all the three countries are small and open economies, however, they differ in the extent to which they are integrated with the global political economy. As shown in the widely quoted annual reports of *Economic Freedom of the World* (Gwartney and

Lawson, various issues), the annual average score for economic openness was 9.2 (out of 10, the highest score) in Singapore over the period 1985–2006, as compared to 7.7 in Malaysia and 7.3 in Thailand in the same period. The systemic-centred explanation would thus posit that Singapore, which has been more economically open than Malaysia and Thailand, has been under greater pressure to reform capital markets. The proposition is certainly plausible, but there remain theoretical and empirical problems. Theoretically, the systemic-centred argument suffers from an endogeneity problem: greater openness in Singapore may have reflected its more consistent and successful efforts to liberalise the financial sector in general and capital markets in particular. Likewise, piecemeal and halting reform processes in Thailand and, to a lesser extent, in Malaysia contributed towards the relatively low levels of economic openness. Furthermore, it would be hard to argue a priori that external market forces would dictate the public-regarding orientation of capital market reforms, although they may play a crucial role in initiating such reforms. As a matter of fact, rapid and radical financial market reforms, which are often launched under intensive systemic pressures, are more likely to create opportunities for patronage and rent-seeking activities and hasten the policy and political pathologies that plague the real economy (Haggard 2000a: 32–38; Lee and Haggard 1995; Lewis and Stein 1997; Zhang and Underhill 2003).

Empirically, there are three key issues. First, while Singapore allowed foreign banks to operate offshore businesses in its Asian dollar market in the late 1960s, it separated the offshore market strictly from the domestic financial sector and maintained regulatory barriers that kept the securities industry closed to new entrants and restricted foreign presence in the capital market (Giap and Kang 1999; Lall and Liu 1997; Tan 2005). Equally importantly, the government had an extensive ownership of the economy, despite the country's economic openness. As regards key reform measures—entry deregulation, brokerage liberalisation and privatisation, Singapore did not have much head start over Malaysia and Thailand in the 1980s when capital market reforms were initiated in the three countries. It would thus be implausible to attribute Singapore's more successful reform efforts to its earlier process of financial opening. Second, while Singapore might have been more economically open, Malaysia and Thailand were similarly exposed to external market pressures. This poses a puzzle of why Malaysian policy-makers made more progress in capital market reforms than their Thai counterparts. Third, systemic factors cannot account for temporal variations in the pattern of market reforms within Thailand. The Thai government became more decisive in initiating important reform measures and more committed to maintaining these measures in the early 2000s. However, there was little discernible increase in the overall level of economic openness in Thailand during this period as compared to the mid- and late 1990s.

The central argument

The preceding discussion of the rival causal variables—policy resources, political regimes, technocratic capacities and systemic factors—clearly shows that these variables have limited application to the comparative analysis of cross-country variations in capital market reforms between Malaysia, Singapore and Thailand. While limited in different ways, they have all paid inadequate attention to the importance of domestic institutional variations in shaping financial policy processes. As a result, they do not fundamentally differentiate the three country cases in terms of different reform approaches and outcomes. The foregoing critical review, in illustrating the limitations of extant explanations, suggests an alternative analytical framework for understanding the divergent trajectories of capital market reforms. This book locates the political sources of financial policy choices and market changes at the complex interplay of two key political party variables—party system structures and internal party organisation.

In this book, politicians and their roles in the design of financial and regulatory policies occupy the proscenium of the political analysis of capital market reforms. While they intervene in the policy process with the ultimate view to holding onto office, politicians differ in their incentives to deliver public-regarding reform policies and in their abilities to initiate market reforms decisively and commit to maintaining them resolutely. The central theoretical proposition to be advanced here emphasises political parties as the primary institutional context within which policy incentives are defined and reform capabilities structured. It posits that the integration of party system concentration and organisational strength offers a powerful perspective on the propensity of politicians to formulate nationally oriented reform policies, as opposed to particularistic ones, in both democratic and electoral authoritarian polities. Equally importantly, party system configurations interact with intra-party organisational structures to shape the ways in which politicians initiate and implement capital market reforms in line with their policy incentives.

More specifically, political party structures create incentives for politicians to be geared towards one reform orientation over the other via their effect on their overriding desire to maintain power. This holds true across electoral democratic and authoritarian regimes in which government politicians are under similar electoral pressures to respond to voter interests and build support bases. Where concentrated party systems exist alongside centrally and cohesively organised parties, elections are more likely to motivate politicians to associate their political careers with the advancement of public welfare. In such circumstances, they are expected to have strong incentives to enact public-regarding reform policies that serve the interests of the general population. By contrast, where fragmented party systems are married to poorly organised parties, elections would press politicians to generate localised and particularised support as a strategically important way to enhance their political careers. They are thus more inclined to oppose capital market reforms that threaten to harm the welfare of their narrow constituencies or capture the reform process as a vehicle for seeking rents for particular private firms, discrete economic actors or special interest groups.

In the cross-national context of electoral authoritarian countries, politicians operating through concentrated party systems and centrally and coherently organised parties are more strongly motivated to be accountable to broader constituencies and have greater incentives to pursue party-focused strategies and policies. As a result, they are more concerned about promoting such public-regarding policies as capital market reforms for which they can claim partisan credit and that can deliver broad benefits to a large swathe of the voting public. More importantly, across the developing world, politicians in electoral authoritarian regimes are more likely than their counterparts in electoral democracies to promote public goods provision if the former operate in concentrated party systems and strongly organised parties. In other words, when elections generate comparable impact on the ability of voters to hold politicians to account and the strategic behaviour of candidates in electoral processes regardless of regime type, countries with more concentrated party systems and more cohesively organised parties should be better positioned to supply growth-enhancing financial policies and orient capital market reforms towards public policy purposes.

Not only do political party structures shape the orientation of capital market reforms, they also bear crucially upon the national pattern of such reforms. Financial and regulatory changes and, indeed, any economic policy reforms are more likely to be successful if they are enacted decisively, often in response to external pressures or policy failures. How decisive politicians are in the initiation of policy reforms is primarily contingent upon the number of veto players or institutional or partisan actors whose consent is required for policy changes. With regard to the impact of veto players on capital market reforms, the most important factor is the number of parties whose agreement is needed for existing market regulations to be altered and for new financial bills to become laws. Party system concentration determines the distribution of veto power exercised by partisan players in regulatory and financial policy processes. Concentrated party systems that minimise the number of partisan veto players and centralise financial policy authority strengthen the ability of governments to initiate capital market reforms decisively. On the other hand, fragmented party structures that scatter veto authority among multiple actors representing heterogeneous interests impede decisive and effective policy changes. The central themes of this argument are well established and have been widely applied across many policy areas (Hallerberg and Basinger 1998; Kastner and Rector 2003; O'Reilly 2005; Roubini and Sachs 1989; Tsebelis 1999 and 2002). However, it is important to emphasise that governments are more able to manage such complex policy processes as capital market reforms that are politically difficult, involve a wide range of actors and require multi-stage implementation when they have centralised decision-making apparatuses.

The strong ability of politicians to initiate swift and decisive financial policy changes may not lead to market reform success, however; public-regarding capital market reforms are unlikely to be implemented in a coherent and effective manner if governments are unable to sustain such reforms over time. The internal organisational configurations of political parties exert a shaping influence on the ability of politicians to enforce policy reforms from formation through to implementation. Centralised and coherent parties that commit party leaders to agreed-on decisions, isolate politicians from particularised interests and enhance government stability produce more resolute and credible reform programmes. By contrast, incohesive and factionalised parties that encourage private-regarding behaviour, subject politicians to private pressures and undermine government stability generate frequent policy changes and compromise reform credibility. When viewed in close interaction with the systemic structure of political parties, the varying degrees of intra-party organisational strength provide important insights into why the policy behaviour of different governments varies significantly between decisiveness and resoluteness.

This book posits that variations in party system concentration and organisational strength produce different reform orientations and patterns in the three countries under consideration. In Singapore, the highly concentrated party system and the centrally and cohesively organised ruling party combined to both generate strong incentives for policy elites to pursue public-regarding market reforms and enable them to initiate and implement these reforms decisively and resolutely. By contrast, the highly fragmented party system, which interacted with poorly organised parties in ruling coalitions, spawned rampant particularism in the reform process and produced incoherent and inconsistent reform policies in Thailand prior to the late 1990s. While the increasingly concentrated party system enhanced the prospects of programmatic and decisive market reforms in the early and mid-2000s, intra-party organisational weaknesses continued to create policy failures. In Malaysia, the mix of public-regarding and particularistic incentives and the middling progress of capital market reforms reflect the fact that inter-party and intra-party structures were arrayed between Singapore and Thailand, in terms of system concentration and organisational strength.

Research design

These three cases are offered as primary evidence illustrating the central thesis about the causal impact of political parties on financial policy choices. They are selected for three main reasons. In the first place, as noted above, each country has a distinct combination of inter-party and intra-party organisational configurations. These configurations differed systematically both across Malaysia, Singapore and Thailand and within Thailand for much of the period under review in this book. Focusing on different combinations of the independent variables gives the central theoretical proposition explanatory leverage. As will be shown in the chapters that will follow, party system structures and internal organisational attributes interacted differently to produce both spatial and temporal variations in the orientation and pattern of capital market reforms in the three countries.

Furthermore, the selection of these three cases serves an important methodological purpose. Singapore and Thailand illustrate opposite ends of inter-party and intra-party organisational structures and provide clear-cut examples of reform success and failure. However, a paired comparison might have left a certain number of national cases occupying ambiguous positions, as they do not neatly rest on the concentrated or fragmented party systems and strongly or weakly organised parties by which reform approaches and outcomes can be differentiated.

Conducting a triangular rather than a binary comparison by adding an intermediate case, Malaysia, would help assess whether mixed organisational structures lead to mixed market reform approaches and outcomes. Evidence that the two party variables can explain different reform orientations and patterns in other cases would increase confidence in the central proposition and findings of this book.

Finally, this book seeks to develop a single analytical approach that can be applied across the three countries that differ in such macro institutions as territorial structures and political regimes, as made clear in the preceding analysis. Singapore, a city-state, is juxtaposed with Malaysia, a federal state, and with Thailand, a unitary state. Similarly, the three countries fall across a broad spectrum of regime types, from electoral authoritarian to electoral democratic polities. Selecting the cases in this manner, this book clearly shows that the party-based explanation travels well through different macro-political structures. It brings the policy effects of political parties to the foreground by examining their independent causal weight in isolation from these structures.

In accounting for divergent market reform orientations and patterns in the three countries, this book employs the method of focused, structured comparison (George and Bennett 2005). The comparative analysis is focused in that the accounts of different political party structures and divergent reform approaches and outcomes are converted for central analytical purposes. In the theory chapter, the focal point is provided by the inter-party and intra-party organisational attributes that are causally important from the theoretical perspective of this book. In the country chapters, the comparative-historical analysis of capital market reforms in the three countries since the late 1980s centres on the deregulatory and regulatory dimensions of capital market reforms identified earlier in this chapter.

To gain methodological rigour, the comparison is also structured in that the same question is asked of the different cases of capital market reforms in Malaysia, Singapore and Thailand: How party system structures and internal party organisations interact to aggregate the interests and actions of politicians in such different ways that the three countries display divergent policy choices and market outcomes? Each country chapter is configured to facilitate a detailed and systematic analysis of the causal linkage between the independent and dependent variables through a chronological narrative of market reform processes. Empirical evidence is then examined and compared in terms of the central theoretical proposition in order to highlight the application of the causal variables to the three case studies.

Organisation of the book

The next two chapters present the independent variables of the book in greater detail. Chapter 2 explains how and why party system structures and internal party organisation interact to create different incentives for politicians to pursue market reform policies and produce divergent abilities to initiate market reforms decisively and follow them through resolutely. Having established the analytical framework, in Chapter 3 the book differentiates and locates Malaysia, Singapore and Thailand on the external and internal organisation dimensions of political parties. The following three chapters provide the case studies of capital market reforms in the three countries from the late 1980s through the mid-2000s. In each case, the orientation and pattern of capital market reforms are linked to the institutional structures of political parties and thus back to the central theoretical claims advanced in Chapter 2. The concluding chapter presents the major empirical findings of this book in a more focused manner. It also reflects on what can be gained in terms of applications to economic policy-making in Southeast Asia and other emerging market countries and evaluates what this book implies about the political underpinnings of market reforms, particularly against the backdrop of recent financial crises, including the global financial meltdown of 2008–2009.

2
Political Parties and Reform Processes

The central claim of this book is that capital market reforms pose different challenges to politicians in different countries. Even when governments are motivated by comparable market and political forces to launch similar reforms, their incentives to harness these reforms to public-regarding policies differ dramatically. Furthermore, disparate incentives vis-à-vis similar capital market reforms are often coupled with divergent abilities to enact reform initiatives decisively and follow them through resolutely in the face of political and institutional obstacles. What accounts for the heterogeneous incentives of politicians and their different abilities to enact market reforms in line with their incentives and commit to maintaining reform processes? This chapter develops a theoretical model that emphasises the complex interaction between party system structures and party organisational attributes as an explanatory approach to examining the question.

Politicians as central actors

This book focuses explicitly on politicians as central actors in the design, initiation and enactment of capital market reforms. More specifically, it deals primarily with the interests and actions of chief executives, party leaders, legislators and political appointees heading economic ministries. The role of politicians in the development of capital markets and the connection between them and market reforms may not seem obvious. This is plausibly because the nature of capital market operations is seemingly technical and the regulation of securities firms appears apolitical and bureaucratic. As noted in the introductory chapter, however, reforms designed to make bank-based financial systems more market-oriented produce a wide array of winners and losers and thereby alter the distributive politics of reforming countries. Equally significantly, they fundamentally change the ways in which governments allocate financial resources and manage national economies. Capital market reforms, therefore, carry with them profound ramifications for the fortunes of politicians and the welfare of their constituents. Politicians are expected to care greatly about capital market reforms.

Arguing that capital market reforms can significantly influence the political prospects of politicians does not necessarily justify an empirical focus on politicians as central actors in the reform process. Many political analyses of market reforms start with reference to social groups and economic interests, precisely because they generate wide-ranging distributive consequences that reverberate across society. However, before social actors are given any analytical attention, the question of whether they have incentives and organisational resources to influence capital market reforms needs to be addressed.

The central political dilemma of capital market reforms lies with the defining features of such reforms as public goods. As mentioned in the preceding chapter, capital market reforms, including both deregulatory and regulatory measures, produce positive externalities that are conducive to the provision of such public goods as economic growth. These growth-enhancing externalities are directly manifest in low capital costs, long-run physical investment and rapid industrial growth. To the extent that reforms can spur capital market growth, they contribute towards the development of more balanced financial systems that in turn constitute a crucial institutional precondition for sustained economic growth. Aggregate economic growth means that absolute poverty declines, although significant improvement in relative poverty may not derive from the growth process per se. Most developing countries have typically had bank-based financial systems and poorly developed capital markets. This suggests that more balanced and efficient financial systems that can improve collective welfare are unlikely to emerge unless reforms that stimulate capital market growth are enacted.

While capital market reforms are public in the sense that virtually everyone in society would benefit from aggregate economic growth, they also involve significant costs to particular groups. Stock market opening, entry barrier deregulation and commission rate liberalisation can generate overall efficiency and growth gains, but incumbent securities firms may be subject to greater competitive pressures. Similarly, while reforms that improve legal frameworks foster the stable and sustained growth of capital markets and promote financial development, private financiers can gain from practices that undermine effective market regulation and can be reluctant to bear the costs of legal reforms if other policy-relevant political actors have little incentive to do so. Conflicting policy goals thus make the trade-off between private and public interests difficult to reconcile and therefore effective collective action among social groups is unlikely to organise.

Not all social groups lose out from capital market reforms; some may benefit from and thereby support specific reform policies. For instance, individual investors can gain from the lower brokerages that come with the liberalisation of commission rates; bankers or industrialists who want to expand into the securities industry would support the deregulation of entry restrictions; both foreign and domestic investors welcome diversified investment opportunities created by privatisation. But these social actors may not be able to act on their interests for three important reasons. First, individual investors, financiers or industrialists are unlikely to be excluded from enjoying benefits produced through capital market reforms, once such benefits are provided and become available for all. This suggests that they would be reluctant to expend the resources needed to organise effective collective action in order to achieve market reforms. As a result, public goods reforms are subject to free riding and are likely to be undersupplied. Second, even if social groups with pro-reform preferences can organise, common interests are hard to discover. The identification of such interests requires the provision of adequate information that is highly costly (Arrow 1985; Lohmann 1998). Not knowing each other's interests, different social actors would pursue their own interests and have little incentive to engage in collective action. Third, to stand a chance of prevailing over losers from market reforms who are often more concentrated and better organised, beneficiaries need to form reform coalitions. But such coalitions are unlikely to be politically effective if the problem of free riding remains rampant, incentives are dispersed and barriers to collective action are significant.

Politicians and political leaders in particular are better positioned to shape the process of capital market reforms. In the first place, politicians make policy choices and design market reforms in line with their political and economic interests, which cannot be reducible to social demands (Ames 2001; Eaton 2002; Geddes 1994). Social groups, no matter how powerful, have to act through executives, political parties or government agencies to achieve their policy goals. Whether they can translate their policy interests into reform outcomes hinges crucially on the interests of politicians in capital market reforms and on the political institutions that not only shape these interests but also define the avenues of societal access to financial policy processes. Furthermore, political leaders exercise overarching controls over state apparatuses and have important institutional resources at their command. They can use these apparatuses and resources to influence the range of economic interests that are represented in government policy-making and change the relative leverage that political actors can wield over market reforms. While politicians may or may not pursue public-regarding policies through market reforms, they are more able than any other actors to influence the approaches and outcomes of market reforms.

Apart from social groups, bureaucrats in general and technocrats in particular may prove to be influential in the process of capital market reforms. Empirical studies (Dominguez 1997; Silva 1998) on the politics of market reforms in developing countries have indeed shown that technocrats are able to acquire significant leverage over reform programmes and gain privileged positions within the hierarchy of state agencies by playing effective roles in changing the rules and procedures that govern economic policy-making. By dint of their policy expertise and informational resources, technocrats in financial and regulatory agencies—central banks, finance ministries and securities commissions—are pivotal to the design of capital market reforms that are often more technical and complicated than other economic policy changes. In many developing and emerging market countries, capital market reforms have generally been accompanied and facilitated by the empowerment of financial technocrats. This has essentially resulted from technocrats being isolated from political pressures and delegated the authority to craft and execute policy reforms (Ghosh 2006; IMF 2005; Litan et al. 2003). Technocrats have thus become not only integral actors but also beneficiaries in the process of capital market reforms.

Economic bureaucrats and financial technocrats remain essential for understanding capital market reforms, but the nature of their influence is frequently misunderstood. As suggested in the introductory chapter, the power of technocrats is politically endogenous, primarily depending upon the incentives of political elites to privilege their position in the policy process. Delegating policy-making powers to technocrats may help increase the credibility of economic policy and improve the quality of policy formulation and enactment. However, delegation does not in itself allow technocrats to create their own autonomy from politicians and gain complete control over the policy agenda. To the extent that technocrats are entrusted with an extensive policy authority, it is because politicians who possess power and set the agenda find it politically rewarding to empower them. Depending upon whether policies advocated by technocrats advance their political fortunes and the welfare of their supporters, politicians can change the institutional position that technocrats occupy in the state apparatus (Bates and Krueger 1993; Haggard 1999a). If politicians and their constituents benefit from capital market reforms, for example, the viewpoints of pro-reform technocrats are likely to prevail in reform processes and their influence over financial policy is likely to be augmented.

In recent years, recurrent financial crises have pushed politicians to grant greater legal autonomy to financial technocrats and capital market regulators across many developing and emerging market countries. But it is misleading to think that such autonomy would be a sufficient condition for technocrats to formulate and implement financial and regulatory policies independently of politicians. In democratic countries, politicians have strong incentives to control and monitor economic technocrats so that they are attentive to the concerns and welfare of politicians and their constituents. Important theoretical and empirical studies (Bawn 1997; Lupia and McCubbins 2000; Miller 2005) have demonstrated that politicians have not only the incentives but also the means to exercise oversight over the behaviour of bureaucratic and technocratic agents. If the policy interests of technocrats deviate from those of politicians, the latter would most likely diminish the power of the former and rescind the delegated authority, albeit at the cost of policy credibility and investor confidence. In authoritarian regimes, technocrats would have even less independent influence over economic policies. Just as state elites can easily structure the political process to empower technocrats as they see fit, they can take back what they have granted, virtually with impunity. In essence, technocrats are little more than agents of ruling politicians who ultimately determine the course of policy in line with their political interests and policy preferences (Duncan 1995; Huneeus 2000; Nunberg 2002).

The above analysis implies that an approach that emphasises politicians as central actors would provide an appropriate point of theoretical departure for understanding the politics of capital market reforms. Despite its merits, however, this politician-centred approach needs to effectively address the policy interests of politicians in capital market reforms. More specifically, it needs to examine whether politicians have an interest in advancing social welfare through market reforms, how their interests diverge with regard to the same set of reform measures and why they have different interests in capital market reforms.

Politicians, interests and reforms

Given that capital market reforms can enhance public goods provision, welfare economists would expect political leaders to provide such reforms. This social planner perspective, which studies economic policy-making from a normative point of view, sees politicians as being benevolent. They are assumed to be concerned with optimising social utility functions and interested in advancing the welfare of the general public through policy reforms. To the extent that politicians fail to implement market reforms, this is either because they do not understand what policies represent the good application of economic principles or because they lack the institutional capacity to carry out the necessary market reforms (Dornbusch and Edwards 1995; Krugman 1999). However, many scholars, both economists and political scientists, do not subscribe to this benign perception of politicians;[1] they deny the existence of benevolent social planners and underscore the discrepancy between the private utility functions of politicians and the public welfare of society.

There are no prior theoretical reasons to believe that capital market reforms can automatically translate into public-regarding policies. Politicians' interests in pursuing such policies cannot be assumed from the characterisation of capital market reforms as public goods. Strong as external political and market pressures can be, politicians may not respond positively to such pressures by initiating policy changes to fashion a more balanced financial system. Political actors in all polities, democratic or authoritarian, face choices regarding the types of economic policies they pursue and the interests they have in enacting their chosen policies. As regards capital market reforms, politicians may be more concerned with retaining various regulatory and policy restrictions as an important way to channel benefits to specially targeted constituencies than with carrying out public goods reforms that benefit broad swathes of the population. As a result, they are not expected to have any strong incentives to marshal the necessary support for initiating and enacting effective reform programmes.

In developing countries, financial policies that support and sustain bank-based market structures have crucial underlying political rationales. They provide politicians with economic and political resources with which to protect and advance their own policy interests, such as nourishing pet development projects, promoting the welfare of favoured constituents or seeking campaign financing (Haggard and Maxfield 1993; Loriaux et al. 1997; Perotti and von Thadden 2006). State-owned banks in particular permit politicians to target selective favours to industrial projects and economic groups and facilitate their ability to dispense patronage and seek rents in the policy process. More decentralised than banks, capital markets are not the preferred mechanisms for pursing particularistic policies. This is primarily because it would be more difficult to influence the decision calculus of vast numbers of individual investors than that of a handful of commercial lenders. Politicians may thus be disinclined to support capital market reforms and encourage a more market-oriented system of resource allocation over which they have less control.

Furthermore, capital market reforms are likely to weaken the ability of politicians to use various policy restrictions to make particularistic distinctions among the recipients of regulatory favours. Stock market liberalisation is likely to strip governments of an important policy tool with which to shield domestic industrial sectors and privileged private firms from external competitive pressures. By the same token, the deregulation of commission rates threatens to deprive incumbent firms of guaranteed profits associated with oligopolistic market structures. Politicians are more likely to resist competitive pressures generated by capital market reforms if they depend upon the securities industry for support or if they themselves have direct stakes in securities firms. In many developing countries, state-owned enterprises under the supervision of economic line ministries are typically considered as assets from which politicians in charge of these ministries can obtain particularistic benefits both for them and their cronies. Privatisation essentially means the loss of a valuable source of patronage and would thus run into opposition from politicians (Megginson and Netter 2001; Opper 2004; Shleifer 1998).

Politicians with private-regarding interests in capital market reforms may be inclined to support deregulatory measures, particularly if such measures can enhance their ability to seek rents and dispense patronage in the reform process. Politicians who have large holdings of listed stocks or direct stakes in securities firms may have narrow pursuits in connection with capital market growth. They may not be so much concerned with long-term and efficiency-enhancing market reforms as with short-term liberalisation measures to bolster share prices and make quick profits. For the same reason, politicians may be keen to support stock market liberalisation but resist consistent efforts to improve market regulation that is likely to make rent-seeking more difficult. The motivation of politicians to advance their private interests is expected to be stronger if their key constituents who benefit from initial market reforms want to block further and thorough reforms that cut against their interests.

However, while capital market reforms can create ample opportunities for political particularism and rent-seeking, not all politicians are equally interested in pursuing private-regarding policies in reform processes. In some developing and emerging market countries, the past two decades' experience with capital market reforms does in fact offer much evidence to suggest that politicians can be steadfast and important reform proponents. Careful empirical studies (de la Torre 2007; Ghosh 2006; Litan et al. 2003; Zhang 2009b) have documented important country cases in which politicians have been keen to push for capital market reforms with a view to fostering a more efficient financial system, expanding the scope of industrial financing and mobilising more resources for national development. While systemic market and political forces have provided important impetuses, these forces have acted through the pro-reform preferences of politicians, which have made them willing to marshal political and institutional support for reforming and nurturing the securities industry. The strong desire of such politicians to improve public welfare through market reforms has limited the play of particularistic interests and steered reform processes towards public-regarding policies. The key questions to be addressed here are: Under what conditions will politicians be motivated to align market reforms with public policy interests? And how they will push public-regarding reforms through to initiation and enactment?

Political parties as key causal variables

Political parties are granted causal primacy in the explanatory approach of this book to examining the above-mentioned questions. Parties are pivotal to legislative, electoral and policy processes in modern democracies. They define the structure of legislative politics (Carey 2009; Cox and McCubbins 1993), organise elections and frame electoral choices, aggregate and articulate social interests, and create political identities and coalitions (Hershey 2006; Karvonen and Kuhnle 2001; Lipset and Rokkan 1967). To the extent that parties can provide voters with effective information about their policy positions and performance, they constitute the crucial institutional mechanism by which the accountability of governments to the electorate is enhanced (Powell 2000; Shugart et al. 2005; Snyder and Ting 2002). Finally and of more relevance to the central concerns of this book, political parties can significantly shape policy choices, outputs and patterns through partisan influences or through the structure of party systems and the internal organisation of parties.

In the 1970s and 1980s, political parties in Western democracies experienced organisational atrophy as a result of dramatic political, social, economic and technological changes. This gave rise to the party decline proposition that regarded these challenges as so serious as to call the existence and survival of parties into question (Lawson and Merkl 1988; Wattenberg 1986). Contrary to predictions about party decline, political parties in Western democracies are clearly and convincingly shown, in recent theoretical and empirical literature, to have adapted themselves to the challenges so effectively that they have remained the most important institutions in democratic systems.[2] The indispensable roles of political parities have been reaffirmed and heightened in the process of democratic transition that has been sweeping across many developing and emerging market countries over the past decades. Not only have parties in nascent democracies performed the standard functions of their counterparts in more established democracies, they have also been of central importance in establishing and consolidating new democratic practices, rules and institutions. It has been argued that political stability and economic governance in newly democratised countries are contingent upon the institutionalisation of party systems and political parties.[3]

Do political parties in authoritarian polities play the same roles as their counterparts in liberal democracies? Parties may not fulfil any meaningful electoral and legislative functions in closed and hard-boiled autocracies where multi-party elections for political executives are not held, the opposition remains banned and political control is maintained through the widespread use of repression. Conventional analyses (Angrist 2004; Brooker 2000: 81–99) have argued that ruling parties in these regimes constitute nothing but political tools with which elites can construct and maintain authoritarian systems. Party organisations are merely a vehicle for autocrats to commandeer state apparatuses and deter organised challenges to their rule. More recent studies have gone beyond this understanding of autocratic parties as crude instruments of suppression and regarded them as more inclusionary institutions. For some scholars (Gandhi and Przeworski 2007), autocratic parties play crucial roles in co-opting opposition by giving outsiders limited control over policy and thereby a stake in the survival of autocrats. For others (Brownlee 2008; Geddes 1999, 2005; Magaloni 2006), parties entrench authoritarian rule by helping solve intra-regime conflicts, build networks of supporters and maintain credible power-sharing arrangements between autocrats and their ruling coalitions. While shedding important light on why autocracies have political institutions similar to those in democracies, these studies have posited that autocratic parties that act as central mechanisms in the survival strategy of authoritarian rulers behave differently in fundamental ways from democratic parties.

However, this proposition does not allow for the empirical possibility of political parties behaving differently in the different varieties of authoritarianism. In electoral authoritarian polities that hold regular, multi-party and contested elections, parties may resemble their democratic counterparts. Such polities differ from closed exclusionary autocracies in that they establish competitive elections as the primary means of obtaining state power.[4] While national leaders are selected through lineage, party decrees or military orders in full-blown autocracies, politicians in electoral authoritarian systems must contest in executive and legislative elections as the official route of access to political authority. It is true that incumbent parties often change and manipulate the rules of the game to ensure that they ultimately prevail in electoral contests. But authoritarian elections are more than façades: they constitute the central arena of political conflicts that define the rules, processes and outcomes of national politics and shape the behaviour and strategies of politicians (Karl 1995; Olcott and Ottaway 1999; Schedler 2006).

Furthermore, unlike pure autocracies that routinely ban opposition parties or disqualify them from national elections, electoral authoritarian systems regularise political opposition and legitimate organised dissidence. However, electoral authoritarian regimes depart from liberal democracies in that they use various illegal measures to harass opposition politicians, restrict the access of the opposition to mass media and campaign resources, and even exclude opposition candidates from entering the electoral arena. As a result, opposition parties are not on a level playing field with incumbent parties and generally stand little chance of winning elections (Diamond 2002; Geddes 2005; Levitsky and Way 2002). While the lack of procedural integrity renders authoritarian elections normatively unacceptable, the principle of legitimate opposition embodied in the formal institution of multi-party competition prevails. As top executive and legislative positions are subject to regular elections that are both competitive and pluralist, authoritarian regimes create an institutionalised channel through which opposition forces pose periodic and significant challenges to incumbent parties. Operating within the arena of perennial contestation, authoritarian rulers and parties have no choice but to take seriously elections, the electoral processes and their opponents (Hadenius and Teorell 2007; Howard and Roessler 2006; Schedler 2006).

Not only are elections under electoral authoritarian rule largely pluralist, they are also broadly inclusive in that they operate on the basis of universal franchise and allow citizens to participate in the process of selecting chief executives and national assemblies. In a departure from liberal democracies, electoral authoritarian regimes may infringe upon the political rights and civil liberties of citizens and even impose some suffrage restrictions on voters. By subjecting the selection of national leaders to electoral confirmation and popular consent, however, the regimes endow citizens with the ultimate control over who can have access to power (Karl 1995; Schedler 2002, 2006: 12–15). While election results may not completely reflect the will of the people, due primarily to electoral controls and manipulations, incumbent rulers and parties have to take into account popular preferences, if only for the purpose of winning enough votes to continue holding onto office. Moreover, in contrast to the heavy and systematic suppression of civil society in full-scale autocracies, there is some political space for interest groups, social organisations and even independent media in electoral authoritarian regimes. While these institutions are unlikely to pose serious threats to the regimes and may be subject to subtle yet considerable repression, they constitute real and potential sites of contestation and dissidence. By simply allowing such sites to exist, electoral authoritarian rulers abandon their attempts to monopolise the definition of public interests and impose uniform ideologies on the populace, and accept social cleavages and ideological conflicts in political processes (Levitsky and Way 2002; Olcott and Ottaway 1999; Smith and Ziegler 2008).

Once it is established that the major forces that determine the activities and strategies of political parties in liberal democracies—competitive elections, legitimate opposition and socio-political cleavages—are present in electoral authoritarian polities, it becomes easier to accept that the roles of electoral authoritarian parties can be very similar to those of their democratic counterparts. Incumbent parties under electoral authoritarian rule have an incentive to regularise legislatures as an important way to take control of state resources and shape national policy processes in their favour. As a consequence, they play a crucial role in defining and structuring the process of legislative politics. Since parties in electoral authoritarian regimes compete for votes, they need to organise supporters into networks and build coalitions in ways similar to what is ordinarily observed in democratic polities. To achieve this, parties have to recruit members utilising various incentives, mobilise voters and aggregate their interests, and educate and socialise citizens to support their strategies (Geddes 1999, 2005; Ottaway 2003: 139–149; van de

Walle and Butler 1999; Ware 1996: 126–143). In electoral authoritarian regimes, as in democratic systems, parties not only obtain information about the extent of their support and its geographical distribution but also provide an essential channel of information from the regime to the general public (Magaloni 2006). More directly relevant to the central concerns of this book, political parties exert shaping influence over the direction, approaches and outcomes of social and economic policies in electoral authoritarian regimes (Haggard and Kaufman 1995; Marsh et al. 1999; Noble 1998; Zhang 2007).

In arguing for the causal impact of political parties in both democratic and electoral authoritarian regimes, this book draws on two influential bodies of scholarship. The first examines political party systems or regular and recurring interactions among political parties within self-contained and clearly identifiable boundaries. Within this body of scholarship, theoretical and empirical analyses have emphasised the number of parties contesting elections and the ideological distance between the extreme parties as the key parameters of party systems (see, for example, Coppedge 1998; Mainwaring and Scully 1995; Mair 1996; Sartori 1976). Party system theorists have investigated the emergence, development and transformation of these structural properties, particularly their sources in electoral institutions and social cleavages.[5] More significantly, they have moved beyond the formation and change of party system properties and explored the effects of these properties on the electoral choices that voters make when they cast ballots, the processes through which legislative and executive majorities come into being, and the stability and survival of different government systems in both developed and developing countries.[6]

In the literature on the policy impact of party system properties, party system concentration and ideological distribution are particularly salient for understanding political behaviour. This book focuses on party system concentration for two key reasons. First, it is difficult to place political parties in developing countries on the same left–right dimension that defines partisan influence in Western European countries; party competition is generally geared towards obtaining political office and policy benefits rather than achieving ideological goals (Blondel 1999; Haggard and Kaufman 1995). Second, even in those developing countries with left and populist parties, party cleavages have not impinged directly upon the trajectories of economic policies and their effects have remained ambiguous. The ambiguity is reflected in the fact that like their rightist counterparts, many left and populist parties that might have been expected to oppose market-oriented policy changes, including financial market reforms, have actually initiated and adopted such changes in the past decades (see, for example, Biglaiser and DeRouen 2004; Bresser Pereira et al. 1993; Weyland 2002).

The second body of scholarship upon which this book draws to advance its explanations emphasises internal party organisation as a primary determinant of the strategies and behaviour of politicians in the policy-making process. This approach has been closely associated with time-honoured studies on the typologies of party organisation, the functions of different organisational structures and changes in these structures.[7] While they are not inherently explanatory and fall short of constituting cumulative theories of party politics, these studies have conceptually inspired empirical research on the impact of intra-party structures, of which two different streams are prominent. One stream has attempted to unravel the internal mechanisms by which party organisations influence party performance, as reflected in electoral success, resource distribution and party competitiveness (Janda and Colman 1998; Sferza 2002; Wellhofer 1979). The other stream of research focuses on the relationship linking parties with governance, democratisation and public policy. Some scholars (Ames and Power 2007; Eaton 2002; Garman et al. 2001; Golden and Chang 2001; Nielson 2003; Nielson and Shugart 1999) have explored the impact of intra-party structures through the mediation of or in conjunction with electoral rules while others (Hankla 2006; Sinclair 2006; Webb and White 2007; Webb et al. 2002) have examined the direct effects of party organisational variations. The precise definitions and the key indicators of party organisation vary in these two streams of studies, but they do converge on intra-party competition, decision-making structures, party leaderships and party–society links as crucial causal variables.

While causal variables identified in the two streams of studies on internal party organisation are important, not all of them are of equal significance. Presumably, some have greater impact on financial policy-making and capital market reforms than others. Taking its cue from theoretical insights provided in the above-mentioned works, this book focuses on the two most causally exogenous dimensions of intra-party organisation—centralisation and coherence. Centralisation refers to the ways in which decision-making authority is distributed within parties and is identical with the notion of organisational centralisation (Duverger 1954: 52–60; Hankla 2006; Janda 1980: 108–117; Samuels 1999). Parties are centralised where party leaders determine party platforms and policies, centrally control candidate nomination and campaign resources, and enforce programmatic discipline on followers.

Coherence concerns the degree of congruence in the strategic, value or policy orientations of party actors and supporters and derives conceptually from 'systemness' (Panebianco 1988: 55–59) or 'structural cohesiveness' (Janda 1980; Janda and Colman 1998). When parties are coherently organised they act as unified collectivities with well-defined and stable policy positions, party members acquire identification with and commitment to party labels, and inter-party rivalries and factional activities are minimal or remain subdued.

In theory, centralisation and coherence are characteristics that are independent of party organisation and have different determinants and differing effects (Janda 1980; Janda and Colman 1998; Nielson 2003). This implies that they may not necessarily go together. For instance, parties that are centralised could be organisationally incoherent, although there could be parties that are high or low on both centralisation and coherence. In practice, however, these two dimensions are likely to be interactive upon each other. In centralised parties, leaders who are delegated great authority to make key decisions about party platforms and impose discipline on party backbenchers are well positioned to protect party labels. Tight controls over candidate selection and campaign financing enable party leaders to align the behaviour of party members with party policies and reduce intra-party divisions, conflicts and rivalries. On the other hand, decentralised party structures deprive party leaders of the institutional leverage to compel individual politicians to support party policies and strategies. Where party leaderships are weak, there is little prospect of enforcing programmatic discipline on party officials and legislators and greater likelihood that party members defect from collective party goals.

Reciprocally, coherently organised parties that commit individual party members to party platforms and labels and encourage high degrees of intra-party congruence in policy and strategic objectives provide party leaders with institutional resources with which to maintain their centralised controls over candidate nomination, campaign finance and policy processes. However, if parties are factionalised and rival groups autonomously control organisational resources, decision-making authority may become scattered across sub-national and atomised party organs and be devolved into the hands of local party officials. Decentralised policy structures and intra-party conflicts that encourage individual party members to seek particularistic interests at the expense of party labels can severely weaken the ability of national party leaders to maintain effective party controls and enforce decisions on party actors and followers. It can thus be argued that it makes more sense to examine the impact of centralisation and coherence by embracing them in one concept—party organisational strength—rather than analysing them separately. Parties are organisationally strong only when they have both centralised controls and policy processes *and* coherent intra-party structures.

This book takes party system concentration and organisational strength as constituting the core of inter-party and intra-party mechanisms by which political parties exert shaping influences over financial policy processes. It seeks to provide an aggregated approach to explaining political behaviour and policy outcomes by blending these external and internal party structures into a single theoretical framework. The central argument is that systemic party structures and party organisational attributes, while analytically distinct, act interdependently in the policy-making process. As will be shown below, the key research questions of this book—why politicians differ in their incentives to achieve public-regarding policies through capital market reforms and in their abilities to initiate reform policies decisively and sustain reform processes over time—cannot be addressed effectively unless party system concentration is considered in tandem with organisational strength.

Political parties and reform orientations

One central proposition of this book is that political parties shape the incentives of politicians over the choice of capital market reforms. It begins with the assumption that politicians, in both democratic and authoritarian regimes, have an overarching interest in holding onto office.[8] By maintaining their position of authority and prestige, politicians have the ability to enact their preferred policies and deliver benefits to social groups, which in turn enhances their prospects of retaining power. This book aims to explore the importance of political parties as key contextual constraints on the strategies that politicians employ to accomplish their ultimate objectives. While politicians everywhere have uniform interests in advancing their political careers, party system concentration and party organisational strength that define their strategic preferences vary across countries. It is these cross-country variations that provide the micro-foundations for different policy choices made by politicians and generate different incentives for politicians that shape financial policy orientations.

The theoretical literature on the strategic preferences of politicians makes a clear distinction between a narrow, distributional or private-regarding orientation and a broad, national or public-regarding orientation (Gilligan and Krehbiel 1989; Myerson 1993). Political parties create incentives for politicians to be geared towards one orientation over the other via their effects on the overriding desire of politicians to hold onto power. Where politicians are motivated by concentrated party systems and cohesive parties to associate their political fortunes with the advancement of public welfare, they are expected to have strong incentives to enact public policies that serve the interests of the general population. By contrast, where politicians are prompted by fragmented party systems and weakly organised parties to generate localised support as a strategically important way to enhance their political careers, they are more likely to oppose those public policies that threaten to harm the welfare of their narrow constituencies or capture the policy process in order to deliver targeted benefits to particular private firms, discrete economic actors or special interest groups.

Party system structures and reform incentives

Party system structures shape the strategic preferences of politicians for public goods policies, first, through their impact on the ability of voters to hold elected officials accountable for retrospective performance. In the normative theory of democratic government (Dahl 1971; Mayhew 1974), elections are the mechanisms through which the accountability of politicians to voters is enforced. The underlying assumption is that citizens consider government outputs, including policy outcomes and economic conditions, to be the significant determinants of their voting decisions. Voters can reward incumbents for good performance by re-electing them or punish incumbents for bad outcomes by replacing them with challengers. However, it has now been well established that competitive elections are a necessary but not sufficient condition for voters to hold politicians responsible for the results of their past actions and policies. Electoral accountability varies with the political context within which voters evaluate the performance of incumbents and make their voting choices and decisions accordingly.

A growing cluster of studies on economic voting (Anderson 2000; Bengtsson 2004; Nadeau et al. 2002) has emphasised the characteristics of party systems as an important element of such political context. The institutional derivatives of concentrated party systems—the small number of effective parties, one-party dominance or majority governments—are expected to enhance the ability of voters to identify those who ultimately control policy-making, assign responsibility to the incumbents and reward or punish them for economic outcomes. The large number of effective parties, minority governments or multi-party coalitions, all of which are associated with fragmented party systems, not only complicate the efforts of voters to gather information about those actually responsible for government outputs but also create opportunities for incumbent politicians to blame those with whom they share control of policy processes. These institutional features thus make it difficult for voters to identify the linkages between the actions of incumbents and economic performance and thus exercise their sanctions effectively. Recent empirical studies (Bengtsson 2004; Samuels 2004; Tavits 2007) have confirmed that party system structures influence the ability of voters to assign responsibility across a broader range of government policies than just economic outcomes.

The central propositions in these works provide important insights into how party system structures generate incentives for politicians to orient towards public-regarding versus private-regarding policies. Voters as a whole prefer more public goods provision over less public goods provision; they would thus reward politicians for any increases in public goods but punish them for any declines in these goods.[9] If voters behave along these lines, incumbent politicians operating in concentrated party systems that are subject to strong electoral accountability and bear clear responsibility for their actions are pressed to deliver public goods policies. Where fragmented party systems obscure clarity of responsibility for incumbent governments and thus weaken the ability of voters to hold them to account for the supply of public goods, politicians are more likely to deviate from the mandate in the best interest of the public and serve only their own narrow goals. Thus, in a cross-national context, given the more credible threat of voters to punish in countries with concentrated party systems, politicians would have stronger incentives to enact public-regarding policies. In countries with fragmented party systems and muted electoral accountability, politicians are expected to pursue economic policies in ways that are counter to public welfare.

Party system structures influence the policy orientation of politicians not only through their impact on voter choices and decisions but also through their constraining effects on the strategies that parties and politicians adopt to seek political support in electoral processes. Political parties in concentrated systems aggregate the interests of voters differently from their counterparts in fragmented systems. The difference is in the extent to which politicians appeal to a broad range of voters or pay close attention to special interest groups. Concentrated systems, with competition organised among a small number of large parties, institutionalise strong incentives for politicians to build broad bases of electoral support. The basic idea is that the more concentrated party systems, the more votes parties need to secure in order to win elections. Parties in concentrated systems that rely upon localised and specialised constituencies for electoral support are most likely to be defeated by parties that converge towards the mass of voters and form alliances across many social groups. If incentives generated by party concentration motivate politicians to mobilise as many voters as possible on the campaign trail, the same incentives are expected to gear them towards promoting the collective interest of broad support bases once in office. As amply evidenced in empirical studies on the impact of party systems on fiscal policy processes (Chhibber and Nooruddin 2004; Perotti and Kontopoulos 2002), concentrated systems are indeed shown to generate strong incentives for politicians to support the allocation of spending on broad public goods.

This argument also suggests that fragmented party systems motivate politicians to target smaller subsets of the electorate than are required for politicians in concentrated systems. The theoretical premise underpinning this proposition is that with a large number of small parties competing in elections, the proportion of votes that each party needs to secure in order to win seats and participate in government would be small. The overriding concern of politicians with holding onto power and getting re-elected is unlikely to lead them to make appeals to a broad range of voters. Instead, they can often do better by mobilising particular segments of society for electoral support and moving towards the formation of narrow coalitions (Cox 1990; Cox and McCubbins 2001; Lizzeri and Persico 2005). Thus, in fragmented systems, parties and their corresponding coalitions of voters are each so small that politicians are keen to pursue goods and services that are targeted to the coalitions. They have little incentive to support public goods policies, primarily because their narrow and localised constituencies cannot enjoy the benefits from such policies, which are typically dispersed across society. Important empirical studies (Bawn and Rosenbluth 2006; Chhibber and Nooruddin 2004; Stasavage 2005) lead to the conclusion that policy outcomes in fragmented party systems may diverge from the preferences of the general public.

It is thus clear that different party system structures generate variations in the incentive of politicians to pursue public-regarding policies through their differential effects on both the ability of voters to hold politicians to account and the strategies of parties and politicians to build electoral coalitions. If this proposition can be accepted, differences in the overall orientation of capital market reforms are expected to exist between countries with different party systems. Concentrated party structures force politicians to pursue financial policies that are pivotal to the mass of voters. In these systems, politicians are more strongly motivated to enact capital market reforms and have little incentive to manipulate reform processes for private-regarding purposes. By contrast, fragmented party systems accentuate the value of specific interest groups to politicians and the importance of delivering target-specific policy favours to the groups. Politicians operating in these systems are not expected to support capital market reforms whose growth-enhancing benefits tend to be widely dispersed among the general population. To the extent that they show an interest in market reforms, they are more likely to capture the reforms as a vehicle for seeking rents for their strategic constituencies.[10]

Internal party organisation and reform incentives

While the proposition that stresses the public goods consequences of party system concentration seems plausible, it may be challenged, at least on the empirical front. In both developed and developing countries, there is no lack of examples of concentrated party systems that nevertheless do not appear to have discouraged private-regarding and rent-seeking behaviour. Malaysia fits the bill, as did India under the Congress Party from 1952 to 1984 (with the exception of 1977), Japan under the Liberal Democratic Party from 1955 to 1993, and Mexico under the Institutional Revolutionary Party until 2000.[11] In these societies, the presence of centralised party systems in which ruling parties dominated the political scene for lengthy periods is not sufficient to account for many policy choices that were far from public-regarding (Chhibber 1995; Gomez and Jomo 1997; Magaloni 2006; Ramseyer and Rosenbluth 1993). On the other side of the ledger, the absence of concentrated party systems in such Western European countries as Denmark, Finland and Sweden have not prevented their governments from producing high-quality public policy and low levels of rent-seeking behaviour; party fragmentation does not appear to have decreased the provision of substantial public benefits (Birchfield and Crepaz 1998; Crepaz 1996).

This ambiguity over the impact of party system structures on politicians' incentives to provide public-regarding policies can be unravelled when these structures are examined in close interaction with the internal organisation of parties. Intra-party organisational structures generate incentives for politicians to pursue public-regarding over private-regarding policies primarily via their effect on the propensity of politicians to use party-centred, as opposed to candidate-centred, strategies to obtain electoral support. Important empirical studies (see, for example, Ames 2001; Golden and Picci 2008; Nielson 2003; Samuels 1999) have focused on the ways in which electoral rules shape the incentive structure of politicians in policy processes. While admitting of the causal importance of electoral rules, this book emphasises more explicitly the direct impact of intra-party organisational features. These features may be a function of specific electoral rules but can vary across countries independently of national electoral systems. Party organisational structures converge across different electoral systems as much as they diverge under similar electoral rules. The ruling parties of Singapore and Malaysia have demonstrated crucial organisational differences, for example, despite the fact that they have been operating within the same electoral system, as will be shown in the following chapter.

Party organisational strength generates incentives for politicians to pursue certain policies over others in several important ways. First, party leaders in centralised and coherent parties are able to exercise tight and effective controls over party platforms, candidate selection and campaign funds. These organisational strengths enable party leaders to enforce programmatic discipline on members and followers and align their behaviour and interests with party policies and principles (Garman et al. 2001; Haggard 1997; Hankla 2006; Nielson 2003). Party leaders who are charged with promoting the collective electoral prospects of their parties and have a greater stake in national policy outcomes than individual politicians can thus acquire the important institutional leverage to limit the play of particularistic interests and privilege party strategies. Even in electoral systems that encourage the personal vote (Cain et al. 1984; Carey and Shugart 1995), centralised parties can compel politicians to stick to the policy appeals that party leaderships dictate (Jacobson 1985; Samuels 1999). In decentralised and incohesive parties, on the other hand, national party leaders lack the institutional resources with which to impose discipline and rein in particularism. In these circumstances, there is less likelihood that party members will follow party-centred strategies and a greater prospect that they will make candidate-focused appeals the dominate strategy for securing electoral support. Geographic or other constituent interests rather than aggregated national interests are most likely to dominate party strategies and prevail in policy-making processes.

Second, strong parties not only develop clear policy positions and party labels but also enhance the ability of party leaders to guard and maintain party positions and labels over time, as noted earlier. It is well established in important studies (Aldrich 1995; Cox and McCubbins 1993; Hager and Talbert 2000) that distinguishable and stable party reputations and labels are the key assets that candidates can draw upon to enhance their chances of being elected. Their affiliation with strongly organised parties and the cues projected by party labels allow them to clearly and credibly convey to voters the party platforms for which they stand. Voters who have little incentive to acquire costly information about candidates prefer those whose policy positions are clearer, better known and more credible. Candidates thus find it electorally optimal to vote for party positions in order to maintain the clarity and credibility of the positions to voters and increase the probability of their holding onto office. The importance of supporting party platforms encourages politicians to link their individual career prospects closely to the fortunes of their parties and subordinate their pursuits to party-determined purposes. By contrast, decentralised and incoherent parties are very unlikely to develop stable leadership structures, clear policy positions and credible party labels. Risk-averse voters are disinclined to support candidates whose policy positions are opaque, erratic and incredible. Supporting party positions often means that candidates would have to vote against their own policy preferences (Ashworth and Bueno de Mesquita 2008; Snyder and Ting 2002). Politicians are unwilling to bear these costs to support party platforms and more inclined to cultivate personal reputations where party labels confer little electoral advantage.

Third, strongly organised parties are also more likely to have rich collective campaign resources, such as co-ordinated and effective electoral networks and abundant and independent financial support (Gibson et al. 1983; Primo and Snyder 2008; Webb 2002a, 2002b). Equally importantly, such parties have a greater capacity to deploy those resources in a way that achieves their overall purpose, particularly electoral effectiveness and success (Crotty 1971; Wellhofer 1979). Strong organisations that provide campaign resources and deliver votes motivate candidates to be attuned to the preferences and priorities of party leaders seeking to pursue the collective strategies of parties. If individual politicians vote against or deviate from party policies, party leaders can take reprisals against them or compel them to fall back in with party strategies by withholding campaign resources from them or by threatening to do so. By contrast, where parties are weakly and incoherently organised, candidates cannot depend upon their parties for electoral resources and party votes. In such circumstances, they must generate their own campaign resources and secure the personal vote by pursuing personal strategies that target narrow and specific constituents (Ames 2001; Samuels 1999).

Finally, when parties are cohesively structured, they act as such unified collectives and party members acquire such strong identification with party platforms that intra-party rivalries are likely to remain minimal. Party leaders are better positioned to commit candidates to privileging party-centred policies and mobilise them around collective party interests in electoral processes. However, intra-party rivalries are expected to be rampant and even institutionalised in poorly organised parties (Cox and Thies 1998; Samuels 1999). If various politicians and factions compete with each other over votes within parties, candidates can find it futile to campaign by making appeals to party labels and platforms. This places a premium on the ability of individual politicians to pursue personalised electoral strategies that distinguish themselves from their co-partisans and project different cues for voters. Such strategies are important in strengthening the weight of competing politicians against each other and the power position of one faction vis-à-vis other factions within parties. Candidate-focused campaigns create significant incentives for politicians to press for particularistic policies, for which they can claim personal credit and that help them build and maintain narrow bases of political support (Cox and Thies 1998; McCubbins and Thies 1997; Persico et al. 2007).

In sum, in centralised and coherent parties politicians who are concerned with the collective interests of parties have strong incentives to align their policy objectives with those of party leaders and claim credit as a party for the broad benefits that public policy can deliver. By contrast, in decentralised and incoherent parties politicians who are strongly inclined to supplant party-centred policies with personal reputations as the dominant campaign strategy have a stronger propensity to use policies that appeal to a specific segment of the population. As a result, weak party organisations should be associated with politicians who are keen to represent the interests of localised constituencies. As particularism and personalism dominates the electoral and legislative processes, politicians become indifferent and even opposed to the overarching policy platforms of their parties.

An observable implication of this proposition is that countries with centralised and coherent governing parties are expected to do a better job at providing such public goods policies as capital market reforms than those with decentralised and incohesive parties. Party officials from strongly organised parties, insulated from particularistic interests and concerned about the impact of financial policies on the collective electoral prospects of parties, are more likely to craft market reform measures that are associated with public goods provision. The goal of forming a positive relationship with a large swathe of the electorate with a view to maintaining broad bases of political support provides an incentive for parties and their members to promote regulatory policy changes that advance economic development and social welfare. On the other hand, politicians in weak and incohesive parties are keen to provide financial and regulatory policies that can be targeted to specific social groups in order to secure the allegiance of their narrow constituencies. They are thus strongly inclined to press for divisible policy favours that are tailored to particular beneficiaries and resist financial policy reforms that threaten to eliminate such favours. The argument here is not that there is no scope for private-regarding market reforms in centralised and coherent party structures. Political particularism in the reform process is certainly possible where parties are captured by powerful interests. Other things being equal, however, parties and the governments they represent in such structures are more likely to orient capital market reforms towards public-regarding purposes.

It may now be necessary to return to the questions of why party system structures generate ambiguous impacts on the different propensities of politicians to provide public goods policies and of how party system concentration interacts with party organisational strength to explain these differences. That the presence or absence of concentrated party systems is inadequate to account for the varying incentive structures of politicians suggests that their effects be examined interactively with those of intra-party organisational structures. If politicians operating in concentrated systems are disinclined to provide public benefits, this is plausibly because the incohesive organisational structures of their parties generate stronger countervailing incentives to seek private goods policies. Empirical research (Chhibber 1995; Nyblade and Reed 2008; Ramseyer and Rosenbluth 1993) has indeed shown that the decentralised or factionalised party structures in India under the Congress Party and in Japan under the Liberal Democratic Party were clearly associated with politicians who were concerned more with rent-seeking activities than with broad public goods provision, despite the one-party dominant systems. On the other hand, politicians in fragmented party systems do not necessarily press for particularised policies and may be oriented towards public-regarding purposes, where their parties are organisationally centralised and coherent. For example, the coalition governments of Denmark, Norway and Sweden have typically consisted of such strongly and coherently structured parties that they have been able to minimise redistributive policies favouring particular groups that stem from party system fragmentation and support policies that approximate the general interest (Birchfield and Crepaz 1998; Crepaz 1996).

Political parties, electoral authoritarianism and reform incentives

The above proposition is developed in the context of democratic systems or on condition that elections act as crucial constraints on the behaviour of politicians. This raises an important question about the extent to which the proposition can be applied in non-democratic polities. It would be theoretically untenable to argue that inter-party and intra-party organisational structures can shape the policy orientation of political leaders in closed, exclusionary authoritarian regimes where multi-party elections are banned, the opposition is virtually non-existent and repression remains widespread and draconian. In electoral authoritarian regimes that hold multi-party elections, regularise political opposition and admit of social cleavages, however, the effects of political parties on the incentive structure of politicians resemble those of parties in democratic polities in that they shape the ability of voters to hold politicians to account for policy outcomes as well as the types of strategies that candidates pursue in electoral processes.

As was made clear in the preceding analysis, authoritarian elections are more than façades as they constitute the central arena of political conflicts in electoral authoritarian countries that define the processes and outcomes of national politics. While lacking in procedural integrity and substantive uncertainty, authoritarian elections effectively determine who eventually carries the day. The playing field between government and the opposition may be uneven and the cards are often stacked against opposition politicians, but the principle of legitimate opposition embodied in the formal institution of contested and pluralist elections prevails. The presence and persistence of these elections create a regularised mechanism by which opposition forces pose periodic and significant challenges to incumbent rulers. More importantly, by subjecting the selection of political leaders and party politicians to electoral confirmation and popular consent, authoritarian elections endow the electoral populace with the ultimate control over the official route of access to political authority. Elections in authoritarian regimes may be useful in producing legitimacy, deterring the opposition, avoiding intra-regime splits or reducing rulers' risk of violent removal from office (Cox 2007; Geddes 2005; Magaloni 2006). However, in electoral authoritarian regimes, as in more democratic systems, competitive elections act as the primary means of obtaining, maintaining and wielding state power.

For these reasons, incumbent parties and politicians in electoral authoritarian regimes are genuinely concerned with electoral processes and outcomes. They invest heavily in the creation of extensive electoral organisations and networks and the organisation of intense campaign activities, with the view to winning by huge margins. Despite the fact that the opposition generally stand little chance of winning office in electoral authoritarian countries, incumbent parties invariably insist on settling for nothing short of super majorities (Geddes 2005; Magaloni 2006; Ottaway 2003). This generates strong incentives for authoritarian leaders to manipulate fiscal and monetary policies to increase the spending power of voters prior to elections in many of the same ways that democratically elected politicians normally do. Both cross-country analyses (Block et al. 2003; Brender and Drazen 2005; Shi and Svensson 2006) and case studies (Blaydes 2006; Gonzalez 2002; Magaloni 2006: 98–121; Pepinsky 2007) have provided ample evidence for political business cycles in developing authoritarian regimes in general and in Southeast Asian electoral authoritarian countries in particular.

Not only do party politicians in electoral authoritarian regimes take elections seriously, they are also under perennial pressure to win popular support. While full-blown autocracies typically win elections simply by proclaiming whatever results they want, electoral authoritarian regimes are very unlikely to have that option. Electoral authoritarian incumbents can pursue manipulations and frauds to ensure their electoral advantages over the opposition, but they ultimately have to obtain real and substantial popular acceptance through competitive elections. While authoritarian elections may not be an effective means by which incumbent governments can be replaced, voters are still able to punish them for bad policy outcomes by withholding their support or by voting for the opposition. Unlike closed exclusionary autocracies, electoral authoritarian regimes allow citizens to enjoy more genuine choice and obtain more effective mechanisms by which to judge incumbents in elections. There is no lack of examples in electoral authoritarian countries, including those in Southeast Asia, in which significant declines in popular votes have encouraged opposition parties to become more assertive, dented the political dominance and governing legitimacy of ruling parties and even created real prospects for incumbents to be ultimately defeated (Case 2002; Ottaway 2003; Posusney 2002; Taylor 1996; Way 2004). These examples clearly show that there are crucial limits to the extent to which electoral authoritarian regimes can win elections and sustain their rule without substantial popular support.

In electoral authoritarian regimes, as in more democratic systems, the battle for winning and maintaining popular support in competitive and pluralist elections plays an important role in forcing incumbent parties and politicians to take into account voter preferences. This does not suggest that politicians in electoral authoritarian regimes are any more responsive to the electorate than their counterparts in democratic polities. Indeed they may wield authoritarian powers to ignore and even repress some social interests, particularly those associated with opposition forces. However, regular and contested elections press authoritarian parties and politicians to respond to popular demands, if only to secure election, retain office and gain continued access to state power. Lindberg (2006) and Van Rijckeghem and Weder (2009) find evidence that elections render incumbents accountable, at least partly, to voters in a wide sample of developing democracies and non-democracies. Important case studies (Chua 1997, 2005; Crouch 1996a, 1996b; Puthucheary and Othman 2005; Sebastian 1997) show that the desire to sustain electoral dominance generates strong incentives for ruling parties to be responsive to popular interests in Malaysia and Singapore. Furthermore, as parties in electoral authoritarian systems compete for votes and respond to the demands of electoral rivalries, they need to craft and implement campaign strategies in order to mobilise supporters and build electoral coalitions. Cross-country empirical research (Brambor et al. 2007; Lindberg 2006; Mozaffar et al. 2003) demonstrates that the impact of elections and electoral rules on the campaign behaviour of politicians is comparable across regime types, particularly in developing and emerging market countries.

In summary, elections in authoritarian regimes resemble those in more democratic polities in that they force political leaders and party politicians to be responsive to voter interests and employ effective campaign strategies to win office. As with elections in more democratic systems, authoritarian elections themselves are necessary but insufficient to explain how politicians adapt to popular demands and what strategies they pursue in the campaign trail; party system structures and party organisational attributes combine to determine whether elections can enhance the ability of voters to hold ruling parties accountable for policy outcomes and whether party labels and appeals supplant personal reputation and appeals in electoral processes. Two important points can be made on the basis of the theoretical accounts of the impact of inter-party and intra-party organisational configurations on the incentive structures of politicians provided in the preceding subsection.

First, in the cross-national context of electoral authoritarian countries, politicians operating through concentrated party systems and centrally and coherently organised parties are more strongly motivated to be accountable to broader constituencies and have greater incentives to pursue party-focused strategies and policies. As a result, they are more concerned about promoting such public-regarding policies as capital market reforms, for which they can claim partisan credit and that can deliver broad benefits to a large swathe of the voting public. Second and more importantly, across the developing world, politicians in electoral authoritarian regimes are more likely than their counterparts in electoral democracies to promote public goods provision if the former operate in concentrated party systems and strongly organised parties. In other words, when elections generate similar impacts on the ability of voters to hold politicians to account and the strategic behaviour of candidates in electoral processes regardless of regime type, countries with more concentrated party systems and more cohesively organised parties should be better positioned to supply growth-enhancing financial policies and orient capital market reforms towards public-regarding purposes.

Political parties and reform patterns

The central proposition advanced in the previous section posits that concentrated party systems and well-organised parties should be associated with politicians who are more concerned about pursuing financial policy changes that can deliver broad benefits to the general public and enacting capital market reforms that enhance the provision of such public goods as economic growth. This holds true across electoral democratic and authoritarian systems in which elections operate similarly with regard to their impact on the propensity of politicians to respond to voter interests and build electoral coalitions. Not only are politicians operating in strong inter-party and intra-party structures more inclined to pursue public-regarding capital market reforms, they are also more capable of acting on their policy incentives decisively and resolutely. More specifically, concentrated party systems increase the ability of government politicians to initiate and enact financial policy reforms that stimulate capital market growth while strongly organised parties enhance their ability to commit to maintaining given reform policies.

Party system structures and reform decisiveness

Capital market reforms and, indeed, any economic policy reforms are more likely to be successful if reform policies are enacted decisively, often in response to external pressures, market changes or policy failures. How decisive government politicians are in the initiation and enactment of policy reforms is primarily contingent upon the number of veto players or institutional or partisan actors whose consent is required for policy changes.[12] When the number of veto players is high, the range of distinctive interests represented in the policy-making process is very likely to be multiple and diverse. As more interests are provided with vetoes, it would become difficult to ensure that every player finds policy changes compatible with their preferences and is thus motivated to accept new policy deals. The wide distribution of policy-making power among different players can undermine the capacity of central authorities to undertake the co-ordinated and effective implementation of policy programmes. Hence the difficulty of changing existing policies and enacting policy reforms increases with the multiplicity of actors and the diversity of their preferences (Cox and McCubbins 2001; Sartori 1997; Tsebelis 1995, 2002; Weaver and Rockman 1993). The implication is that countries with few veto players are more capable of formulating and enacting new policies swiftly and effectively whereas countries with many veto players are more likely to have indecisive and ineffective policy-making. In the latter scenario, policy stalemate or gridlock is bound to result, with few and incremental policy changes, if at all. The number of veto players has been empirically shown to be causally important in the design and making of economic policies in both democratic and non-democratic countries (Frye and Mansfield 2003; MacIntyre 2003; Mansfield et al. 2007).

With regard to the impact of veto players on capital market reforms, the most important factor is the number of parties whose agreement is needed for existing market regulations to be altered and for new financial bills to become laws. The crucial institutional configurations that determine the distribution of veto power exercised by partisan players in regulatory and financial policy processes are party system structures. Concentrated party systems that minimise the number of partisan veto players and centralise financial policy authority strengthen the ability of governments to initiate capital market reforms in line with their policy incentives. On the other hand, fragmented party structures that scatter veto authority among multiple actors representing heterogeneous interests impede decisive and effective policy changes in the development and regulation of capital markets. The central themes of this argument are well established and have been widely applied across many policy areas (see, for example, Hallerberg and Basinger 1998; Kastner and Rector 2003; O'Reilly 2005; Roubini and Sachs 1989; Tsebelis 2002). However, it is important to emphasise that governments are better able to manage such complex policy processes as capital market reforms that are politically difficult, involve a wide range of actors and require multistage implementation, when they have centralised decision-making apparatuses. Overarching controls of financial policy processes enable governments to plan regulatory changes and market reforms decisively, particularly in circumstances where external pressures demand rapid responses.

The ability of government politicians to initiate and enact financial policy changes quickly and decisively may not lead to market reform success, however; public-regarding capital market reforms are unlikely to be implemented in a coherent and effective manner if governments are unable to sustain such reforms over time. Important theoretical and empirical studies (Cox and McCubbins 2001; MacIntyre 2003; Tsebelis 2002; Weaver and Rockman 1993) have suggested that there are trade-offs between institutional capabilities generated by party concentration and fragmentation. Concentrated party systems that promote capabilities for enacting decisive policy changes by centralising veto authority are likely to undermine capabilities for following given policies through. Conversely, fragmented party structures that generate institutional barriers to decisive and rapid policy changes also reduce the likelihood of policy instability or irresoluteness. This tension has led some scholars (MacIntyre 2003; Spolaore 2004) to argue that the intermediate configurations of party systems or political structures that foster both decisiveness and resoluteness can deliver policy success. Others (Hicken and Ritchie 2002; Yap 2003) have contended that governments with a centralised veto authority may be able to achieve policy stability if deep and broad coalitions or regularised bargaining mechanisms between state elites and key owners of economic resources credibly commit governments to maintaining given policies.

For the most part, however, the contrast between institutional capabilities generated by party system structures for decisiveness and resoluteness may not be as rigid as portrayed in the extant literature. The changing patterns of capital market reforms in the three countries under consideration in this book appear to contravene the trade-off proposition. Singapore is reputed to have been able to carry through capital market reforms, despite its one-party rule. Thailand's highly fragmented party system accompanied chronic policy instability for much of the democratic period; the increasingly concentrated system in the early 2000s facilitated rather than hampered the implementation of reform measures. While having a more concentrated party system, Malaysia displayed a stronger ability to be resolute than Thailand in the key reform areas. More generally, many governments operating in concentrated party systems are shown to have been able to both enact decisive policy changes and market reforms and maintain these changes and reforms over time (Haggard and Kaufman 1995; Weaver and Rockman 1993). On the other hand, there are important examples in which countries with fragmented party systems do not always suffer from indecisiveness and are largely able to implement effective policy reforms (Bowler et al. 1999; Strom 1990b). This book argues that the key to understanding these puzzles lies in the consideration of the structure of party systems in close interaction with the internal organisation of political parties themselves.

Internal party organisation and reform resoluteness

Strong political parties, with centralised controls over candidate selection and organisational resources and high congruence in policy orientations, can not only work powerfully for the initiation of public-regarding market reforms, as made clear in the preceding analysis, but also facilitate the maintenance of such reforms. There are specific causal pathways through which intra-party organisational configurations bear strongly on reform policy resoluteness.

In the first place, empirical studies (Gerring and Thacker 2008; Grossman and Helpman 2006; Hankla 2006; Mainwaring and Shugart 1997) have related party centralisation and coherence to the convergence of policy positions among party members and the limited number of actors involved in policy-making processes within parties. At a more theoretical level, Tsebelis (1995, 2002) has argued that high degrees of party cohesiveness restrict deviation from agreed-on party decisions and increase policy stability. This implies that centrally and coherently structured parties are more likely to sustain economic policy reforms once party leaders have made commitments to such reforms. Conversely, low degrees of intra-party organisational centralisation and unity, which tend to multiply the number of actors and expand the diversity of interests within parties, are more likely to upset policy agreements and decrease policy resoluteness. In decentralised and incohesive parties, shifts in personal or factional controls within the party caucus can lead to leadership changes and, concomitantly, policy instability

(Giannetti 2008; McCubbins and Thies 1997). Party leaders may still fail to implement reform agendas even if they have strong incentives to push for market reform policies.

The theoretical analysis of this book has so far emphasised the importance of centralised and coherent parties in enabling party leaders to enforce programmatic discipline on their followers, prioritise party-focused platforms and pursue the policy objectives of the entire party. It is argued that intra-party organisational strength not only empowers but also constrains party leaders. While party leaders may have broader policy concerns than party members, they still have personal goals that set them apart from party strategies and national interests. This is particularly the case where they have an interest in maintaining the loyalty of their constituents and use particularistic policy favours to that end. The critical question is thus whether the propensity and ability of party leaders to achieve broad national policy goals are credible. The party organisation normally possesses internal mechanisms, such as selection and dismissal power, to control party leaders and orient their incentive structures towards party-centred objectives. But centralised and cohesive parties that can deliver the votes of their members of parliament and ensure electoral success act as a more powerful constraint on the behaviour of party leaders (Linz 1994; Mainwaring and Shugart 1997). The desire of party leaders to keep their parties coherent and unified in order to maintain parliamentary support and govern effectively prevents them from deviating significantly from the collective interests of party members and supporters while pursuing their own personal goals.

Furthermore, one crucial source of policy instability stems from the private capture of party leaders and politicians by special interest groups. When this happens, government policy processes are likely to succumb to the whims of powerful individuals and to the shifting preferences of particularised interests, compromising policy resoluteness and credibility. Strong intra-party organisations can circumvent the problem by generating constraints on the behaviour of party politicians and limiting the play of particularistic groups. As noted above, in centralised and coherent parties politicians who are motivated to be concerned with the collective interests of parties and responsive to the broad voting public have strong incentives to maintain encompassing electoral coalitions. In such coalitions, broad and diverse interests tend to prevail and particularistic ones are unlikely to dominate. As a consequence, politicians are less dependent upon special interest groups and more able to isolate economic policy-making from interference by private market agents. This has the effect both of facilitating the maintenance of support for agreed-on decisions and of preventing departures from given policies. Once economic policies, such as capital market reforms, that promote the welfare of the general public are enacted, it would be difficult for special interest groups to tamper with or alter them.

On the other hand, decentralised, incohesive and faction-ridden parties that foster candidate-focused strategies and appeals to specialised constituents encourage politicians to build and operate in small and narrow coalitions of supporters. Politicians and parties that represent such coalitions are likely to be beholden to a few influential private pressure groups. They are more inclined to change, dilute or even abandon given market reform programmes that threaten the interests of specialised economic groups. As the result of government politicians being responsive and obligated to particularised interests, private market agents are able to gain enhanced entrée to financial policy processes. The political obstacles to which private capture gives rise are likely to yield financial policy reforms that are more erratic and less resolute than would be the case in a country with strong parties, broad coalitions and few particularistic influences.

Finally, intra-party organisational structures impinge directly on government stability, which in turn influences policy resoluteness. Governments and cabinets composed of centralised and coherent parties tend to be more durable and stable (Chambers 2008; Druckman 1996; Lijphart 1999; Saalfeld 2008).[13] Government and cabinet durability and stability enhance the ability of decision-makers to ensure that policies are enacted as intended and that the policies themselves are sustained (Huber 1998; Sartori 1997: 111–114; Spiller and Tommasi 2003; Warwick 1994: 134–140). This is crucial for the successful implementation of capital market reforms, which is typically contingent upon the stability and solidarity of financial policy elites. Equally importantly, government and policy stability allows private market agents to incorporate regulatory rules in their behaviour and ensures that the objectives of reforms are more likely to be fulfilled. Where ruling parties are decentralised, incoherent and fluid, governments tend to experience chronic instability. Even if governments are dominated by one party but the party itself is incohesive and factionalised, this may lead to rapid cabinet reshuffles. In such circumstances, financial policy-makers are not expected to be able to develop the institutional cohesion and consistency necessary to follow through on implementing financial policy reforms over time.

It is clear from the above that the internal organisational configurations of political parties exert a shaping influence on the ability of politicians to enforce policy reforms from formation through to implementation. Centralised and coherent parties that commit party leaders to agreed-on decisions, isolate politicians from particularised interests and enhance government stability produce more resolute and credible reform programmes. By contrast, incohesive and factionalised parties that encourage private-regarding behaviour, subject politicians to private pressures, and undermine government and cabinet durability generate frequent policy changes and compromise reform stability and efficiency.

Political parties and reform processes: A synthesis

In this book, politicians and their roles in the design of financial and regulatory policies occupy the proscenium of the political analysis of capital market reforms. While they intervene in the policy process with the ultimate view to holding onto office, politicians differ in their incentives to deliver public-regarding policies through capital market reforms and in their abilities to initiate market reform policies decisively and sustain them over time. The central theoretical proposition developed in this chapter emphasises political parties as the primary institutional context within which policy interests are defined and reform capabilities are structured. It posits that the integration of party system configurations and party organisational attributes offers a powerful perspective on the propensity of politicians to formulate nationally oriented financial policies, as opposed to particularistic ones, in both electoral authoritarian regimes and more democratic polities. Furthermore, the external and internal organisational dimensions of political parties have crucial bearings on the ways in which politicians shape the patterns of capital market reforms in line with policy incentives. In developing and emerging market countries, the inter-party and intra-party structures identified in the book can vary significantly. Table 2.1 characterises heuristically the different combinations of these two structures and their respective policy effects.

When concentrated party systems exist alongside well-organised parties (Cell I), governments are expected to display strong incentives to harness capital market reforms to public-regarding purposes and strong capabilities both to initiate market reforms and follow them through to the end. High degrees of organisational centralisation and coherence within the majority party generate such powerful stabilising effects that they can commit party leaders to given reform programmes and overcome the problem of policy instability associated with centralised veto authority. The systemic concentration and internal organisational

Table 2.1 Political parties and reform processes

		Party system concentration	
		High	Low
Party organisational strength	High	**I** High propensity to provide public-regarding reforms; strong abilities to both initiate and sustain such reforms	**II** Moderate/high proclivity to seek public goods reforms; weak/moderate abilities to initiate but strong capabilities to follow through such reforms
	Low	**III** Weak/moderate incentives to supply public goods reforms; strong abilities to enact but weak abilities to sustain such reforms	**IV** Weak incentives to provide public-regarding reforms; weak abilities to both initiate and implement such reforms

strength of parties combine to make it possible for governments to be decisive and resolute simultaneously. On the other hand, where party systems are fragmented and parties themselves are poorly organised (Cell IV), politicians are strongly inclined to seek particularistic policies through capital market reforms. Reform processes are more likely to lapse into indecision, delay and gridlock that stem from dispersed veto power, and experience the chronic instability and inconsistency that are associated with organisational decentralisation and incoherence. Governments with such party configurations thus suffer the worst of two worlds: they can neither initiate swift and effective market reforms nor ensure that reforms, if enacted at all, are durable.

In the case of fragmented party systems co-existing with centralised and coherently structured parties (Cell II), high degrees of intra-party cohesion enable party leaders to rein in the rank and file in line with the collective interests of parties and the broad concerns of their electoral coalitions. Party-centred rules and strong party leaderships are likely to restrain the proclivity of politicians to seek private goods engendered by party system fragmentation and mitigate the particularism that plagues the provision of such public goods policies as growth-enhancing capital market reforms. While multiple partisan players in fragmented systems may subject policy processes to indecisiveness, the organisation centralisation and coherence of these players reduces the number of actors in both inter-party and intra-party policy negotiations and enables them work out stable agreements. Intra-party organisational strength thus increases the probability that reform policies, once hammered out among various partisan veto players, are more likely to be implemented as intended.

Finally, where concentrated party systems are married to decentralised and incoherent parties, weak party controls over candidate selection and financial resources, candidate-focused strategies or rampant factional activities encourage party officials and members to seek personal votes and appeal to narrow constituencies so strongly that they are likely to counteract the tendency for parties in concentrated systems to provide public-regarding market reforms. Politicians in such mixed organisational structures may be more inclined to support public goods policies than their counterparts in fragmented systems coupled with poorly organised parties. But their incentives to do so would be weaker than would be the case in centralised and coherent parties operating within concentrated systems. Equally importantly, while concentrated party systems may be conducive to the formulation of decisive policy reforms, weak intra-party structures are inimical to the sustained enactment of such reforms. Decisive policies are thus likely to be quickly changed or even reversed before they can be fully implemented. Despite the centripetal effects of party system concentration on policy processes, party leaders who confront a party or a legislature full of atomised and wayward politicians are more constrained in their ability to deliver consistent and resolute reform outcomes than their counterparts in governments composed of multiple yet cohesive parties.

3
Variations in Political Party Structures

In order to explore the central argument of this book regarding the impact of political parties on capital market reforms, this chapter presents an analytical account of cross-country variations in party systems and organisational structures between Singapore, Malaysia and Thailand. It first discusses the analytical measures of party system concentration and organisational strength and then differentiates and locates the three countries on these two dimensions. The purpose is not to provide a full account of inter-party and intra-party configurations in the three countries but to highlight their variations as the primary determinants of different reform orientations and processes.

Comparative tools and measures

Given the causal importance of party system concentration and organisational strength in the process of capital market reforms, as was made clear in the preceding chapter, these two dimensions need to be measured accurately. In comparative politics literature, the number of political parties has traditionally been employed as the basic variable to examine how concentrated party systems are. Counting the number of parties precisely has proved far from easy, however, and several different yet interrelated indices have been developed in comparative party studies. One of the earlier efforts to classify party systems and measure the number of parties was represented in the works of Kesselman (1966) and Wildgen (1971). Known as the Kesselman–Wildgen or hyper-fractionalisation index, this has been criticised for being excessively sensitive to the presence of small parties and therefore overstating party system fragmentation (Kuster and Botero 2008; Molinar 1991). As a result, the index has all but passed into disuse in the literature.

Another measure of party system concentration, which has been so widely accepted and employed that it has become the standard criterion in the comparative analysis of party systems, is the effective number of parties index (N or ENP) developed by Laakso and Taagepera (1979).[1] While it accords some weight to all parties, the index weights parties with large vote or seat shares more than parties with small shares. In this respect, it has overcome the problem inherent in the Kesselman–Wildgen index by highlighting the importance of large parties. Furthermore, the index ranges from 1 (if one party captures all of the votes or seats) to infinity (if n parties have equal vote or seat shares). The empirical implications of a given number of effective parties for the concentration or fragmentation of party systems are more directly observable using this index (Laakso and Taagepera 1979; Taagepera and Shugart 1993). It has offered an easily calculable and understandable indicator of party system concentration and has had few rivals in measuring the number of parties in electoral and legislative processes.

However, the Laakso–Taagepera index has not gone unchallenged and has been subject to some scathing reviews (Blau 2008; Dumont and Caulier 2005; Dunleavy and Boucek 2003). These reviews have converged on one prominent problem with the index—high ENP scores tend to provide misleading information about competition for government, particularly where the winning party holds a majority of votes or seats. For instance, with the largest party winning 65 per cent of the votes in a five-party system and three parties 10 per cent each and the smallest party 5 per cent, the ENP score is 2.2. This gives an impression that the system has two relevant parties but masks the fact that the largest party dominates and faces no viable competitors.

Among the scholarly efforts to critically examine and improve the original Laakso–Taagepera index, Molinar's approach (1991) stands out as a more successful one, particularly with regard to its ability to give fuller attention to one-party dominance.[2] While the Molinar index (NP) derives from the Laakso–Taagepera index, it counts the winning party differently from other parties and therefore captures situations of dominance by one major party where ENP indices still indicate a multi-party constellation. NP gives values around 1.16 to the above example of a five-party system, clearly showing the distinction between the winning party and the rest and more accurately reflecting the concentrated structure. While inclined to underrate the relevance of small parties for coalition formation (Dunleavy and Boucek 2003; Taagepera 1999), the Molinar index serves well the purpose for which it was originally designed. It strongly complements the Laakso–Taagepera index as an alternative measure of the effective number and size of parties and the concentration of party systems.

It is more difficult to measure and compare intra-party organisational strength, primarily because there are no widely accepted and methodologically convincing approaches to quantifying the concept. Existing approaches (see, for example, Gibson et al. 1983; Mayhew 1986; Rice 1925) are either too narrow in their measurements of organisational strength or emphasise the intra-party dimensions that are only marginally relevant to the empirical focus of this book— organisational centralisation and coherence. To provide a comparative context for Malaysia, Singapore and Thailand, this book devises a coding scheme on party organisational strength, mainly following Carey and Shugart (1995) and Janda (1980). The scheme sums the coding of the variables that constitute the essential attributes of centralisation and coherence. As informed by the theoretical accounts provided in the preceding chapter, centralisation is operationalised with reference to policy-making structures, candidate selection, fund collection and allocation, and imposition of discipline; coherence is measured through party labels, loyalty and party switching, and intra-party competition and factionalism. The index that combines the variables ranges from the weakest score of zero to the strongest score of 24. A full explanation of the coding scheme is provided in the appendix to this chapter.

Political parties in the same country tend to display similar or convergent internal organisations; common political, social and institutional settings may generate homologising effects on the propensity and ability of parties to develop comparable organisational structures. In developing countries, however, parties operating in the same national context are empirically shown to have different attributes (Samuels 1999; Webb and White 2007). In Malaysia and Singapore, the ruling parties have been much better organised than most of opposition parties. While Thai parties have generally been decentralised and incoherent, there are a number of prominent parties that seem to be partial exceptions to the rule. This book therefore focuses on the ruling parties and treats their internal organisational structures as national characteristics when coding centralisation and coherence in the three countries. Such an approach is justifiable because it allows inferences to be drawn connecting the organisations of ruling parties that control financial policy with capital market reforms. In case of multi-party governments, the central tendency of the parties' intra-party organisational attributes will be coded.

The coding scheme on organisational strength in Malaysia, Singapore and Thailand covers the 1988–2006 period during which time most market reforms were enacted. While it covers an 18-year time span, the scheme gives an aggregated measurement of centralisation and coherence in each country. But the coding scheme is also variable across different parties and time periods, in line with organisational developments that are significant enough to justify major adjustments in scoring parties. It can reflect the different organisational structures of incoming ruling parties as a result of government turnovers or changes in the organisational attributes of the same ruling parties across years. Coding the changing configurations of intra-party organisations in different parties and across years requires the collection of comparable and reliable data from multiple sources. This book relies upon primary and secondary sources gleaned from author interviews, national archives, country case studies and cross-sectional analyses that provide relevant information for coding the eight ordinal variables mentioned above.

Variations in party system structures

Malaysia, Singapore and Thailand differ significantly in terms of party system concentration measured by the number of effective parties, using both the Laakso–Taagepera and Molinar indices. As shown in Table 3.1, the two indices give virtually the same scores for the party system structure of Singapore, clearly revealing the predominance of the People's Action Party (PAP) and the weak position of opposition parties in political processes. The Laakso–Taagepera index indicates that the Malaysian party system resembled a near two-party structure in some years, thus apparently overstating the relevance of opposition parties. The Molinar index corrects this bias, more precisely reflecting the fact that one umbrella party, the Barisan Nasional (BN), always won a majority of votes. Overall, the two indices clearly suggest that the party systems of both Singapore and Malaysia were more concentrated than that of Thailand for much of the period under consideration here. In Thailand, constitutional reforms enacted in the late 1990s significantly centralised the party system, as illustrated in Table 3.1. Once again, the Molinar index pays more attention to the fact that the TRT dominated the multi-party coalition over 2001–2005. It formed a single-party government following the 2005 election before it was toppled in the September 2006 coup.

In Malaysia, the BN, while comprising a dozen organisationally separate and ethnically based parties, was formally registered as one party

Table 3.1   Party system concentration[a]

	Laakso–Taagepera index	Molinar index
Malaysia		
1986	1.4	1.0
1990	1.9	1.1
1995	1.4	1.0
1999	1.7	1.1
2004	1.2	1.0
All years	**1.5**	**1.0**
Singapore		
1988	1.0	1.0
1991	1.1	1.0
1997	1.1	1.0
2001	1.1	1.0
2006	1.1	1.0
All years	**1.1**	**1.0**
Thailand		
1986	6.1	4.0
1988	7.8	5.2
Sept 1992	6.1	5.3
1995	6.2	5.1
1996	4.3	3.4
All years	**6.1**	**4.6**
2001	3.1	1.7
2005	1.7	1.1
All years	**2.4**	**1.4**

Sources: Author calculations, based on data provided in *EIUCR*-Malaysia (various issues), *EIUCR*-Singapore (various issues), *EIUCR*-Thailand (various issues), Nelson (2001), Rieger (2001) and Tan (2001).
[a] In calculating the two indices, this book uses vote shares.

in electoral processes. It contested elections with a single slate of candidates who campaigned under the same party label and platforms. More importantly, it nominated candidates in each constituency in such a highly co-ordinated manner that they not only avoided competition with each other but also won cross-ethnic votes (Crouch 1996b: 115–119; Lim and Ong 2006: 68–69). In parliament, as in elections, the various constituent parties of the BN co-operated so closely that they actually formed a single parliamentary party group. Disputes did arise among the member parties over procedural and substantive issues, but the BN was able to act as a tightly organised bloc in legislative processes. Finally, the leaders of most of the BN parties were represented in the cabinet, which provided an important forum through which inter-party consultations were maintained and strengthened.

The cohesion and dominance of the BN rested most crucially with the preponderant position of the United Malays National Organisation (UMNO), the huge Malay party, in the ruling coalition. It always functioned as primus inter pares among the constituent parties, because it maintained a massive membership, established stable and broad support bases, operated extensive organisational networks, held the lion's share of BN seats in parliament and had rich financial resources at its disposal (Case 1996b; Gomez 1998; Gomez and Jomo 1999). While the leaders of the BN parties often had latitude in nominating their BN candidates, the UMNO president had the final say over which candidates would be selected and how seats would be apportioned between the member parties of the BN. Equally important were the extensive and effective controls over the legislative processes exercised by UMNO leaders and politicians to whom the other smaller parties delegated decision-making power and whose legislative proposals and motions they seldom disputed. Despite the formal equality of party representation in the cabinet, senior UMNO politicians invariably secured and controlled the important portfolios of foreign affairs, internal security, finance, defence and education while the smaller constituent parties had to content themselves with what was left over. The UMNO presidency and deputy presidency were always attached as ex officio posts to the prime ministership and deputy prime ministership of Malaysia.

The subordination of the junior parties in the BN derived primarily from their heavy reliance upon the UMNO for financial resources to compete against the opposition in elections and for cabinet positions to access state resources. While they had their own policy interests to pursue and were geared towards their particular supporters, they joined and operated in the BN under the UMNO's terms. They challenged these terms at the risk of their being politically ostracised in the BN and even forced out of it.[3] The Malaysian Chinese Association (MCA) and the Malaysian Indian Congress (MIC), the second and third largest parties in the BN respectively, had substantial bargaining power vis-à-vis the UMNO in the Alliance during the 1950s and 1960s; however, their influence was dramatically diluted and weakened in 1974 when the Alliance was reconstituted into the enlarged BN. In policy-making processes, the priorities and preferences of the UMNO almost always prevailed over those of the other constituent parties (Gomez and Jomo 1999). The BN and its main governing body, the Supreme Council, merely acted at the behest of top UMNO leaders and were 'in effect a façade for UMNO rule' (Crouch 1996a: 34).

In Singapore, the highly concentrated party system meant that political power was extremely centralised. One-party rule by the PAP, which had been installed since independence in 1965, remained a central defining feature of the Singapore polity in the subsequent decades. The opposition was too fragmented and ill-organised to challenge the hegemonic position of the ruling party. The parliament operated largely under the aegis of the PAP and exercised little oversight over its leaders. Although the ordinarily passive presidency acquired new powers in the 1990s, it nevertheless did not have effective checks on the prime minister. For all practical purposes, the party operated as a single veto player in national political processes. This contrasts with their UMNO counterparts who, while invested with exclusive veto authority, were clearly constrained by the need to maintain support within the BN. While both Malaysia and Singapore had centralised political frameworks, the PAP was more dominant than the UNMO in overall electoral, legislative and policy processes.

In sharp contrast to Malaysia and Singapore, Thailand had a highly decentralised political framework that stemmed primarily from its fragmented party system, an essential institutional hallmark of the Thai polity for much of its more democratic era through the late 1990s. From 1988 to 2001, there were often as many as 16 political parties running in an election, and the number of parties winning seats in parliament hovered at around ten. With so many parties represented in parliament, coalition governments that typically comprised six or more parties became the rule. In Thailand, the lower house of parliament, the House of Representatives, carried veto authority and the upper house, the Senate, had the power to delay rather than block legislation. However, multi-party coalition governments in which the consent of all the parties—who had different interests, constituencies and agendas—was needed for legislative or policy changes significantly diffused veto authority and generated a highly decentralised political structure (Hicken 2002; MacIntyre 2003).

This changed in 2001–2006 when constitutional reforms enacted in the late 1990s drastically reduced the number of political parties and centralised the party system structure in Thailand.[4] The TRT, which won more than 40 per cent of the popular vote and nearly half of parliamentary seats in 2001, the first election under the new constitution, formed a coalition government with two much smaller parties. The electoral and legislative dominance of the TRT was enhanced in the 2005 election in which it secured more than 60 per cent of the vote and 75 per cent of parliamentary seats. While the Senate became fully elected and more active in the political scene, its formal powers regarding legislation remained unchanged. Together with the enhanced leverage of the prime minister over coalition partners, an increasingly concentrated party system centralised policy authority in the hands of TRT leaders. Thailand under the TRT became a de facto dominant-party system over 2001–2005, despite the existence of a coalition government, and had a single-party government during the period 2005–2006.

Variations in internal party organisations

Malaysia, Singapore and Thailand also differ systematically with regard to party organisational strength. In examining cross-country variations along this dimension, this book combines qualitative judgements and quantitative indicators. It first provides a focused analysis of party organisational strength in each country for the 1988–2006 period. The analysis is structured around the four variables that operationalise organisational centralisation—policy-making structures, candidate selection, fund collection and imposition of discipline—and the four variables that operationalise coherence—party labels, loyalty and party switching, intra-party competition and factionalism. The book then provides an overall index of organisational strength in each country by using the coding scheme developed in the appendix.

As was made clear in the previous section, party organisational strength often differs across political parties of the same country, although national tendencies are sometimes in evidence. The comparative analysis therefore focuses on the ruling party that controls government processes and shapes financial policy. In Singapore, this means the PAP, which ruled the country continuously during the period in question. While the BN was the ruling coalition in Malaysia, it was the UMNO that de facto controlled the government. From 1988 to 2000, all the successive governments in Thailand were multi-party coalitions. The empirical discussion focuses on the average organisational structures of all the constituent parties in each coalition government rather than the organisational attributes of each individual party. During 2001–2005, the government led and dominated by the TRT was a multi-party coalition in all but in name. The TRT thus provides the analytical focus.

Malaysia

The UMNO was the leading political force in the Malaysian government since the attainment of independence in 1957. It established itself as the backbone of the Alliance and saw its dominance in the national political system greatly enhanced in the BN. From its inception in 1946, the party developed as the principle vehicle of Malay political aspirations and presented itself as the champion of the Malay community, particularly in rural areas. The organisational structures of the UMNO gradually evolved and changed in the early post-war period, amidst incessant and significant social, political and economic transformations.[5] These structures had become consolidated by the 1980s and displayed a high degree of continuity over the ensuing decades.

In the UMNO, the locus of policy-making power in determining both campaign strategies and substantive issues of government was an important indicator of organisational centralisation within the party. The UMNO was structured hierarchically, from branches that formed the basic organisational units through divisions and state liaison committees to the Supreme Council, the highest decision-making body of the party. Policy inputs were often sought from across all levels of the UMNO and policy deliberations conducted through the general meetings of branches and divisions and particularly at the triennial general assemblies of the party. However, major policy positions were made and announced by the Supreme Council; these positions constituted official party policies without the need for approval by any other party organs. At the epicentre of the Council was the UMNO president who appointed one-third of its members and was given extensive powers to call its meetings and set their agenda. This centralisation of authority, which had typified the policy-making process of the UMNO in the 1960s and 1970s (Funston 1980: 168–184), was greatly enhanced from the early 1980s when Mahathir Mohamad became the president and the prime minister (Lim 2002; Slater 2003).

Centralised policy-making structures within the UMNO contributed to significant party controls over candidate selection in the process of parliamentary elections. Not only did UMNO leaders have the final say over the selection of candidates from the various constituent parties of the BN, as noted earlier, they also exercised great discretion in the final selection of UMNO candidates. While divisions and state-level organisations nominated candidates to the Candidates Selection Committee at the national level, party leaderships eventually decided which candidates would stand for parliament. The formalised method of submission and nomination provided a strong measure of elitist controls in the selection of legislators (Case 1996b; Gomez 1998: 257–258). However, this does not suggest that party leaders could make decisions in isolation and without pressure from local and intermediate party organisations. The desires of party leaders to reduce dissensions and maintain party unity disposed them to take full account of local suggestions about candidates. The centralised nomination procedures within the UMNO were thus tempered by local preferences and influences. This trend, which was manifest in the process of candidate selection in the 1960s and 1970s (Musolf and Springer 1979: 81–88), appears to have strengthened over subsequent decades. Mahathir and his successor, Abdullah Badawi, were often under intense pressures to modify their choices of UMNO candidates (Gomez 1996a: 18–20; *NST* 17 November 1994: 5, 13 April 2003: 3; *ST* 10 February 1995: 23).

Within the UMNO, party finances, including campaign funds, were managed in a relatively centralised manner. During the early years of its operations, the UMNO were often financially constrained and had to depend upon the richer member parties of the BN for support of its activities, particularly electoral campaigns. In the 1970s and 1980s, the financial independence of the UMNO increased significantly, as the party acquired growing and large corporate assets and formed close ties with private businesses (*FEER* 5 July 1990: 48–50; Gomez 1990, 1991). While the actual processes through which the UMNO raised funds remained opaque, important empirical studies (Gomez 1994, 1996b) have clearly shown that the party derived much of its financial support from UMNO-owned firms, business nominees who held enormous corporate assets in the name of the UMNO or big companies controlled by Chinese and foreign interests but closely linked to senior UMNO politicians. Despite the diverse sources of party finances, central party organs were largely responsible for allocating them in line with the policy goals and priorities of the party.

However, it is important to note that in parallel with the efforts of the UMNO to achieve financial self-sufficiency through direct involvements in business activities, individual politicians and local and intermediate party organs also owned or controlled business concerns and established patron–client relations with *bumiputera* or Malay and non-*bumiputera* corporate figures and private entities. This gave them considerable latitude, not only in collecting but in using funds in ways that were more attuned to their preferences and priorities than those of the UMNO and party leaders. Furthermore, competitions within the UMNO for leadership positions across all levels of the party remained fierce during the period under review, as will be detailed below. In these competitions, politicians and factions lavished money to secure the party positions that would provide them with direct and enhanced access to state resources and economic rents (Gomez and Jomo 1997: 117–165; Lim and Ong 2006; Teh 2002). The prevalence of money politics instigated politicians to explore, develop and maintain their autonomous sources of campaign funds. These politicians and their factions, with their own business interests and corporate backers and their own mechanisms of collecting funds, seldom depended upon centralised party leaderships for funding support and operated increasingly independently, at least in financial terms, of national party organs (Gomez 1994: 290–293).

Centralised policy-making structures and relatively effective controls over candidate selection and party finances strengthened the power of UMNO leaders to impose programmatic discipline on party officials and members. They had an array of disciplinary techniques to motivate individuals to conform to party principles and policies. They screened out undesirable mavericks and punished rebellious politicians by denying them access to party resources, removing them from party office or even expelling them from the UMNO. The administration of major disciplinary actions was centralised in the UMNO Disciplinary Committee, the Supreme Council and the party president. In the 1980s and 1990s, local organisations and state party organs were playing an increasingly significant role in monitoring and disciplining the behaviour of their own members.[6] However, the effectiveness of disciplinary actions was often called into question. For instance, while UMNO politicians who became independents or crossed over to the opposition after failing to secure nominations for parliamentary contests were generally expelled immediately, such practices continued unabated (*NST* 14 September 1991: 4, 16 November 1994: 2). Likewise, vote-buying and corruption remained rampant in the electoral and policy processes of the UMNO, despite the fact that party leaderships sometimes took severe disciplinary actions against infamous perpetrators, some of whom were senior UMNO politicians.

The key defining features of intra-UMNO organisation, particularly the elitist nature of policy formulation and candidate selection, provided party leaders with crucial institutional resources to promote and protect the party label. Among the major political parties both in the BN and the opposition, the UMNO stood out due to its ability to develop and maintain relatively strong party reputations. During election campaigns, it was the party label and reputation that provided the key assets for UMNO candidates and were instrumental in assisting them to achieve electoral success. As UMNO leaderships were generally able to control access to such assets, most party officials and members were willing to toe the party line and adopted UMNO-centred strategies (Gomez 1998; Lim and Ong 2006). This by no means suggests that particularism was absent in electoral and policy processes. Indeed, local influences over candidate nomination and weakened party controls over the collection and allocation of funds generated incentives for UMNO politicians to eschew party-oriented strategies. Increasingly, it was the ability of individual politicians to raise money as much as party labels and platforms that delivered votes. However, particularly in general elections, adopting a label-promoting strategy was still able to help candidates reap considerable electoral advantages that money could not buy easily.[7]

Relatively strong organisational controls enabled UMNO leaders to ensure that party members were concerned with party reputation. Most of them remained loyal to the party; party switching, while not absent, happened mainly during the critical junctures of party realignments and splits or in the aftermath of severe factional infightings. Many party members stayed closely affiliated with the UMNO, not so much because of ideological convictions and policy orientations as because of ethnic affiliations (Brown 1994: 206–257) and, more importantly, materialistic interests. In the 1980s and 1990s, party leaderships increasingly used patronage to ensure loyalty. Party membership was widely perceived as a key avenue for upward mobility and wealth generation, either by moving up the party ranks or by being first in the line for state largesse (Crouch 1996a: 36–43; Gomez and Jomo 1999: 237–238). To defect from the UMNO was to be not only consigned to the political wilderness but also denied all the attendant commercial opportunities. However, UMNO politicians who were left out or bypassed on patronage did defect to the opposition or contested as independents against UMNO candidates in general elections (*NST* 14 September 1991: 4, 16 November 1994: 2; *ST* 11 June 1995: 17).

In Malaysia, the electoral system of single-member districts with plurality voting tended to encourage politicians to campaign on the basis of party affiliation. The largely party-centred rules were more heavily geared towards committing politicians to co-operating rather than competing with co-partisans in general elections. However, it is in the process of party elections in which intra-party rivalries within the UMNO manifested themselves most clearly and intensely. Competitions for branch and divisional posts, Supreme Council seats and the three vice-presidencies remained open and sometimes fierce (Case 2002: 111–119; Crouch 1996b; *FEER* 30 September 1993: 18–21). Even the party president and deputy president were frequently challenged in

UMNO general assembly elections, particularly in recent decades. UMNO politicians jostled for leadership posts in the party apparatuses, especially at the local and intermediate levels, primarily because these posts provided direct entrée to state positions and business opportunities. For the most part, intra-party competitions were concerned more with controls over political power and patronage resources than with ideological and policy differences (Case 1994; Muzaffar 1989: 17–24).

Intra-party rivalries gave rise to the emergence and persistence of factions in the UMNO. During the period in question, the party remained severely factionalised, with factional leaders competing for state resources to develop their power bases and move up the party hierarchy. As a result, factional conflicts often became so open and untoward that they erupted into party splits or purges. The most serious of these conflicts were the challenge to Mahathir's leadership by his finance minister, Tengku Razaleigh in 1987, the defeat and replacement of Ghafar Baba, the then deputy president, by Anwar Ibrahim, a UMNO vice-president in 1993, and the clash between Mahathir and Anwar, his one-time protégé in the wake of the Asian financial crisis of 1997–1998, which was followed by the purge and imprisonment of the latter.[8] Intra-party fighting was not subdued after Mahathir stepped aside in autumn 2003. The party under Abdullah was spared major splits, but factional rivalries raged on among up-and-comers within the UMNO (*FEER* 7 October 2004: 18, July/August 2008: 30–34; Mauzy and Barter 2008). While roughly distinguished by leadership styles, administrative capacities and generational memberships, UMNO factions were seldom based on disagreements over governmental philosophy, substantial issues or party strategies. Factional activities centred almost exclusively on the struggle for access to economic rents associated with control of party and state apparatuses (Gomez 2002; Gomez and Jomo 1997).

Factional activities and clashes within the UMNO tended to become rampant both when the party gained new benefits to dispense and when resources became more scarce. This was particularly the case because factional conflicts were largely structured around the distribution of state rents and there were no clearly and rigidly demarcated boundaries between different factions. It was not uncommon for members and even leaders of factional cliques and groups, notably at the branch and divisional levels, to change their allegiances across elections and over time, with a view to securing ascendancy in the UMNO hierarchy and maximising access to patronage. This might have prevented factions from becoming strong and powerful enough to disintegrate the

UMNO. At the same time, party procedures also ensured that while factions competed fiercely, they did not undermine basic intra-party cohesion (Case 2005; Muzaffar 1989: 1–5). But the fact remains that the UMNO was perennially susceptible to factional rivalries and centrifugal effects they generated on intra-party organisations. While a relatively centralised structure might have enabled the UMNO to survive major intra-party clashes (Brownlee 2008), the intensity of factional conflicts and associated internal rifts rendered the party less than coherent.

Singapore

Born out of the struggle for independence in 1954, the PAP started out as a radical and anti-colonial coalition of left-wing pro-communist forces and English-educated moderates. This union of temporary political convenience in which the pro-communists mobilised mass electoral support through their organisations and the moderates largely comprised the leadership saw the PAP elected to power in 1959. However, an unprecedented split in 1961 when the pro-communists defected and formed a new party, the Barisan Sosialis (Socialist Front), stripped the party of much of its social base and organisational capacity. The collapse of the merger with the Federation of Malaysia in 1965 left in tatters the government plan to access a prospective common market, a central plank of the PAP development strategy. However, not only did the party survive these political and economic crises, it also succeeded in establishing its hold on power by co-opting the upper echelons of the bureaucracy and thus fusing party and state instrumentalities. Equally importantly, it fostered grassroots para-political institutions as an important way to disseminate and achieve party policies and secure and broaden political support.[9] In the 1960s and 1970s, PAP elites consolidated centralised and co-ordinated political apparatuses that facilitated the control of society and the dominance of the party.[10] These underpinned the uninterrupted rule of the PAP, first under the leadership of Lee Kuan Yew, then from 1990, Goh Chok Tong, and from 2004, Lee Hsien Loong—the eldest son of Lee Kuan Yew. The party exercised such a pervasive influence over the country that it defined the character of the political regime and shaped a political economy that was supportive of that regime.

A centralised and coherent organisational structure within the PAP began to emerge during its formative years and was strengthened over subsequent decades. A salient defining feature of such a structure was the extremely high centralisation of policy authority. The basic units of the party were branches organised to coincide with electoral constituencies and clustered around district committees. Not only did branches and indeed the whole party bureaucracy remained limited in their functions, they also had little say in party policies and strategies, reflecting the desire of PAP leaders to prevent the pro-communists from capturing grassroots organisations to dominate the party, particularly in the 1960s (Chan 1989: 71–82; Milne and Mauzy 1990: 84–88). Electoral participation and support were promoted more through parapolitical organisations, as noted earlier, than through party branches. More significantly, policy formation was detached from the wider party organisation and became the total preserve of the Central Executive Committee (CEC) of the PAP. While local party organisations were rejuvenated and their roles were enhanced in the 1980s (Chan 2000), their policy influence within the party remained minimal.

Unique to the internal organisation of the party was the cadre system through which the CEC appointed cadre members, who in turn elected most CEC members. Cadre members, whose number was believed to stand at about 1000 in the late 1990s (*ST* 4 April 1998: 3), fulfilled crucial organisational functions and constituted the backbone of the PAP. The system, which was designed to stem any hostile takeover attempts by the pro-communists, significantly contributed to the development of a cohesive party caucus (Pang 1971: 58–59; *WSJ* 7 November 1990: A14). However, the cadre operated under the aegis of the CEC, which consisted of 12 members elected at bi-annual party conferences and a maximum of six co-opted members. The committee, which largely overlapped with the cabinet in terms of membership and exercised direct control over the parliamentary-ministerial wing, was the epicentre of power in the PAP (Chan 1985; Mauzy and Milne 2002: 40–44). The most powerful position within the CEC and indeed the whole party was that of the secretary-general, who was concurrently the prime minister. He played a leading role in shaping and determining major policy positions, in consultation with a small subgroup of the CEC. The preponderance of his authority derived primarily from his dominance over the formation of the CEC, the appointment of cadre members and the selection of parliamentary candidates, as will be made clear below.

The organisational centralisation of the PAP was maintained through an extremely rigorous and highly centralised process through which its election candidates were selected. From the 1970s, PAP leaders developed and refined a formal and institutionalised method of short-listing and fielding the best people to stand in general elections. The multistage process comprised several rounds of formal and informal talks and interviews in which the track record, character, commitment and capacity of prospective candidates were thoroughly and extensively examined by senior party officials and the selection committee of PAP ministers. Those who went through all these stages were finally interviewed and selected by the PAP secretary-general and his close associates before the CEC endorsed the selected candidates (Mauzy and Milne 2002: 46–49; Ooi 1998: 371–373; *ST* 18 August 1988: 14, 12 October 1996: 34). The entire process was so centralised that party branches and district organisations had no say in the nomination of candidates. Similarly, PAP leaders formalised and centralised their approach to gleaning the most loyal and promising candidates for the cadre from the regular membership rolls. Potential cadre members were first vetted by members of the CEC and then subjected to a battery of psychological tests before the secretary-general himself made final decision on their promotion to cadre status (*ST* 4 April 1998: 3; *WSJ* 7 November 1990: A14).

The strong effects of centralised power structure and candidate selection on the organisational cohesion of the PAP were also reinforced by the highly controlled manner in which party finances were managed. From its inception, the PAP derived much of its finances, including campaign funds, from regular contributions by its members of parliaments and ministers, while it also received political donations from other groups and individuals. In comparison to other political parties in Singapore, the PAP was able to secure stable and independent sources of funds and maintained a healthy financial position. As a growing number of PAP members of parliament became top executives and directors in the corporate sector in the 1980s and 1990s, they made enhanced contributions to the party coffers (*ST* 10 December 1994: 32). The PAP headquarters was directly responsible for collecting and allocating funds strictly in line with the dictates of the CEC and the secretary-general (Mutalib 2004: 261; Ooi 1998: 373–378; Pang 1971: 29–31; *ST* 22 July 1989: 3, 15 January 1992: 27). PAP branches raised their own funds mainly by providing a range of social services, and most of them managed to attain financial self-sufficiency. However, the headquarters exercised controls over the fund-raising and other activities of branches, not only because local members of parliaments who were cadre members chaired branch committees but also because the CEC approved all committee members.

Tight and effective controls over the policy apparatuses of the PAP, selection of election candidates and cadre members and allocation of funds enabled party leaders to impose discipline on party backbenchers. These controls provided them with crucial institutional instruments with which to compel party officials and members, both ordinary and cadre, to toe the party line and align their preferences and priorities with those of the party. Party leaders strictly enforced the PAP's disciplinary code of conduct, traditionally through the party whip that mandated members to side completely with the party position in electoral, legislative and government policy processes. The PAP was thus able to prevent members from defecting from its collective goals and rein in particularism, while promoting policies that benefited the party as a whole. This does not suggest that party members and PAP members of parliament had no disagreements with party leaderships; indeed, some openly criticised legislative motions, party policies or government bills and even abstained occasionally in parliamentary votes (*BT*-Singapore 25 August 1986: 1; Mutalib 2002). However, they eventually had no choice but to fall in with the party position or face the prospect of being denied career advancement, promotion to cadre status or access to financial resources, or even being expelled from the party (*BT*-Singapore 28 August 1994: 2; Ho 2003: 196–197; Mutalib 2004: 281).

The centralised intra-party organisational configurations of the PAP accompanied and indeed contributed to the high internal cohesion of the party. Extremely strong leadership and concentrated policy authority lent PAP elites powerful leverage with which to make party officials and members privilege party-centred strategies and therefore cultivate a strong and distinct party label. From the time of its inception, the PAP attached great importance to the development of clear party reputations and evolved, over the ensuing years, into the only coherent and cogent party with well-defined and stable policy objectives in the Singapore political arena (Chan 1985, 1989). While avowedly non-ideological, the PAP was able to craft and sustain programmatic and durable platforms on bureaucratic development, social progress and economic advancement that gained the party considerable credibility with the electoral populace. The ability of PAP leaders to promote and protect the value of the party label and reputation remained crucial to their efforts to maintain the hegemonic position of the PAP government (Mauzy and Milne 2002: 51–65; Milne and Mauzy 1990: 109–114).

PAP politicians, particularly cadre members and members of parliament, were highly concerned with the party reputation and with platforms that delivered their electoral success and advanced their political careers. They demonstrated strong and long-term loyalty to the party; party switching, while not uncommon among many opposition parties, never happened within the PAP during the period under consideration in this book. In the one-party dominant system in which the PAP controlled enormous institutional and political resources while the poorly organised and funded opposition enjoyed little prospect of ever winning power, defections from the ruling party amounted to being politically suicidal. However, it should be noted that party members were unpaid volunteers and received no fringe benefits, although grassroots leaders received such rewards as housing and school admission priority and limited parking in Housing Board estates (Mauzy and Milne 2002: 41). The loyalty of ordinary members did not guarantee promotion within party ranks or candidacy in general elections, as ministerial and electoral candidates were often recruited from outside the party and directly elevated into the leadership positions of various levels. PAP members nevertheless contented themselves with this arrangement and remained long-standing and staunch party supporters.

The organisational coherence of the PAP also manifested itself in the absence of intra-party rivalries, with the exception of the late 1950s and early 1960s. Party-centred electoral rules were an important contributing factor. Prior to 1988, Singapore operated with the electoral system of single-member districts with plurality voting. Strongly encouraging campaigns on the basis of party affiliation, this system committed party members to prioritise PAP strategies and placed a premium on party unity. Since then, Singapore has combined a handful of single-member districts with Group Representation Constituencies (GRCs), each with three to six seats.[11] GRCs could only be contested by teams of candidates from the same party; voters cast a single vote for a team rather than for individual candidates. This minimised any inter-candidate competition, typical of multi-member electoral systems, which might have weakened party unity.

The importance of electoral rules should not be overemphasised, however, as opposition parties that operated under the same system remained far less unified and were often plagued by severe intra-party clashes. It was centralised organisational structures rather than anything else that fostered the allegiance of individual politicians to party-centred strategies and enabled PAP leaders to mobilise party members to throw their weight behind their policy priorities. The highly controlled process through which cadre members were selected helped screen out those who had different world views and might deviate from party platforms; strong party discipline, strictly administered through the party whip, also deterred potential mavericks from going against the party line. While disputes did occur among cadre members and within the CEC, they were usually concluded with unanimous decisions, largely through reasoned consensuses. More often than not, these disputes were not so much over general policy principles and goals as over imple-mentation specifics.[12] The central decision-making apparatus of the PAP was so compact and coherent that it enhanced the acculturation of pol-icy values and interests among party elites.[13] The resulting institutional cohesion invariably subdued major disagreements and prevented them from developing into open, full-blown intra-party conflicts.

Closely associated with high degrees of party unity within the PAP was the lack of rival cliques or factions that were either based on ideologi-cal differences, policy disagreements, strategic divergences or leadership conflicts. Infighting with the pro-communists in the late 1950s and early 1960s and the associated party splits had had such a traumatic impact on the development of PAP organisations that party leaders made every effort to nip factional activities in the bud (Bellows 1970; Pang 1971). Party controls were so tight, policy processes so centralised and disci-plinary procedures so effective that party members developed a strong sense of the common identity and purpose, and factionalism was thus virtually absent. While the expansion and globalisation of state capi-tal, more specifically government-linked companies (GLCs), might have given rise to diverse interests within the Singapore state, particularly in the 1990s (Worthington 2003), the ruling party itself remained unified and devoid of significant factional rivalry (Ho 2003; Mauzy and Milne 2002; Ooi 1998).

Thailand

For much of the period between the overthrow of the absolute monar-chy in 1932 and the late 1970s, Thai political parties ebbed and flowed, as the country alternated between military and civilian rule. But they began to experience stable development in the 1980s when Thailand gradually retreated from the shadow of long-standing authoritarianism and embarked on the solid yet tortuous process of democratisation. It is the consensus of virtually every scholar of Thai politics that typical political parties, during both authoritarian and more democratic peri-ods, lacked clear and durable platforms, well-funded apparatuses and coherent organisations; instead, they were little more than loose and temporary alliances of factions formed around powerful individuals who worked primarily to win elections.[14] While the Democratic Party, the oldest in Thailand, has often been cited as a partial exception, particu-larly given its relatively wide branch network and clear policy positions, the party was invariably subject to rampant factionalism, poor disci-pline and organisational paralysis. The weaknesses of Thai parties were mainly attributable to the country's long-running military rule, chronic political instability and unpropitious social structures and cultures, and candidate-centred electoral rules.[15]

Formally, Thai political parties comprised branches as the basic organisational units and administrative committees as the central decision-making bodies. Annual party conventions in which party leaderships were selected and policy changes were determined were attended by members of administrative committees, members of parliaments and representatives of party members. In practice, however, responsibilities for formulating and implementing party policies and strategies were significantly diffused throughout the parties. As will be detailed below, all Thai parties featured multiple, long-standing and institutionalised factions that essentially acted as veto players; while party leaders might be heads of the largest factions within parties, they were merely the first among equals. With every major faction exercising veto power over party decisions, the policy-making structure of parties was highly dispersed and the authority of party leaders severely constrained. Furthermore, politicians and factional leaders enjoyed considerable autonomy from administrative committees, primarily because they were more directly dependent upon provincial patrons, personal networks and factions than on parties for electoral and other support (Bowie 2008; Ockey 1994; Sombat 2000; Suchit 1990). This decentralised and localised decision-making authority, and often scattered policy apparatuses among several contending centres of power within parties.

Nowhere was this organisational decentralisation more manifest than in the nomination and selection of candidates in general elections. While administrative or electoral committees were given the formal authority to oversee the recruitment and selection of candidates, parties and party leaders actually exercised weak control over the process. Specific selection procedures might have varied across parties but a general tendency was in evidence: decisions over candidate selection largely rested with factions and regional electoral and vote-canvassing networks. In some parties, local organisations, such as branches or regional committees, were heavily involved in candidate nominations (Anusorn 1998: 425–426; King 1999; Ockey 2004: 32–33). Regional personages who led factions and provincial fixers who controlled electoral networks had the major say in who would be fielded to stand for parliament; so did powerful financiers who supported candidates and factions and even the strongest candidates of parties, who bore crucially upon candidates' electoral performance. Candidate selection was so decentralised that popular and financially robust politicians who expected to run strong campaigns often nominated themselves into the parties of their choice (Anusorn 1998: 425; Hicken 2002: 54).

The manner in which party finances and campaign funds were collected and allocated was similarly decentralised. In theory, Thai political parties derived their income from membership fees and political donations (Anusorn 1998: 427). But in actuality, these only contributed meagrely to party finances, partly because of fluid, unstable and thin membership and partly because of the dearth of close ties between parties and social groups who could provide funds.[16] As a result, the financial position of many parties that typically lacked independent and reliable funding sources was precarious for the most part. While some candidates, particularly new candidates, did receive funds from their own parties, these were barely sufficient to cover the costs of electoral campaigns and other activities. Vote-buying remained endemic and rendered campaigns an increasingly expensive business (Arghiros 1995; Bowie 2008; Callahan and McCargo 1996). More often than not, most politicians depended heavily upon factional bosses and financiers for their financial needs; some teamed up with wealthy members of parliament as an important way of financing their electoral campaigns. Even in those parties in which finances were co-ordinated through party leaderships, the management and allocation of such finances remained firmly in the hands of factional leaders and their regional networks (Chambers 2006a; Hicken 2002; Ockey 1994, 2004: 26; Sombat 2000). The lack of party-generated funds strongly motivated politicians to cultivate and maintain their personal mechanisms of securing funds, weakening the development of centralised party organisations.

The absence of centralised decision-making apparatuses and effective party controls over candidate selection and party finances deprived party leaders of the institutional means by which to impose discipline on backbenchers and rein in the rank and file. The several constitutions effected prior to the late 1990s required party members, particularly members of parliament, to obey party rules and resolutions and respect administrative committee decisions; but in practice it was extremely difficult for party leaders to enforce these requirements. Members in most Thai political parties disobeyed the will of the party majority, routinely and openly defied party leaderships and voted against their own parties in electoral processes, virtually with impunity, particularly when party decisions and strategies threatened to harm their personal interests. To the extent that party leaders tried to subject dissenting and rebellious politicians to disciplinary action, most of these politicians either fought back fiercely or simply switched parties, depending on their popularity, financial strength and ability to secure votes (Anusorn 1998: 442–443; Chai-Anan 1986: 255–256; Chambers 2005; McCargo 1997; Suchit 1987: 70–71).

Decentralised organisational structures that typified Thai political parties conformed with and indeed reinforced their structural incoherence. This was manifest, first and foremost, in their weak party labels and murky policy reputations. As controls over financial management, electoral campaigns and career development within parties were highly decentralised and personalised, party leaders were in a very weak position to force members to follow the party line and promote the value of party labels. This strongly encouraged individual politicians to wantonly pursue their particularistic interests but discouraged them from privileging party labels and principles (Hicken 2002: 43–51; King and LoGerfo 1996: 112; Kuhonta 2004; Suchit 1990). Furthermore, the Thai electoral system that featured multi-seat and multi-vote plurality prior to the 2001 general elections fostered intra-party electoral rivalries, generated incentives for developing personalised strategies and enhanced particularism. Politicians did not campaign on partisan platforms and reputations but on candidate-focused appeals, with the view to differentiating themselves from their co-partisans and building their narrow bases of electoral support (Ammar and MacIntyre 2001; Hicken 2002: 38–57). The labels of political parties were so weak and their informational content was so diluted that the majority of voters had little familiarity with leading parties and their platforms. As a result, voters voted on the basis of personal strategies rather than party labels; they invariably split their votes for candidates from different parties, disregarding their party affiliations (Anusorn 1998: 443; Hicken 2002: 52–57).

Coupled with weak party labels was the enduring lack of clearly defined and substantive policy positions, let along ideologies, among Thai political parties. Party platforms were notable for their absence of credible and distinctive policy content; to the extent that some platforms did have policy content, they were essentially parochial in character. The manifestos of most parties were so similar that they did not display any clear distinctions and were largely interchangeable. Party platforms were kept vague and non-committal so that politicians were able to change them in line with their erratic and whimsical interests. While some parties campaigned on detailed policy platforms during elections and even announced policy statements following the opening of new parliaments (King and LoGerfo 1996; Murray 1996), these were largely campaign tools designed to woo voters and did not represent genuine policy commitments. They had little constraining effect on the opportunistic behaviour of politicians who would throw their policy platforms and statements to the winds as the occasion demanded (McCargo 2000: 103–106).

The absence of strong party labels and durable and credible party platforms suggested that individual politicians could not depend upon partisan reputations and appeals for securing votes and advancing political careers. Atomised campaign organisations and personalised party finances needed to pursue candidate-centred strategies discouraged politicians from developing long-term party identification and institutionalised strong and perennial centrifugal tendencies among Thai parties. As a direct result, most politicians had little incentive to remain loyal to their parties once elected; they were far more faithful to their factions and vote-canvassing networks (Anusorn 1998; Chambers 2005; Hicken 2002: 52–53). They regarded party affiliations as the expedient way to win elections, seize cabinet portfolios and pocket state resources. They thus jumped ship when offered more lucrative deals by other parties or factions; they could be easily bought or lured away by promises of gaining the best material rewards. The upshot was that party switching by both candidates and factions, particularly prior to elections, remained prevalent. In each election between 1983 and 1995, for instance, an average of 38 per cent of members of parliament switched parties; elections in 1996 and 2001 also saw the massive defection of individual candidates and factions (King 1997; Murray 1997; Ockey 2003).

Low levels of organisational coherence among Thai parties were also an important function of intra-party rivalries between leaderships, factions and individual members. Prior to the late 1990s, the electoral system that comprised multi-vote and multi-seat districts allowed voters to vote for candidates rather than parties and pitted candidates from the same party against each other in electoral processes, as noted earlier. While parties nominated an entire slate of candidates and encouraged them to campaign as a team, candidates often campaigned against their co-partisans, primarily because it was the number of votes they garnered individually that was crucial to their election (Anusorn 1998; Hicken 2002). Electoral competition was particularly fierce in multi-member districts, in which individual candidates competed with more members both of the opposition and their own parties. Furthermore, intra-party rivalries may have reflected a lack of elite cohesion not only within parties but also within the military, bureaucracy and business community. As suggested by Case (2002: 150–165), relatively favourable systemic environments and weak independence movements contributed to elite-level disunity and even warring in Thai political parties as in other key socio-political organisations.

Intra-party rivalries both derived from and contributed to the rise and persistence of party factions. Factions were institutionalised in that they had their distinct constituent bases of support, maintained dedicated regional electoral and vote-canvassing networks and ran their candidates in general elections, sometimes under their own labels. While Thai factions tended to be organisationally fluid, they were far more cohesive than highly unstable and short-lived parties and tended to stick together despite their frequent switches across parties. Members, particularly core members, of those factions that were based on close personal ties, common electoral networks and shared financial support tended to be loyal to their factional leaders (Ockey 1994, 2004: 34–37). Furthermore, factions and factional strife constituted a primary defining feature of virtually every Thai party. The Democratic Party, the oldest and best organised of any party in Thailand, split numerous times under both authoritarian and more democratic regimes, mainly because it could not control internal factionalism (*BP* 10 March 2005: 6; McCargo 1997: 122–124; Neher 1988: 197–198). Factions were so ubiquitous in the Thai political arena that they significantly outnumbered parties in parliament at any given time. Between 1979 and 2001, for example, there were more than 20 parliamentary factions, as compared to about six parliamentary parties (Chambers 2005: 500).

In the early 2000s, party organisational structures displayed profound changes, although important continuities existed. These changes were embodied in the TRT. One crucial change was that policy authority became increasingly centralised in the hands of the TRT leader, Thaksin Shinawatra, who essentially ran party affairs in conjunction with a small coterie of advisors. Some scholars (Chamber 2005; Hicken 2006, 2009) have attributed growing policy centralisation to the provisions of the 1997 constitution, which gave greater powers to party leaders over factions and significantly reduced the veto power of factions over party policies. Others (Ockey 2003) have emphasised the importance of the financial crisis of 1997–1998 that enervated the financial positions of factional leaders, strengthening the ability of Thaksin, arguably the country's wealthiest tycoon, to rein in their behaviour. While the debate is certainly interesting, the consensus of most analysts of Thai politics has been that the TRT had a more concentrated policy-making structure than all of its counterparts in the past (see, for example, Kuhonta 2008; McCargo and Ukrist 2005; Pasuk and Baker 2004). For the most part, policy formulation was centralised through the increased power of Thaksin as both the party leader and prime minister rather than through the strengthening of formal party organisations. In the TRT, as in other Thai parties, the roles of the administrative committee and party conventions in the policy process remained weak.[17]

However, the centralisation of policy authority was tempered by at least two old institutional patterns. First, Thaksin achieved electoral success in large part by convincing many factions with existing electoral networks to run under the TRT banner. While his formidable financial resources increased the party's leverage over factions, Thaksin failed to build an effective and extensive electoral organisation of his own, particularly in provinces, and had no choice but to rely upon factional leaders and their local networks for ensuring his electoral victories. The policy influence of factional leaders and provincial politicians who controlled the votes thus remained potent within the TRT. Second, the TRT was heavily imbued with internal conflicts among a dozen factions over party executive positions, legislative posts and cabinet portfolios. Thaksin's strategy to craft a grand, multi-faction coalition limited the ability of any single faction to destabilise his government (*BP* 31 January 2002: 2; Ockey 2003). But to hold such a coalition together and ensure that it functioned as an effective and cohesive governing body would have meant that Thaksin was under constant pressure to concede to the demands of major factions (*BP* 31 July 2002: 9, 22 March 2005: 3, 2 August 2005: 3; Chambers 2006a, 2006b).

While policy-making processes within the TRT were considerably centralised, party controls over candidate selection were less so. The new constitution of 1997 introduced a mixed-member and two-tier system, with 400 of the parliament's 500 seats elected from single-member districts by plurality rules and the remainder chosen from a single nationwide constituency by proportional representation. TRT leaders had much say in the nomination of national list candidates and largely controlled the order in which these candidates were elected. However, party controls were much weaker when it came to the selection of single-member district candidates. Given that electoral networks remained largely in the hands of factions and regional groups, factional leaders, financial backers and local notables were still influential in the selection of candidates in their own areas and were able to field their hand-picked politicians. Many TRT members of parliament, elected from single-seat constituencies in the 2001 and 2005 elections, were either former members of parliament or their relatives and close aides who were nominated and supported by factions and local networks (Croissant and

Dosch 2003; Croissant and Pojar 2006; Nelson 2005; Ockey 2003). This strongly suggests that factional leaders and provincial barons still held sway over who would stand for parliament.

The same holds true for the manner in which party finances were managed. Unlike the average Thai political party, which was financially strapped, the TRT boasted enormous and stable resources; it lavished money on member recruitment, electoral campaigns and populist projects. However, this reflected not so much the development of formal and effective party apparatuses to collect and manage finances as the immensity of Thaksin's personal wealth. While the TRT provided more campaign funds to its candidates than any other parties, particularly to those who had close ties with the upper echelons of the party leadership, many TRT politicians had to secure their own funds. As in the past, most of these funds came from factional bosses, provincial barons and local network leaders (Nelson 2005; Somchai 2008: 114). Despite the electoral reforms of the late 1990s, money politics and vote-buying, albeit conducted in a more careful and subtly different manner, remained alive and rampant, bringing pressure upon politicians, including those from the TRT, to develop and maintain their own source of funds (Callahan 2005; Ockey 2003, 2004: 44–45). Thus, the key roles of factions and electoral networks in financing the campaigns and other activities of many of their candidates did not change significantly. Funds continued flowing directly from financial backers to individual politicians, largely bypassing the TRT headquarters and the formal party organisation remained secondary to personal and factional networks in the collection and allocation of party finances.[18]

The subdued influence of factions over party policies, enhanced party controls over the selection of candidates and Thaksin's financial power appear to have strengthened the hands of TRT leaders to impose discipline on party officials and members. As politicians obtained electoral advantages by campaigning under the TRT banner and were partly dependent upon the party for funds, they had incentives to be attuned to the preferences and priorities of party leaders. On the other hand, however, the continued influence of factions and local networks on party strategies, the selection of constituency candidates and the collection of party finances emboldened factional leaders and even individual politicians to challenge party positions when they threatened to undermine their personal interests. For example, when the deputy leader of a small constituent party of the coalition was denied a cabinet seat after the 2001 election, he went on the offensive, openly criticising the policies of the Thaksin government (*BP* 26 February 2001: 1; *Nation*

7 February 2001: 7); rival factions continuously accused each other of engaging in corruption and vote-buying, defying the repeated warnings from Thaksin that he would take disciplinary action against the mudslingers (*BP* 16 November 2002: 5, 17 March 2004: 3, 1 April 2005: 1); the leader of a powerful faction who was marginalised in TRT policy processes lashed out, in public, at the incompetency of Thaksin's close associates and even the authoritarian leadership style of Thaksin himself, much to the chagrin of the latter (*BP* 22 March 2005: 7, 5 June 2005: 2).

Concomitant with enhanced organisational centralisation, the TRT also became increasingly cohesive. This was reflected primarily in the ability of TRT leaders to build and protect the party label and in their proclivity to stake out clear policies on salient socio-economic issues with which voters were concerned. While some scholars (Nelson 2007; Pasuk and Baker 2004, 2008) see these policies largely as campaign tools to attract voters, many others (Albritton 2006; Hicken 2006; Kuhonta and Mutebi 2006; Orathai 2002) contend that these signified a crucial departure from normal Thai party behaviour. In electoral processes at least, not only did the TRT differentiate itself from other parties by developing distinctive policy platforms, it also campaigned seriously on these platforms. Stronger party controls over policies, legislative careers and finances enabled TRT leaders to align the preferences of candidates to party-centred strategies and promote partisan appeals as the primary cue for voters. On the other hand, the sustained electoral victories of the TRT, which were partly attributable to the efforts of its leaders to establish credible policy reputations (McCargo 2002; Somchai 2008), generated incentives for TRT candidates to privilege the value of the party label.

However, the increased importance of party reputations and policies by no means suggests that particularism and personalism were absent in electoral and legislative processes. While national list candidates had greater incentives to campaign on party platforms and concentrated their energies on issues of national importance, their constituency counterparts who represented local districts were still motivated to cultivate personal support bases and pursue candidate-centred strategies. Such motivation was further enhanced by a dramatic reduction in the size of electoral districts and the average number of votes needed to win a parliamentary seat brought about by the 1997 constitution. Smaller districts placed a premium on the ability of politicians, particularly those who had been little known in previously bigger electorates, to build and maintain local support (Hicken 2006; Somchai 2008: 112). The continued dependence of many TRT candidates on factions and local networks for campaign funds and electoral support ensured that incentives to supplant party-focused platforms and strategies with personal appeals remained. As a result, both national list and constituency politicians pursued particularistic interests on the campaign trail and in office at the cost of party reputations (McCargo and Ukrist 2005; Mutebi 2008; Thanee and Pasuk 2008).

The growing organisational coherence of the TRT was also a function of individual politicians and factions being unable and unwilling to switch parties in the run-up to general elections. Some scholars (Chambers 2006a, 2006b; Hicken 2006) who emphasise the causal importance of formal electoral rules argue that the provisions of the 1997 constitution placed new restrictions on defections from the TRT.[19] Others (Nelson 2007; Ockey 2004; Pasuk and Baker 2004), who look to socio-economic factors for explanations, contend that the effective campaign strategies and widespread popularity of the TRT and Thaksin's enormous financial resources created such powerful centripetal effects that they propelled various factions and politicians into hanging together. Whatever the reasons, the TRT became the first party in the post-war history of Thai politics that did not suffer any significant defections. However, this should not be taken to suggest that individual politicians and factions developed long-term loyalty to the TRT and its leaders. They joined and stayed with the TRT not so much because they shared policy concerns but because the party provided them with greater prospects of winning seats and gaining access to state resources. When the TRT ceased to offer these material deals, politicians were likely to switch parties. Indeed, many factions defected and joined new parties following the dissolution and re-organisation of the TRT in May 2007.

The strengthening of party cohesion within the TRT stemmed further from the sharp decline of intra-party competition in electoral processes. Under the provisions of the 1997 constitution, Thailand moved to a two-tier electoral system—single-seat constituencies combined with a national party list, as mentioned above. This system encouraged voters to focus more on parties and their policies and prevented co-partisans from competing with each other for votes, significantly reducing the intra-party rivalries that had instigated personalised campaign strategies (Hicken 2006).

While intra-party competition on the campaign trail became subdued, factional infighting within the TRT remained very much alive. Despite the enhanced powers of TRT leaders over factional bosses, factions continued struggling over various government, party and parliamentary posts and opportunities to seek rents for themselves and their local constituencies. No sooner had the TRT come to power following the 2001 election than its different factions got embroiled in intensive conflicts over cabinet portfolios and legislative positions. Equally importantly, the rival factions of the party ran against each other in local government elections and differentiated themselves by different campaign colours and suffixes to the party label (Nelson 2005; Pasuk and Baker 2004: 192–195). Inter-faction conflicts persisted throughout the first Thaksin administration and intensified prior to the 2005 elections when the total number of factions in the TRT swelled to 15. Such conflicts encouraged factional leaders and their key members to develop faction-focused rather than party-oriented strategies that centred on the maintenance of their local networks and the delivery of benefits to their local supporters. These strategies strengthened the weight of rival factions against each other within the TRT but worked against the efforts of its leaders to develop a more coherent political party.

Variations in party strength

The preceding discussions highlight variations both across Malaysia, Singapore and Thailand and over time in Thailand in terms of the two key intra-party dimensions—organisational centralisation and coherence—that constitute party strength. During the period under consideration in this book, the PAP, the long-standing ruling party in Singapore, remained highly centralised, as it exercised tight and effective controls over party policies, candidate selection and party finances and was able to impose effective discipline on party members. High levels of organisational centralisation enabled PAP leaders to protect the party label, prevent defections and maintain party unity, contributing to the structural cohesion of the party. Thai political parties fell at the other extreme prior to the late 1990s. Factional leaders and local political barons played a crucial role in determining policies, selecting candidates and managing campaign funds. Concomitant with organisational decentralisation was the lack of intra-party coherence; the average Thai party was plagued by weak labels, frequent defections and rampant intra-party and factional conflicts. However, these intra-party patterns experienced important changes in 2001–2006 when the TRT developed into an organisationally stronger party. While the TRT was more centralised and coherent, its strength was compromised by continued factional influences over party strategies, candidate nominations and financial management and by persistent and intensive inter-faction rivalries. For much of the period under review here, the UMNO, as the dominant party in the Malaysian ruling coalition, was arrayed between its Singaporean and Thai counterparts. In the early 2000s, both the UMNO and TRT were organisationally similar in that they displayed a mixed pattern of intra-party centralisation and coherence.

The focused and structured comparison of intra-party organisations in the three countries helps to quantify their variations, using the coding scheme contained in the appendix to this chapter. Table 3.2 shows the quantitative indicators of these spatial and temporal variations on the basis of the eight ordinal variables that are used to operationalise party organisational strength, and provides a summary of cross-country differences. The PAP had the strongest organisation, the UMNO was in the middle and Thai parties on average had the weakest intra-party structure. Over the 2001–2006 period the TRT was moving towards the middle of the intra-party organisational spectrum.

Table 3.2   Party organisational strength

	Malaysia	Singapore	Thailand	
	1988–2006	1988–2006	1988–2000	2001–2006
Organisational centralisation				
Policy-making structure	3	3	1	3
Candidate selection and nomination	2	3	1	1
Fund collection and allocation	2	2	0	2
Imposition of discipline	2	3	0	1
Organisational coherence				
Party labels	2	3	0	2
Loyalty and party switching	2	3	0	2
Intra-party competition	1	3	1	2
Party factionalism	1	3	0	1
Overall score for party organisational strength	15	23	3	14

While relatively crude, these calibrations point to basic and highly consequential variations among the party organisational configurations of the three countries.

Central hypothetical propositions

This chapter has measured and compared Malaysia, Singapore and Thailand with regard to their variations in party system centralisation and party organisational strength. Table 3.3 clearly demonstrates that the three countries differed systematically in terms of these inter-party and intra-party dimensions. These differences both across countries and over time lead to three central propositions on the basis of the theoretical arguments about the impact of political parties on the orientation, decisiveness and resoluteness of capital market reforms developed in the preceding chapter.

First, the highly concentrated party system combined with the cohesively organised PAP to generate strong incentives for political elites in Singapore to pursue public-regarding policies through capital market reforms. UMNO politicians were likely to have weaker incentives to do so than their PAP counterparts, as the less centralised and cohesive UMNO would temper the strong reform incentives that might have derived from the concentrated party system in Malaysia. Prior to the late 1990s, Thai politicians would be expected to have the weakest propensity to enact growth-enhancing market reforms, primarily because of the fragmented party system and decentralised and incoherent parties in coalition governments. To the extent that they were interested in market reforms, they were more likely to use reform processes as a vehicle for seeking rents for their strategic constituencies. While their propensity to provide reforms would increase in 2001–2006 when the party system

Table 3.3 Variations in inter-party and intra-party structures

		Party system concentration		Party organisational strength	
		Quantitative indicator[a]	Qualitative judgement	Quantitative indicator	Qualitative judgement
Malaysia	1988–2006	1.0	High	15	Medium
Singapore	1988–2006	1.0	High	23	High
Thailand	1988–2000	4.6	Low	3	Low
	2001–2006	1.4	High	14	Medium

[a] This refers to the Molinar index.

was increasingly concentrated and the TRT became more cohesive, incentives to pursue particularistic interests were expected to remain.

Second, the more concentrated party systems in Singapore and Malaysia would render their political leaders more capable than their Thai counterparts to initiate market reform policies decisively and effectively. But the ability of Thai policy-makers to introduce and enact quick and decisive market reforms was likely to be greater in the early 2000s, as the Thai party system became significantly more concentrated. Third, the centralised and coherent organisational structure of the PAP was most likely to generate a consistent and successful reform of the capital market in Singapore. While the intra-party weaknesses of Thai parties created little commitment to market reforms prior to the late 1990s, the increased cohesion of the ruling party was likely to lead to greater reform resoluteness in 2001–2006. In Malaysia, the mixed organisation structure of the UMNO that was more centralised and coherent than Thai parties but less so than the PAP was expected to produce a middling record in sustaining capital market reforms over time.

The theoretical model of this book that considers the effects of party system structures in close interaction with those of party organisational attributes provides a powerful perspective on the causal linkage between political parties and financial policy changes. As will be shown in the following three chapters, variations across Malaysia, Singapore and Thailand and over time within Thailand in the processes and outcomes of capital market reforms closely followed the hypothesised policy patterns for different inter-party and intra-party organisational configurations.

Appendix

The index of party organisational strength is the sum of eight separate indices of organisational centralisation and coherence. The codings are based on a four-point scale and permit a total range of the index of the lowest score of zero to the highest score of 24. The coding rules are as follows:

Organisational centralisation

Policy-making structure

0. Party leaders or national committees have little or no control over policy formulation; responsibilities for making major policies are diffused throughout the party.

1. Major policies are formulated by party leaders at the national level, but they are subject to significant influence by local organs, intermediate organisations or factions.
2. Party leaders formulate and determine major policy positions through party congress and national committees or in consultation with local or intermediate party leaders.
3. Party leaders determine major policies on their own or sometimes in consultation with a small coterie of national committee members; they have the final say in the policy process without any participation from other party organs or factions.

Candidate nomination and selection

0. Candidates are nominated and selected by local organs or factions; party leaders have no or little control or influence over the nomination and selection processes.
1. Party leaders and national committees select candidates in consultation with local party organs or factions and may defer to the preferences of local party or factional leaders on the selections.
2. Local party organisations or factions may be able to nominate candidates, but party leaders make final decisions on the selection of candidates through candidate selection councils or national committees.
3. Party leaders select candidates with no or little participation or influence by local organs, factions or even national committees and party councils.

Fund collection and allocation

0. Party funds are collected and managed primarily by local party organs or factions with no or little control by party leaders or party headquarters.
1. Both local organs and headquarters are responsible for collecting funds; funds are allocated through co-ordination and consultation between local organs and party headquarters.
2. Funds are collected and allocated primarily by party headquarters, but local organisations or factions have some or considerable latitude in managing their own finances.
3. Party headquarters exercise primary responsibility for collecting, allocating and managing funds.

Imposition of discipline

0. Party leaders or executive committees are devoid of disciplinary means; there are no or little centralised and effective mechanisms by which party members can be subject to disciplinary action.
1. Party leaders have some disciplinary techniques and means at their disposal, but the administration of discipline is neither centralised nor effective.
2. Party leaders or party committees possess a range of disciplinary techniques and administer them either largely independently or in co-ordination with other party organs; the imposition of disciplinary actions is relatively effective.
3. Party leaders or party committees administer a whole range of disciplinary means and techniques in a centralised and effective manner.

Organisational coherence

Party labels

0. Party labels are vague and erratic; there are strong incentives to pursue personalised strategies and particularistic interests in electoral and policy processes.
1. Party labels are moderately weak and ambiguous; the pursuit of party-focused policies and interests is impeded by relatively strong incentives to resort to personal strategies and appeals on the campaign trail as well as in office.
2. Party labels and platforms are largely clear and stable; while party-focused rules and strategies often obtain, incentives to pursue personal interests remain.
3. Party labels are clearly-defined, stable and credible; there are no or few incentives to cultivate personal reputations and privilege candidate-oriented interests in electoral and policy processes.

Loyalty and party switching

0. Party members have no loyalty to parties; party switching is rampant.
1. Party members have relatively low loyalty to parties; they switch parties whenever the occasion demands.
2. Party members remain largely loyal to parties; party switching takes place occasionally during the critical junctures of major party realignments or splits.

3. Party members have long-term loyalty to parties; party switching rarely or never happens.

Intra-party competition

0. Intra-party competition is fierce and persistent across all levels of the party organisation during both national and party elections.
1. Rivalries among party leaders and members remain at all levels of the party organisation during either national or party elections.
2. Intra-party competition occasionally occurs at some levels of the party organisation during either national or party elections.
3. There is little or no competition among co-partisans during both national and party elections.

Party factionalism

0. Factions are highly organised, independent and long-standing; there is persistent infighting among multiple factions within the party. The party acts merely as a multi-party façade and remains highly divided.
1. Factions are somewhat institutionalised and independent; frequent conflicts between a large number of factions weaken party unity.
2. Factions are ephemeral and loosely organised; factional rivalries are so infrequent and moderate that the party remains largely unified.
3. No or little factionalism; the party is so centralised and unified as to preclude factions.

4
Singapore: Market Reform Success

This chapter examines how party system structures shaped capital market reforms in tandem with internal party organisations in Singapore from the late 1980s to the late 2000s. The central claim is that the highly concentrated party system and the centrally and coherently organised PAP combined to both generate strong incentives for political elites to pursue public-regarding reform policies and enable them to initiate and implement these policies decisively and resolutely. The first section briefly describes the development of policies and regulations concerning the capital market in Singapore prior to the late 1980s to provide a foundation for examining market changes and reforms over the ensuing two decades. The second section explores the process through which major market reforms were enacted from the late 1980s to the mid-1990s, and the third section focuses on further and more significant reforms following the Asian financial crisis of 1997–1998. The fourth and final section concludes.

The pre-reform capital market: Policies and regulations

By the mid-1980s, Singapore boasted a more open and robust financial sector than most developing economies in East and Southeast Asia. This was an important function of consistent and successful government efforts to prioritise financial development as a strong complement to industrial growth, and to develop the city-state into a regional and even global financial centre. From the late 1960s when the Asian dollar market in which domestic and foreign banks engaged in offshore businesses through their Asian currency units was established, the Singapore government made steady progress in liberalising and internationalising the financial system. Over the 1970s and early 1980s, it deregulated interest rates, dismantled exchange controls and reduced barriers to foreign entry into the domestic financial sector in a quick succession. In parallel to these liberalisation efforts, the government enacted a wide range of preferential regulatory and fiscal policies to encourage foreign participation and boost the growth of the offshore banking sector. So much so that Singapore had emerged as an eminent international financial hub by the 1980s, rivalling such East Asian counterparts as Tokyo and Hong Kong.

However, policy reforms and market changes were primarily centred on the expansion of commercial and offshore banking businesses; regulatory reforms designed to spur capital market growth were few and far between. The prototype of the Singapore equity market dates back to the beginning of the twentieth century during the colonial era. It was founded as a more formal institution in 1960 and acted as a joint securities market for both Singapore and Malaysia over the following 14 years. It was not until 1973 when parity exchange between the Singapore dollar and Malaysian ringgit terminated that the Stock Exchange of Singapore (SES), as an independent market, came into being. Despite its long history, the stock exchange was not particularly large and active in the1980s. For instance, the average annual ratio of stock market trading to gross domestic product (GDP) was 0.26 in 1981–1985 while the average annual ratio of private credit by deposit money banks to GDP was 0.81 in the same period (MAS, *Annual Reports*, various years). This suggests that loans extended by banking institutions were nearly four times as large as total shares traded on the SES.

The domestic bond markets were also underdeveloped. While the Asian dollar bond market, part of the Singapore offshore financial sector, grew apace, the government and corporate bond markets were lacking in depth and breadth. The primary market for government securities was essentially captive, in that new securities were usually purchased and held until maturity by various financial institutions to fulfil their statutory requirements. New bond issues were not made to finance public-sector deficits, mainly because the Singapore government budget was constantly in surplus. As a result, trading in government securities was sluggish, leading to an inactive secondary market. By the same token, the corporate bond market, albeit long-existing, was small in size and low in trading activity and thus remained on the periphery of the capital market. This was partly because individual investors tended to favour stocks and partly because firms preferred indirect financing through bank loans and offered few bond issues (Lee 1984a: 274–278; Lim et al. 1991: 348–349).

The development of the capital market was particularly hampered by the fragmented regulation of the securities industry. Prior to the mid-1980s, responsibilities for regulating securities and related businesses had been scattered across several agencies, with the Registrar of Companies (ROC) administering the securities industry and company acts; the Securities Industry Council, a consultative body that advised the finance minister on securities-related policies, overseeing the takeovers and mergers of listed companies; and the SES regulating the stock market and stockbrokers. However, the roles of the ROC in the regulatory process remained limited, due to the lack of resources and expertise; the SES was granted the de facto authority to manage and regulate the securities sector in an essentially self-regulatory framework (Tan et al. 1989; Teo 1991). While the Monetary Authority of Singapore (MAS), established in 1971 to fulfil all the central banking functions except currency issuance, was invested with overall financial regulatory powers, it had little formal authority over the regulation of the securities industry. It was only in 1984 when the Securities Industry Act came under the purview of the MAS that it acquired such authority. No sooner had the MAS taken over than it moved to reform the inadequate and ineffective securities regulatory framework. However, the reform effort met with strong resistance from stockbrokers who jealously guarded their operational freedoms and the privileges associated with self-regulation (*FEER* 31 July 1986: 66; MAS, *Annual Report 1985–86*: 34).

The growing prominence of Singapore as an international financial centre in the 1980s also belied the dualistic nature of its financial system—it was world-class competitive for offshore transactions yet heavily dirigiste domestically. From the late 1960s, a whole range of regulatory barriers was erected and maintained to separate the international financial sector structured around the Asian dollar market from the domestic financial system dominated by state-owned institutions and local commercial banks (Bryant 1989; Skully and Viksnins 1987: 61–66; Walter 1993). This approach derived from the desire of policy elites to protect domestic banks and other institutions from excessive external competitive pressures and maintain financial system stability. More importantly, it also reflected the broad objectives of the MAS to retain monetary control over the economy by preventing the internationalisation of the Singapore dollar and to insulate the domestic market from global financial volatilities (Lee 1984b; Lim et al. 1991: 354).

Like the overall financial structure, the capital market in Singapore had both international and domestic components. As noted earlier, the international component, mainly confined to the Asian dollar bond market, was fully liberalised and competitive. By contrast, the domestic component, consisting of the equity and bond markets, was more protected and less competitive. Despite the open capital account regime in Singapore, a plethora of regulatory restrictions had long existed in the securities sector prior to the late 1980s. In the first place, while foreigners were allowed to purchase locally listed securities and remit funds from the securities they bought, various ownership limitations were imposed on stocks in listed firms. Foreign institutional holdings of individual companies' shares were generally capped at a maximum of 49 per cent; the by-laws of specific listed firms often restricted foreign ownership to varying degrees. Equally significantly, foreign brokerage operations in the SES were restricted and majority ownership of local securities companies and stockbrokers by foreigners was disallowed (Holmes and Wong 2001: 375–376; Lim and Fong 1991: 80).

Furthermore, the securities sector had remained largely closed to foreign stockbroking firms and securities houses as well as to domestic banks and non-bank financial institutions in the late 1980s. Regulatory authorities considered the sector to be saturated and were worried about the impact of excessive competition on its stability. The SES and its members constituted the core of an interest alliance that preferred the status quo. Operating as a private club, the local stockbroking community resisted regulatory changes in entry restrictions. Stock exchange rules constrained competition, limited off-exchange dealings and ensured high profit margins, resulting in an oligopolistic market structure (*AF* 15 January 1986: 52–53). Government regulations abetted these developments by preventing other segments of the financial industry from fully participating in the securities markets. Limited market access and little competition turned the SES into one of the 'most profitable cocoons in the world' (*FEER* 23 October 1986: 152).

Not only was market entry restricted, there was also no price competition in the stockbroking industry. The structure of stockbroking commission rates had remained rigid prior to the reform of the equity market. For many years through to the late 1980s, stockbrokers had charged a fixed 1 per cent fee on stock transactions—the highest in the world—regardless of trade volumes (*WSJ* 2 June 1987: 1). While rigid commission rates reflected the desire of regulatory authorities to discourage undue price competition and maintain stability in the securities market, it was also linked to the oligopolistic formation of the stockbroking community. The relatively high degree of industrial concentration in the securities sector led to the cartel-like organisation in which stockbrokers collectively, through the co-ordination of the SES, set commission rates. This practice caused commission rates to respond slowly to market conditions and kept them at an artificially high level, increasing the costs of stock investments, hurting the interests of investors and impeding market growth.

In sum, the capital market of Singapore in the 1980s was less open and developed than its increasingly eminent status as an international financial centre would suggest. The overall financial market structure remained unbalanced, with the rapid expansion of offshore and commercial banking juxtaposed to the lacklustre growth of equity finance. More crucially, there existed a range of regulatory barriers that restricted foreign presence in the capital market, kept the SES closed to new entrants and stifled inter-firm competition in the securities industry.

Market reforms from late 1980s to mid-1990s

In the late 1980s, the Singapore government moved to enact significant regulatory reforms in the securities sector. Market-oriented changes in securities rules liberalised the capital market and began to internationalise the stockbroking industry. These changes involved fostering greater price competition for services, lowering entry obstacles to foreign firms, dismantling regulatory barriers between sectors of the financial industry and privatising government-linked companies (GLCs). The deregulatory measures were not independent of the efforts to strengthen capital market regulation; indeed the former invariably followed or invoked the latter.

The initial move towards capital market reforms was made in the wake of the global recession of the mid-1980s, which generated an unprecedented economic downturn in Singapore. In response to the adverse market shocks, the government made crucial policy revisions that recognised the perils of over-reliance on the manufacturing sector for long-term development and prioritised the capital market and other services industries as the new engine of growth (Ng 1987). The more immediate impetus behind the initiation of market reforms was the securities market crisis that was triggered by the collapse of a major listed company in late 1985. While moving swiftly to stabilise the stock market through short-term measures, the government also enacted long-term policy reforms to strengthen market regulation, increase competition and efficiency in the domestic securities industry and divest state assets as an important way to boost capital market growth (MAS, *Annual Report* 1985/86 and 1987/88).

Economic pressures for capital market reforms were overlain with Singapore's foreign policy imperative of jockeying for regional economic influence and foreign capital in competition not only with Japan and Hong Kong but also with Taiwan, Malaysia and Thailand that began to actively promote their capital cities as the business hubs of Asia-Pacific in the early 1990s. Reforming and fostering the capital market were pivotal to the Singapore government's strategy for maintaining the status of the city-state as an international financial centre. It linked an open and internationalised capital market with its global ambitions so closely that successful market reforms became a linchpin of the strategy (Bryant 1989; Ngiam 1996).

The impact of market pressures is undeniably important, but they fall short of accounting for the direction and outcomes of capital market reforms in Singapore. While external shocks and market crises played a crucial role in prompting the government to initiate market reforms, they did not shape political elites' incentives to pursue public-regarding policies through such reforms. Nor did they directly influence the ability of policy-makers to enact reform programmes decisively in response to adverse economic conditions and, equally importantly, to carry these programmes through to the end. As will be demonstrated in the following analysis, the policy effects of external market forces were mediated through political party structures that ultimately determined the public-regarding orientation and effective approach of capital market reforms in Singapore.

Public-regarding incentives

In Singapore, financial technocrats, especially in the MAS, were often portrayed as the main architects and strong advocates of financial liberalisation in general and capital market reforms in particular. For the most part, however, PAP leaders led rather than followed technocrats in charting an overall and long-term reform strategy (Lim 1998; Tan 2005). While MAS technocrats played a crucial role in the process of market reforms, they received the sustained backing and guidance of political elites who oversaw financial policy and regulatory processes. Richard Hu, a business executive-turned-politician who took the helm of both the MAS and the finance ministry from 1985 to 1997, was a senior figure in the ruling party and a chief lieutenant of Lee Kuan Yew and his successor, Goh Chok Tong. He played a leading role in formulating legal and regulatory changes, enacting market reforms and shepherding reform programmes to effective implementation. More importantly, from the moment when capital market reforms were thrust onto the government agenda, they engaged the full attention of top PAP leaders who were willing and able to marshal the necessary political and institutional support for a coherent and consistent reform effort (Lee 2000: 76–82; Lee 2009).

The policy priorities of political leaders that were closely aligned with national development imperatives defined the orientation of capital market reforms. PAP elites who headed financial and regulatory authorities had strong incentives to pursue reform policies that reflected long-term policy goals rather than immediate political concerns. They had sustained interests in pushing for capital market reforms with a view to fostering a more efficient financial system, expanding the scope of industrial financing and mobilising more resources for economic development (Ghesquiere 2007; Lall and Liu 1997; Lim 1998). Efforts to develop a more market-based and balanced financial structure were thus oriented to enhance the provision of public goods at the national level. The strong desire of political leaders to deliver these public-regarding policies motivated them to put in place reform programmes that limited the play of particularistic interests; official concerns over institutional development and regulatory enforcement constantly prevailed over sectoral demands for policy favours in the reform process (Montes and Tan 1999; Zhang 2003).

The public-regarding orientation of reform policies ensured the stable and sustained growth of a robust capital market in Singapore, with long-term and salutary consequences for the financial sector and the wider economy. Market reforms that were geared towards national development increasingly transformed a traditionally bank-based system into a more market-oriented yet balanced structure in which both banks and equity markets played equally important roles in financial intermediation. Such a structure boosted the provision of long-term industrial financing and the efficiency of resource allocation, which in turn helped to sustain high economic growth in Singapore during the late 1980s and early and mid-1990s (Ariff and Khalid 2000: 110–146; Tan et al. 1989; Walter 1993: 87–112). Furthermore, the well-guarded approach to prioritising regulatory efficiency over market liberalisation fostered a strong and resilient capital market that helped to tide Singapore over a succession of regional and global financial crises in the period under review (Chia 1999; Lim 1999).

Why did Singaporean political leaders and financial policy-makers have strong incentives to enact public goods policies through capital market reforms? Extant scholarly accounts have emphasised the structural power of key economic agents, the policy capabilities of technocrats or the constraining effects of systemic pressures as the major determinants of public-regarding orientation in Singapore's economic policy processes. While not specifically developed to examine the politics of financial policy reforms, they are all minded to address the same question of why PAP elites committed themselves to promoting national development and public welfare and did not take advantage of the concentrated political structure to pursue private-regarding policies. These accounts need to be assessed before the central proposition of this book, which prioritises the causal weight of political parties, can be convincingly advanced.

In her efforts to account for the political sources of rapid and sustained growth in post-war Singapore, Yap (2003) has argued that the PAP government's commitment to economic development was an important function of real and potential threats posed by producers to withdraw economic resources; such threats were more likely to be credible and effective, particularly when policy performance was less than optimal. While theoretically fresh, this argument may hit a number of empirical snags if applied to explain the public-regarding orientation of capital market reforms in Singapore. In the first place, decisions made by key economic agents to withdraw resources would require collection action. The private sector in Singapore was highly fragmented among multinational companies, GLCs and local private firms, which were each organised along different sub-sectoral preferences vis-à-vis specific market reform measures.[1] This resulted in a multiplication of policy interests in the industrial sector and was likely to doom any attempts to make coherent decisions to launch investment strikes, organise effective collective action or constrain the behaviour of financial policy-makers in the reform process.

Furthermore, even if private market agents were able to overcome collective action problems and aggregate their interests effectively, there would be no guarantee that they would mobilise their economic and organisational resources to press for public-regarding policies. As will be demonstrated below, private financiers and industrialists were more prone to pursue particularistic interests and seek regulatory rents through policy changes. If they had had their own way in the process of capital market reforms in Singapore, such reforms might have been growth-impeding and even produced serious market failures. Finally, with the policy influence of private business on the rise in the 1980s and 1990s (Chalmers 1992; Rodan 1997), public officials were indeed faced with growing political constraints. However, these constraints were more apparent in the area of industry policy, where decisions involved line ministries closely linked to their industrial constituencies and thereby susceptible to their influence, than in financial policy where decisions were made in a largely insulated environment. While policy inputs were actively sought from private economic agents in the formation of capital market reforms, financial policies remained controlled and centralised in the hands of political elites.

This last point underscores the importance of looking to the state agencies that dominated the financial and regulatory arenas for the political sources of public-regarding reform policies in Singapore. In her path-breaking research on the governance roles of central banks in Southeast Asia, Hamilton-Hart (2002) has attributed financial stability and economic growth in Singapore to the capacity of MAS technocrats to constrain rent-seeking and pursue corporate goals, a capacity that was developed and entrenched through historically grounded organisational structures such as meritocratic recruitment processes, long-term career paths and rewards, and rationalised policy-making norms. This argument is reminiscent of the administrative state thesis (Chan 1975) that has focused on the apparent shift in power to the bureaucracy that resulted from deliberate government efforts to resolve development problems and promote public welfare through the rational application of decision-making rules and techniques.[2] While different in empirical concerns, these two approaches have both emphasised the importance of bureaucratic organisational structures in orienting the behaviour of individual office-holders towards public policy objectives and in underpinning the success of development strategies in Singapore.

Both of these propositions contain important elements of the truth but are at the same time subtly misleading. Most crucially, they have relegated the ruling party virtually to the edge of political processes and have overemphasised the role of bureaucrats, who were ultimately the agents of politicians. While economic technocrats were co-opted into PAP leadership positions and delegated significant policy authority, such co-option and delegation served to expand and deepen the ruling party's control over the state apparatus. The bureaucracy as a whole remained subordinate to PAP elites who set the overall direction and agenda of economic policies; it was integrated into the wider system of the PAP government that shaped the capacity and status of technocrats as it saw fit.[3] The most dramatic demonstration of party control over the bureaucracy is the re-organisation of the MAS in 1981 and again in 1998 when PAP leaders saw such changes as indispensable to their efforts to reform and develop financial markets (*BT*-Singapore 4 April 1998: 2; Lee 2000: 80–82; Soon and Tan 1993: 27).

In an important comparative study of the origins of developmental states in East Asia, Doner and colleagues (2005) have causally linked the sustained interests of the Singapore government in promoting growth-oriented institutions and policies to the simultaneous presence of extreme geopolitical insecurity, widespread racial riots and severe resource constraints in the 1950s and 1960s. PAP elites confronted these systemic threats not only with political repression but also with significant incentives and capacities to provide public goods necessary for national development. While shedding important light on the political source of developmental commitments in Singapore during the early post-war period, this argument has a depreciating value in explaining the public-regarding orientation of capital market reforms in recent decades.[4] With the end of the Cold War and a significantly improved regional security environment, the construction of a largely harmonious inter-ethnic relationship, and sustained economic growth and enormous financial resources, PAP leaders do not appear to have faced imminent systemic threats during the period under consideration here. The dramatic reduction of both external and internal threats deprived the ruling party of many of the justifications for its politically repressive regime (Haggard 1999b). While challenges posed by globalisation have remained a crucial factor, systemic explanations beg the question of how market forces translated into public-regarding policy outcomes, as is made clear in the preceding analysis.

One political institution that has often been invoked as the crucial intervening variable that rendered PAP politicians strongly inclined to enhance the welfare of their citizenry is elections. Singapore regularly held competitive elections during the period under review, although the freedom and fairness of the electoral process was compromised by structural and institutional obstacles. Some Western observers (Means 1998; Rodan 1996a) have contended that elections in Singapore were merely the trappings of democracy and exerted little pressure on PAP politicians to be accountable to the general public. However, many other scholars (Bellows 1993; Chua 2005; Ghesquiere 2007; Lim 1999; Sebastian 1997) have opined that electoral contestations, while tempered by weak oppositions, tight media controls and contrived electoral barriers, institutionalised incentives for political elites to be responsive to the wishes of voters. At the very least, elections that acted as referenda on the performance of the ruling party forced the PAP government to behave responsibly. Given that the PAP drew crucially on the existence of elections for claiming its governing legitimacy and maintaining its public acceptance, popular demands could be ignored only at serious political cost to the party.

As is clearly shown in these empirical studies, elections in Singapore were more than façades: they constituted the central avenue of political conflicts that shaped the behaviour and strategies of PAP politicians and defined the process and outcomes of national politics. For these reasons, the ruling party invested heavily in the maintenance of extensive and effective electoral networks and the organisation of intense campaign activities. In all general elections, it fought ferociously for every vote even though its victory was already assured on nomination day and the opposition stood no chance of winning office (Chua 1997; *EIUCR*-Singapore 4th Quarter 1996: 11–12; Lim 1999). More importantly, PAP elites were under mounting pressure to maintain political support, particularly in the 1980s and 1990s when the ruling party's margin of electoral victory constantly fell below 70 per cent of the popular vote and when the opposition posed a more significant challenge to the incumbent ruler. The government responded not only with several institutional reforms to the political system but also with an array of policy changes.[5] It can be argued that these reforms and changes merely reflected the efforts of the PAP to bolster its systemic dominance in the face of the sustained electoral decline. However, they were also designed to address a broad range of public concerns and demands from the different sectors of the electorate (Chua 1997; Ho 2003; Vasil 2000).

While electoral politics was certainly associated with institutional arrangements that pressed for accountability on the part of PAP politicians, elections were necessary but insufficient to account for the public-regarding orientation of economic policies in Singapore. Electoral pressure by itself did not preordain whether it would motivate politicians to respond to narrow and localised constituencies or to promote the interests of the broad public in Singapore, as in many other emerging market countries that featured regular and contested elections. The mere presence of electoral contestations was thus inadequate to explain the nature of political choices in the economic policy-making process. This chapter posits that the impact of elections on the incentives of PAP elites to provide public goods policies through capital market reforms was mediated through the configurations of both inter-party and intra-party structures in Singapore.

The institutional profile of political parties provided in the preceding chapter clearly shows that the party system structure in Singapore remained highly concentrated in the 1980s and 1990s. One-party rule by the PAP, which had been installed since independence in 1965, was a central defining feature of the Singapore polity in the ensuing decades. The party established and exercised such a long-running and pervasive control over the country that Singaporeans closely identified the PAP with the government. In the eyes of the general public, the ruling party was not only the national movement but also the sole custodian of the Singapore government and its policy-making efficiency (Vasil 2000). Voters thus held the PAP and its leaders responsible for the impact of government policies and rewarded or punished them for economic outcomes. The PAP largely depended upon the policy performance of the government for sustaining its wide electoral support and its leaders drew readily on the success of economic policies for their political legitimacy (Lim 1999; Low 2006: 32–84; *ST* 17 April 1992: 25). If government policy processes produced suboptimal or negative socio-economic outcomes, the ruling party would have nobody to blame but itself and would thus be held solely culpable. For these reasons, party concentration that forced the PAP to take both the credit and the blame for policies and enhanced the ability of voters to punish the ruling party in elections generated incentives for political leaders to be more civic minded.

This is not to suggest that Singaporean voters enjoyed a completely genuine choice of candidates, mainly because of the lack of a strong opposition and a viable political alterative to the ruling party. Nor does this imply that the lines of vertical accountability between voters and their representatives were as strong in Singapore as those in liberal democracies. Yet given that elections were the central avenue of political contestation and that the PAP sustained its hegemonic position on the basis of the economic policy performance of the government, the concentrated party system singled out the PAP as being ultimately responsible for policy outcomes and provided voters with effective institutional mechanisms by which to exercise their voting power. Voter choices and preferences could be ignored only at the expense of the electorate shifting its political support to the opposition and the PAP losing votes in general elections, as mentioned above. While this might not be suggestive of a change of government, the prospect of declining support pressed PAP leaders to take into account the interests of Singaporean voters and live up to their expectations. 'If we had betrayed the people's trust', Lee Kuan Yew sternly warned (2000: 121), 'we would have been rejected.'

Elections emboldened the voting public to hold political elites answerable for their policies not only through the concentrated party system but also through the strong internal organisation of the PAP. As made clear in the previous chapter, the PAP featured a highly centralised and coherent organisational structure. This structure enabled PAP leaders to develop and maintain clear party labels and provided the electorate with consistent and unequivocal information about the ruling party's position on a range of public policies. Most Singaporean voters were predisposed to choose the PAP over the opposition, primarily because the former maintained the reputation of staking out much clearer and more credible policy programmes. While distinct and stable policy positions helped the ruling party to garner significant electoral advantages, they also made it easier for voters to hold PAP leaders responsible for policy outcomes. Because the PAP developed coherent and credible policy positions, the electorate obtained clear standards by which to judge ruling politicians in elections. Voters easily detected any departures from the long-established and consistent platforms of the PAP and punished the party for policies inconsistent with their preferences by withholding their support. To the extent that the electorate as a whole preferred such public goods policies as capital market reforms, which stood to enhance social welfare, the government had a strong incentive to initiate and enact these policies.

Not only did the concentrated party system and the internal organisational strength of the PAP combine to enhance the ability of the electorate to hold political leaders accountable for the supply of public goods policies, these inter-party and intra-party configurations also reinforced such policy behaviour through their impact on the disposition of PAP elites to seek broad electoral support. While the PAP experienced electoral declines in the 1980s and 1990s, the concentrated party structure was still able to deliver more than 60 per cent of the popular vote. The ability of this structure to win elections with high percentages in the dominant party environment sustained the strong incentive for PAP leaders to mobilise support across all social groups. Centripetal pressures generated by party concentration forced political elites to build and maintain a large coalition of supporters to stay in office. This is attested to in the observation that the Singapore state drew long-running significant support from its broad socio-political base (Crone 1988; Khong 1995). In such a broad coalition, PAP leaders had to pay attention to the mass of Singaporean voters in the middle, or 'to straddle the middle ground' in the words of Lee Kuan Yew (2000: 131). The need to appeal to a wide range of social actors and interests left party leaders with no choice but to fend off the intense preferences from particular interest groups in order to pull more voters together and buttress the PAP's base of political support.

It is thus clear that the concentrated party system that generated large majorities in electoral returns institutionalised the strong inclination of the ruling party to pursue the median voter outcome through its political and policy actions. The resultant large and necessarily cross-cleavage alliance not only motivated PAP politicians to enact policies that mattered to the electorate but also shielded them from political influences by any one particular social group. In other words, as the high degree of party concentration dictated that a majority of the popular vote be required to secure elections, PAP leaders were pressed to be attentive to the broad and diverse preferences of their supporters and restrain the play of particularistic interests in the policy-making process. This explains in part why the Singapore government formed economic policies with the well-being of the general population rather than that of localised constituencies in mind. It invariably aimed at collective national policies that benefited large swathes of the voting public, such as public-sector reforms, low fiscal deficits and technological developments (Jones 2003; Koh and Koh 2002; Lee and Haque 2006) as well as capital market reforms.

On the other hand, PAP elites were fully aware of the consequences of catering to particularised social groups and deviating from public interests; any attempt to make direct overtures to narrow segments of society would undercut the support base of the ruling party and weaken the public acceptance of its governing legitimacy. In office, as on the campaign trail, the desire of the PAP to nurture the broad-based coalition thus led the government to equate accountable policy-making processes with the sustained ability to implement economic strategies for the long-term public good, even if they harmed the interests of specific social groups and were unpopular in the short term. 'As a custodian of the people's welfare, it [the government] exercises independent judgement on what is in the long-term economic interests of the people and acts on that basis...', Goh Chok Tong asserted when expounding a trustee model of government in Singapore. 'The trustee model of democracy that Singapore has subscribed to enabled it to pursue the tough policies necessary for economic development. Indeed, the concept of the government as the trustee went hand in hand with democratic accountability' (*Sunday Times* 24 September 1995: 3).

While party system concentration motivated state elites to be public-regarding, the centralised and coherent structure of the PAP also provided them with political resources with which to align the policy objectives of party members with the corporate interests of the party. Most crucially, PAP leaders who exercised tight controls over party platforms, candidate selection and campaign funds were well positioned to enforce programmatic discipline on the rank and file. They thus acquired the important institutional leverage to orient PAP members and supporters towards promoting public goods policies that enhanced the collective electoral prospects of the PAP (Ooi 1998: 362–373; Singh

2007: 42–47). Furthermore, the PAP, endowed with well-established and effective electoral networks and abundant and independent resources, was able to achieve and sustain electoral effectiveness and success. The strong internal structures that delivered votes and provided financial support ensured that party members were attuned to the priorities of their leaders (*ST* 6 August 1986: 16; Pang 1971: 50–69; Vasil 2000: 30–44). Individual PAP politicians deviated from party platforms at the risk of being kicked out of the party; to defect from the PAP was not only to be consigned to the political wilderness but also to lose various material benefits. The importance of supporting PAP-determined policies encouraged ordinary members to link their career prospects closely to the fortunes of the party and subordinate their individual goals to the dictates of PAP leaders.

This does not mean that the pursuit of localised interests by politicians was completely absent. In Singapore, members of parliament, who acted as mediators between the government and constituents, often found themselves torn between the need to follow PAP-centred strategies and the impulse to pursue the interests of their local constituents (*BT*-Singapore 25 August 1986: 1; Ho 2003: 198–202). Pressures to cater to particularised preferences was mounting in the 1980s and 1990s when many PAP politicians took up executive positions in the corporate sector (*BT*-Singapore 14 February 1991: 1; *ST* 10 December 1994: 32). But in practice, party members in general and members of parliament in particular were concerned more with pursing party strategies than with defending particularistic interests. In financial and regulatory processes, as in social, fiscal and industrial policy arenas, it was the policies and principles of the PAP rather than the private ends of individual politicians that dominated and prevailed (*BT*-Singapore 27 November 1995: 2; Ghesquiere 2007: 49–98; Ho 2003: 232–248; Zhang 2009b). The internal organisational strength of the PAP strengthened the hands of its leaders to constrain any particularism that might have weakened the public-regarding orientation of these policies, and committed PAP politicians to claiming credit as the ruling party for the broad benefits that capital market reforms could deliver.

Decisive market reforms

Not only did PAP leaders have strong incentives to provide public-regarding policies through capital market reforms, they were also capable of initiating such reforms decisively in the face of political obstacles. In Singapore, the concentrated party system that centralised policy authority in the PAP government greatly facilitated the swift and effective enactment of regulatory changes. Given the dominant position of the PAP as the single veto player in the policy process, its leaders operated virtually without any considerable institutional checks on their power to pursue market reforms in line with their policy interests. In the formation of financial market changes, top PAP leaders and technocratic elites made key decisions about the design of legislative strategies and reform programmes. These characteristics of party organisation played a pivotal role in overcoming distributional conflicts associated with the introduction of stock market liberalisation and enabling the government to take new reform initiatives.

Centralised policy-making apparatuses contributed enormously to the ability of the Singapore government to respond quickly to economic and political pressures for capital market reforms at critical junctures. Within two years from late 1986, financial officials introduced bold and comprehensive liberalisation measures, following growing weaknesses in the securities sector amidst the severe economic slump and the associated stock market crisis. They decontrolled commission rates to increase competition, reduce transaction costs and stimulate public demands for equities; they permitted foreign securities houses to acquire substantial equity stakes in the member firms of the SES; and they desegmented financial services to give banks the licence to undertake stockbroking business.[6] These liberalisation measures, which were designed to foster capital market growth and fashion a more balanced and stable financial system, posed a threat to the vested interests of local brokers. Having long enjoyed comfortable earnings guaranteed by high entry barriers and fixed commissions, they strongly resisted these regulatory changes to the securities sector. However, top MAS technocrats, driven by the desire to see a more market-oriented financial structure and supported by PAP leaders, were determined to transform the clubby SES, and liberalised investment business in defiance of political resistance (*BT*-Singapore 14 May 1987: 1; *FEER* 22 January 1987: 48; *WSJ* 1 June 1988: 16).

An intense period of capital market reforms followed in the early and mid-1990s, when PAP policy-makers were under mounting external pressure to further liberalise the financial sector, as mentioned earlier in this chapter. In further changes to SES entry regulations, existing foreign partners of local securities houses were allowed to raise their stake from 49 per cent to 70 per cent. More significantly, major foreign brokers entered the SES as 'international members' in early 1992 and were no longer forced to trade through local stockbroking firms. While initially restricted to dealing for Singapore residents with large contracts (but no minimum transaction requirements on deals for non-residents), foreign brokers brought large-scale business to Singapore and improved the liquidity and efficiency of the stock market (*EIUCR*-Singapore 2nd Quarter 1993: 20–21; *FEER* 2 April 1992: 78). The decline of formal regulatory impediments to foreign participation coincided with the further removal of barriers that had segmented the financial services industry. In late 1993, major local banks were permitted to broaden the scope of share trading through their newly established sales centres. These centres allowed investors without trading accounts with brokers to buy and sell shares, widening the investor base of the SES and bringing stability to stock transactions.

Entry liberalisation and market desegmentation reduced the fat profit margins associated with the old SES hierarchical structure and undermined the profitability of many local brokers. At the same time, continued reforms greatly stimulated the growth of the capital market, sucking in investable funds from the banking sector. Together with the decision to allow members of the Central Provident Fund (CPF, Singapore's social security programme) to withdraw up to 80 per cent of their funds for stock investment in early 1993, this significantly enervated the deposit bases of banks, squeezed their interest spreads and irked private bankers (*ST* 25 September 1993: 48). While resorting to ingenious capital instruments, new services and technological innovations in order to cope with an increasingly competitive market, private financiers also organised themselves to exercise their voice. Industrial professional associations served as an effective channel to lodge grievances with financial authorities.[7] In the reform process, MAS policy-makers timed the enactment of liberalisation measures in such a way that the safety of the securities sector was not compromised; they even afforded a measure of protection to local firms, primarily for prudential reasons, when lowering entry barriers. While mindful of the concerns of private financiers, policy elites never allowed particularistic interests to block market liberalisation and decisively enacted reforms that stood to enhance financial development.

A similar degree of decisiveness was also manifest in the process of GLC privatisation, which gained momentum in the late 1980s. Given that most GLCs were efficiently run and that the Singapore government had strong coffers, one primary objective of privatisation was to foster the growth of the capital market, as announced in the report by the Public Sector Divestment Committee (PSDC) in 1987.[8] Privatisation, which invariably entangled many other developing country governments in a web of political obstacles, was enacted in a swift yet well-planned manner at the wake of the mid-1980s recession. It was pursued with greater vigour in the early 1990s when the delinking of the Kuala Lumpur Stock Exchange from the SES depressed trading activities in the latter and when the influx of numerous individual investors into the stock market required the enhanced supply of new shares. PAP policy-makers perceived privatisation as a crucial strategy to broaden and deepen stock transactions and to put capital market growth on a stable and solid footing (Low 2006: 216–224; Ng 1989). While occasional resistance arose among civil servants and public-sector employees, PAP ministers were able to overcome obstacles and push ahead with the divestment process (Lee 1995; Milne 1991; *ST* 14 January 1992: 24).

It is in capital market regulation that the impact of a concentrated party system on policy decisiveness was most manifest. The centralised system of government, derived from the systemic dominance of the PAP, helped to put in place the legal and political structure necessary to strengthen prudential controls in line with market liberalisation. In Singapore, laws that authorised market regulation, set the clear outlines for regulatory reforms and gave the process legitimacy were top priorities for PAP leaders. All legislation that mandated new securities rules, improved market infrastructures and enhanced the policy authority of the MAS was invariably carried out in a determined and timely manner. In the aftermath of the 1985 stock market crisis, financial policy-makers moved swiftly to craft a new securities industry bill that would depart from backroom self-regulation and grant the MAS broad powers over the SES. Calling the bill 'overly restrictive' and 'a very badly drafted law', stockbrokers, merchant bankers and corporate lawyers joined in strong opposition. While holding consultations with private market agents to allay their concerns, financial authorities decisively pushed the new securities bill through parliament (*FEER* 31 July 1986: 65 and 23 October 1986: 156; MAS *Annual Report* 1985/86: 34).

More often than not, financial policy elites took proactive measures to reform and rejuvenate the regulatory framework governing the capital market. Market liberalisation was often preceded by the vigilant efforts of the MAS to enhance oversight over capital market operators, both local and foreign. In the late 1980s and early 1990s, the accelerating pace of commission rate liberalisation, entry deregulation and functional desegmentation intensified price competition, diversified the SES membership and exposed the securities industry to external shocks. The MAS took the initiative to tighten up listing requirements, raise business standards in the stockbroking sector and, most importantly of all, strengthen the capital bases of securities firms. From early 1990, it frequently raised minimum capital requirements for SES members, often over vociferous opposition from the latter in alliance with their foreign counterparts (*ST* 17 January 1992: 48 and 24 February 1994: 32; *WSJ* 2 August 1993: B7). Protected by the exclusive political structure and supported by PAP leaders, MAS officials fended off particularistic pressures and effectively enacted regulatory and legislative changes that served to enhance capital market governance.

Resolute and coherent implementation

While party system concentration enabled the Singapore government to decisively initiate capital market reforms, the organisational centralisation and coherence of the PAP hardened the ability of financial policymakers to resolutely implement the reforms. Most crucially, strong party controls exercised by PAP leaders over key economic and financial policy arenas limited the number of actors involved in the policy-making process within the government. This was mirrored in the highly centralised decision-making structure of the cabinet that operated under the aegis of the ruling party. The tightly controlled and disciplined party apparatuses rendered the formation of financial and regulatory policies exclusive and ensured the consistency of capital market reforms. Members of parliament representing the financial community often faced intense pressure from stockbrokers and merchant bankers to slow down market liberalisation, particularly entry deregulation. However, financial policy-making was so centralised in the hands of PAP ministers that members of parliament and their business constituents had little entrée to those policy processes that shaped market reforms.[9] As a result, entry barriers were reduced steadily. Local members of the SES increased from 24 in 1987 to 33 in 1996 and foreign members jumped from 12 to 49 over the same period.

Centralised party controls over economic policy-making also buttressed the sustained process of privatisation in Singapore. The foundation of the privatisation programme was the finance ministry, which was charged with overseeing and carrying out the divestment of state assets. While top PAP leaders were not deeply involved with privatisation plans, they were fully committed to following the plans through to the end (Heracleous 1999; Milne 1991: 330–331). This limited attempts by legislators, GLC management or line ministries to resist the centralisation of divestment decisions and the implementation of privatisation. The government launched the privatisation programme decisively in the late 1980s, but dissenting voices and policy disputes often arose in the process of carrying out the programme. Concerns of their constituents about the prices and quality of privatised services made law-makers plead with the government to, for instance, delay some privatisation plans (*ST* 14 March 1987: 15, 14 January 1992: 24 and 8 March 1994: 2) while line economic agencies sometimes found themselves embroiled in disputes over the speed and mode of divestment (*EIUCR*-Singapore No. 2 1990: 13). However, the organisational cohesion of the PAP that enabled its leaders to control the career paths of legislators forced the latter to be more concerned with such broad national policies as privatisation. Equally importantly, the centralised party apparatuses helped policy elites to resolve inter-agency conflicts and prevent them from undermining the coherent enactment of privatisation plans.

By the early 1990s, it had become clear that privatisation was bound to take longer than initially envisioned by PAP policy-makers for a variety of reasons, including the complex nature of many transactions and the weak ability of the stock market to absorb new share issues. However, the high degree of party centralisation and cohesiveness restricted departures from the agreed-on privatisation plans and kept the plans firmly on the national agenda. The strong intra-PAP organisation provided policy elites with the political resources to reduce discretionary decision-making by individual politicians and state agencies and ensured the integrity of the process, which yielded significant progress. For example, more than 60 per cent of the GLCs slated for divestment in the initial five-year plan announced in the PSDC report had been privatised by the end of 1990 (Ghosh 2000). The sustained privatisation of GLCs significantly bolstered the trading activity and market capitalisation of the SES (Low 2006: 221–224). While the continued process of privatisation did not reduce the pervasive role of the state in the national economy, this was attributable to the desire of PAP leaders to achieve important commercial and political objectives through GLCs rather than their inability to keep the policy in place (Haggard and Low 2002).

Nowhere was the impact of strong intra-party organisational structures on the resoluteness of reform policies more manifest than in the enforcement of capital market regulations. As the capital market was significantly liberalised in the late 1980s and early 1990s, securities laws were not only progressively revised and upgraded, as mentioned in the preceding analysis, but also enforced strictly. While the MAS was often given credit for vigorously regulating the securities sector, its ability to do so derived from the strongly organised ruling party. On the one hand, tight and centralised controls over government processes by the PAP created a highly favourable policy environment in which financial regulators effectively checked malfeasance and fraud in the capital market in isolation from distributive demands. On the other hand party cohesion enabled PAP leaders to orient individual politicians and state agencies to the collective interests of the government and prevent them from bringing particularistic interests to bear upon the MAS and weakening its regulatory authority.

These institutional advantages greatly strengthened the capacity of financial technocrats to act harshly towards the violators of securities market rules. In December 1990, January 1991 and July 1996, for example, many prestigious local and foreign securities companies were heavily fined or stripped of their licences for failing to observe account requirements and reporting standards (see *BT*-Singapore 10 January: 3; *EIUCR*-Singapore No. 2 1991: 29 and 3rd Quarter 1996: 20–21). In early 1988 and early 1997 respectively, a business leader and a ranking government official were arrested and handed down long-term sentences for engaging in insider trading and share price manipulation (*EIUCR*-Singapore 2nd Quarter 1997: 21; *WSJ* 12 January 1988: 6). On many occasions, top PAP leaders intervened to protect the autonomy of the MAS when it faced strong political pressure to lower regulatory standards or to be forbearing to rule violators, particularly from foreign firms (Ghesquiere 2007: 107–108; Lee 2000: 73–76). These sustained efforts resulted in the rigorous enactment of securities laws and rules throughout the process of capital market reforms. Singapore regulators were rated top by a 1993 survey of securities market regulation in eight East Asian economies, scoring the highest mark for rule enforcement (*AMF* February 1993: 55–60).[10]

The capacity to keep particularistic interests at bay and therefore maintain reform resoluteness also derived from broad PAP–society linkages. As argued in the preceding chapter, PAP politicians who were motivated by the centralised and coherent intra-party structures to be concerned with the corporate goals of the ruling party had strong incentives to maintain an encompassing political coalition. In such a coalition, a broad range of diverse interests was represented and particularised pursuits rarely dominated. This caused PAP politicians to remain aloof from special interest groups and protected them from interference by such groups. While policy-makers consulted with private market agents over the design and implementation of stock market liberalisation, privatisation and regulatory changes, they were able to prevent such agents from capturing the policy process and aggregating a wide array of interests into a public-regarding reform programme. The encompassing PAP–society ties structured by intra-party organisational strength thus provided political leaders with considerable capacity to foil any attempts by specialised interests to temper with or alter the existing course of capital market reforms, and maintained support for given liberalisation policies.

Finally, party centralisation and cohesiveness contributed to resolute market reforms through their impact on the durability of the cabinet and the stability of core decision-makers in the MAS and the finance ministry. As shown in Table 4.1, the government was much more durable in Singapore than in Malaysia and, more importantly, in Thailand during the period under review; politicians and technocrats who headed the key state financial agencies had much longer tenures than their Malaysian and, to a greater extent, Thai counterparts. Richard Hu was at the helm of both the MAS and the finance ministry continuously for more than 12 years. Top Singapore financial officials thus had sufficient time to obtain market information, develop technical expertise and create institutional resources to implement market reform programmes consistently. The stability of government and financial policy elites provided the organisational cohesion and continuity necessary to maintain the reform trajectory.

The stability of core state financial agencies was, in the final analysis, built on the political party structure. The systemic dominance

Table 4.1 The stability of government and financial policy-makers

	Malaysia	Singapore	Thailand
Average cabinet duration (in months)	37.3 (1976–2004)	46.0 (1978–2001)	16.3 (1992–2005)
Average turnover (per year)			
Central bank governor	0.22 (1985–2008)	0.13 (1985–2008)	0.33 (1984–2008)
Finance minister	0.26 (1985–2008)	0.13 (1985–2008)	1.18 (1986–2008)
Securities commission head[a]	0.20 (1993–2008)	0.13 (1985–2008)	0.42 (1993–2004)

Sources: Author calculations, based on data provided in Croissant (2006), EIUCR-Malaysia (various issues), EUICR-Singapore (various issues) and EUICR-Thailand (various issues).
[a]This refers to the chairman of the Securities Commission of Malaysia, the chairman of the Monetary Authority of Singapore and the secretary-general of the Securities and Exchange Commission of Thailand.

and intra-party organisational strength of the PAP enabled its leaders to wield virtually unrestricted command over the bureaucracy and to mould the structure of state economic institutions in such a way that their policy objectives could be effectively achieved (Ho 2003; Koh 1997). Seeing capital market reforms both as an important objective in themselves and as an indispensable strategy to promote economic development, PAP leaders were willing to delegate enormous power to the MAS and the finance ministry and established a cohesive and solid cohort of technocrats to lead the two agencies. In order to create a clear and coherent sense of policy direction, they often intervened to ensure that there was institutional solidarity both between and within the two agencies. In mid-1997, Prime Minister Goh Chok Tong moved quickly to resolve emerging disputes among top MAS technocrats over the pace of capital market reforms that might have undermined the stability of financial policy elites and thus the resoluteness of reform programmes (*EIUCR*-Singapore 3rd Quarter 1997: 24).

Market reforms since the Asian crisis

The pace of capital market reforms accelerated and their scope broadened following the Asian financial crisis of 1997–1998. Foreign access to the stock market further increased, commission rates were completely liberalised and securities laws and rules significantly strengthened. More importantly, market reforms expanded into the transformation of corporate governance practices and the promotion of government and corporate bond markets. These were also complemented by new initiatives that opened up some CPF accounts to buttress fund management, allowed cash-rich GLCs to issue bonds to nurture debt market growth, and liberalised guidelines on the internationalisation of the Singapore dollar to facilitate the listing of foreign shares on the stock market. Not only did reform programmes closely tie in with such collective national policies as financial development and economic growth, they were enacted in a swift yet well-planned manner and, equally crucially, implemented resolutely and consistently.

The Asian crisis and the major external shocks that followed in the early 2000s precipitated a strategic reappraisal of the trajectory of financial development by PAP policy elites. While Singapore was not as adversely affected as neighbouring countries by the crisis, it was not completely unscathed. Economic growth dropped sharply, as the worsening financial woes in the region took their toll. Manufactured exports, which were traditionally the engine of industrialisation in Singapore, slumped significantly, raising unemployment levels. After having staged a dramatic recovery from the Asian crisis in 2000, the economy slipped into a severe recession in no less dramatic fashion the ensuing year when a global economic downturn hit Singapore manufacturers particularly hard (*FEER* 6 September 2001: 62–62, 15 November 2001: 40–45). These regional and global economic shocks laid bare the real and potential dangers of acute dependence on manufacturing and stimulated Singapore policy-makers to push ahead with their long-term plans to prioritise the growth of financial services in general and equity markets in particular.

The economic shocks also geared up the long-running contest among East Asian countries to develop their capital cities into regional financial centres as an important strategy to attract and retain foreign capital. The inter-state rivalry for regional economic status and foreign capital sustained pressures for Singapore to deepen and broaden capital market reforms in order to stay ahead of the competition (*EIUCR*-Singapore June 2005: 16–17; *ST* 12 March 2001: 16). While systemic market pressures were powerful stimuli to continued capital market reforms, they need to be viewed in interaction with domestic political institutions, more specifically political party structures, to explain the orientation, approach and outcomes of such reforms. In the late 1990s and early and mid-2000s, as in the past, the concentrated party system and the organisational strength of the PAP shaped both the incentives of Singapore policy-makers to pursue public-regarding interests through market reforms and their ability to initiate and carry out reform policies effectively.

Reforms and development imperatives

As argued in the preceding section, party system concentration and PAP organisational strength combined to translate electoral pressures into strong incentives for political elites to harness capital market reforms to public policy objectives. The same logic of Singapore's political party structure asserted itself in the formulation of reform policies in the post-Asian crisis period. While the PAP managed to arrest the erosion of its electoral support and even increase its popular vote share in the 2001 general election, it was unable to restore the systemic monopoly that had characterised the polity in the 1960s and 1970s. The renewed opposition continued to pose significant challenges to the incumbent party and kept electoral contestations alive and rejuvenated. The PAP government was thus under constant pressure to be attentive to the wishes of the electorate in order to maintain its public acceptance and popularity. At the same time, the political space expanded and the modes of political participation multiplied, allowing the different sectors of the electorate to enhance their voices in public policy and forcing PAP politicians to be responsive to their demands.[11]

The impact of electoral pressures on government policy was mediated through the concentrated party system and the cohesively organised ruling party. As elaborated in the previous section, party concentration not only strongly predisposed political leaders towards maintaining a broad electoral coalition but enabled Singaporean voters to hold the PAP government accountable for policy performance. This stimulated PAP politicians to favour the broader citizenry over narrow and specific interests in the policy-making process. Such centripetal forces were reinforced by the internal organisational centralisation and coherence of the PAP, which strengthened the incentive of its leaders to protect party labels and reputations through the provision of public goods at the national level and align the policy pursuits of individual politicians closely to corporate party objectives. In offering public goods policies, PAP leaders were no less driven by the desire to retain power than their counterparts in other electoral authoritarian regimes or more democratic polities. But the aggregative party structure rendered them more willing to do so by providing broad and programmatic policy platforms to the general public. In a recent cross-national survey of the responsibility of elected politicians to represent public interests in the formulation of policies in six Southeast Asian countries (Carlson and Turner 2008),[12] PAP leaders were rated the highest. This may not be entirely surprising, given that Singapore had the most concentrated and cohesive party structure in the region.

The argument, which resonates with the central proposition of this chapter, is that party concentration and organisational strength translated the electoral imperatives of the PAP into institutionalised responsiveness and even accountability to the voting public for whom economic growth was the paramount concern. Singapore's embrace of deeper and broader capital market reforms in the aftermath of the Asian crisis had more to do with the inter-party and intra-party institutions that shaped the orientation of financial policy than with the external market pressures that confronted them. Prior to the Asian crisis, the Singapore government had already decided that it needed to further restructure the capital market to fashion a more balanced and efficient financial architecture. On the eve of the crisis, a meticulous plan to further liberalise the financial sector in general and the securities industry in particular was crafted. The difficult economic conditions that prevailed at the wake of the crisis only reinforced the official resolve to foster a more robust capital market.

While capital market reforms were embodied in specific plans to increase the competitiveness of the securities sector and promote Singapore as a world-class financial services centre, they were all submitted to broader policy goals—financial development and economic growth that would enhance general social welfare. Despite successful efforts to reform the securities industry in the late 1980s and early 1990s, the capital market had remained relatively small, and the overall financial structure was still largely bank-oriented by the mid-1990s. For instance, the average annual ratio of stock market trading to GDP was 0.72 in Singapore during 1993–1998, as compared to 1.02 in the US, a prototype of marketised financial capitalism, over the same period; more crucially, the average annual ratio of private bond market capitalisation to GDP was a mere 0.12 in Singapore while it was 0.85 in the US.[13] The majority of Singapore industry firms, including many GLCs, continued to depend on banks for much of their financing.

The Asian crisis exposed the real hazards of excessive reliance on bank-based financing, which had encouraged private businesses to recklessly use short-term capital to finance long-term investment projects. The massive bank failures that were primarily associated with the defaults and bankruptcies of highly leveraged firms devastated the real economy in many of Singapore's East Asian neighbours. These weaknesses heightened the importance of avoiding overdependence on bank credit and developing a more market-based corporate capital structure. While a well-capitalised and well-regulated banking sector helped Singapore overcome some of these structural problems and tide it over the crisis, a fully developed capital market was seen as a key alterative source of capital that would diversify industrial financing and help the domestic financial sector cope with the challenges posed by an increasingly volatile global market. There was a renewed consensus among PAP policy-makers that the robust growth of *both* banks and equity markets would be conducive to the development of a more efficient financial system (Fock and Wong 2001; Hew 2005).

Public-regarding policies to be achieved through capital market reforms were not merely related to financial development; they were also overlain with the PAP government's long-term strategy to expand the external sources of Singapore's economic growth. Launched in the early 1990s and pursued more vigorously at the wake of the Asian crisis, the strategy was designed to overcome the limitations of a small domestic market, maximise opportunities afforded by globalisation and put national development on a sustained footing (Mahizhnan 1994; Tan 2003). Capital market reforms facilitated the achievement of these objectives primarily because they loosened the overall regulatory regime and bolstered a more conducive environment for multinational companies who played a key role in developing the external economy. Equally importantly, market reforms optimised the corporate capital structure of local enterprises, particularly GLCs, that spearheaded the drive to enhance Singapore's growth potential and strengthened its ability to expand regionally and even globally (Chong 2007; Rodan 2004a).

Finally, capital market reforms were associated with the PAP's efforts to spread the benefits of growth and manage inequality. While Singapore achieved equitable development for much of the post-independence period, income gaps between the rich and the poor began to widen in the early and mid-1990s. The Asian crisis and the fuller integration of the Singapore economy with the global market only served to reinforce the trend towards the unequal distribution of incomes in the late 1990s and early 2000s. Among the many policy responses to increased inequalities, the government distributed nearly S$1.68 billion in the form of CPF top-up schemes, mainly targeted at the lower income groups of the population, between 1993 and 2000 (Thangavelu 2009: 234). As more and more CPF funds were allowed to invest in stocks in the 1990s, the performance of the equity market directly impacted the financial health of the CPF and consequently the social welfare of lower middle-class Singaporeans. The post-crisis reform initiatives were thus intended to boost stock market growth and lend support to the government's efforts to contain inequalities.

Furthermore, to stem rising material inequalities at the wake of the Asian crisis, the government initiated New Singapore shares in 2000 and Economic Restructuring shares in 2002, both of which were angled towards the lower-paid. While some cashed in their shares, many held onto them for capital gains. These two schemes further swelled the pool of shareholders in Singapore, which had already become the largest in the world by the mid-1990s, mainly as a result of the privatisation of big GLCs (*ST* 22 May 1995: 52). The wide holding of shares by a broad array of social groups who constituted the PAP's coalition motivated the government to further develop the capital market through more significant reforms. Reform successes that were instrumental in increasing the income levels of most Singaporeans and thus reinforcing the bases of the PAP's electoral support had a direct bearing upon the political fortunes of the ruling party.

Swift and effective policy responses

In response to the Asian financial crisis and external economic shocks in the early 2000s, PAP policy elites initiated and enacted decisive capital market reforms closely in line with their policy interests. Recall from the preceding section that Singapore's concentrated party system heavily centralised policy power in the PAP, and that the PAP was the only veto player. With the ruling party exercising supreme authority over virtually all major economic policies, the political framework was highly conducive to very swift and flexible policy action. Decisions by top PAP leaders had a powerful and prompt impact; since no other political actors could constrain the process, their decisions could be translated quickly and effectively into reform policies. There was thus a strong connection between the concentrated party structure and the PAP government's overall policy posture in response to external market pressures and challenges. As PAP elites faced no institutional checks on their decision-making power, they were well positioned to direct and change financial and regulatory policies in such a powerful and rapid manner that their policy objectives could be effectively achieved.

During the first half of 1997, top PAP leaders decided to further liberalise and develop the capital market, in view of new market challenges facing Singapore (*Asiamoney* June 1998: 21–36; Lee 2000: 80–82). They exerted political will with particular force in the key policy areas that covered stock market liberalisation, corporate governance reform, debt market development, fiscal incentives, institutional infrastructures and legislative changes. They set up well-crafted procedures and organisations to ensure the effective and satisfactory design of market reform plans. The plans were meticulously yet rapidly deliberated among a wide range of individuals and entities under the auspices of three government-sanctioned specialised committees comprising private-sector actors and MAS technocrats. But final decisions on whether proposals that emerged from the deliberations were enacted rested with the Financial Sector Review Group headed by Deputy Prime Minster Lee Hsien Loong, who had taken over the MAS chairmanship on the eve of the Asian crisis. This ensured that the institutionally complex and multi-faceted reform plans were formulated in a centralised and co-ordinated manner.

The market reform programmes that had been hatched at the wake of the crisis were turned into quick policy actions thereafter. More manifestly, the MAS moved swiftly to open up the stock market to more qualified stockbrokers, both domestic and foreign, and deregulate commission rates across the full spectrum of transaction values; it established a clear and specific time frame for the completion of liberalisation measures. These were accompanied by government efforts to boost the position of stockbroking firms by allowing them to provide new products and expand into other securities-related areas. At the same time, the government continued pushing for the divestment of state assets, particularly in the utilities sector, in which state monopolies tended to prevail. This was designed both to support the strategy to develop the external economy of Singapore that was underpinned by more competitive GLCs and to supply tradable shares to an ever-growing stock market (Tay 2001: 282).

Equally significantly, regulatory barriers to foreign participation in the capital market were quickly reduced or completely removed. Not only were more foreign stockbrokers able to gain access to the equities markets, foreign ownership limits in full SES member firms were raised to 70 and even 100 per cent. Furthermore, in order to facilitate the development of government and corporate debt markets, financial authorities permitted international securities houses and investment banks to participate in the issuing and underwriting of bonds. These liberalisations made the debt markets more attractive to investors and coincided with the government's efforts to push local industrial firms, particularly GLCs, to use more debt instruments to finance their investments (*Asiamoney* March 1999: 14–15). The MAS also moved to liberalise Singapore dollar listing for foreign firms. While a few foreign firms with substantial businesses in Singapore had been listed in the currency prior to the Asian crisis, many others had to issue foreign currency-denominated stocks. In the aftermath of the crisis, swift decisions were made to give foreign firms considerable latitude in choosing the currency in which their shares traded on the stock market.

Local stockbrokers, merchant banks and institutional investors had strong reservations that liberalising commission rates or lowering entry barriers in the equities markets would generate new competitive pressures in the market segments in which they still enjoyed some special privileges. Because of their stronger financial positions, Singapore capital market operators were better able to withstand the fallout from the Asian crisis than their counterparts in many other East Asian economies. But sharply declining trading activities in the SES, at least in the wake of the crisis, ate into their profit margins and racked their capital structures. They pressed hard for the gradual and cautious liberalisation of the capital market and actively lobbied for regulatory favours that could ease the pinch of increased competition (*BT*-Singapore 4 February 1998: 4;

ST 19 February 1998: 53 and 13 August 1998: 66). PAP policy-makers defiantly ruled out an incremental reform stance and initiated a series of bold reform measures throughout 1998. In early 1999, they even set out to speed up the process of market liberalisation (*BT*-Singapore 30 January 1998: 3; MAS *Annual Report* 1999/2000: 40).

Having set in motion various initiatives to liberalise the capital market, financial policy elites turned to upgrade corporate regulatory regimes in both the financial and non-financial sectors. Lee Hsien Loong and his close associates decided that drastic measures were needed to reform corporate governance practices in Singapore and policy action closely corresponding to their rhetoric followed swiftly. They identified the key areas of corporate governance in which they believed Singapore was lagging, set the shape of corporate reform policies and orchestrated broad and rapid consultations with the private sector through three specialised committees. In less than a year, they developed a comprehensive corporate governance framework covering accounting standards, information disclosure, investment protection and bankruptcy procedures, all of which were crucial to the sustained development of the equities markets (*EIUCR*-Singapore 1st Quarter 2000: 13–14). And this framework was quickly legislated into the Code of Corporate Governance in early 2001, through the joint efforts of the MAS, the finance ministry and the Registrar of Companies.

In parallel to rapid and extensive liberalisation programmes, the Singapore government acted expeditiously to enhance market infrastructures, strengthen supervisory capabilities and upgrade securities laws. The Asian crisis brought home the importance and indispensability of underpinning capital market reforms with tenacious institutional building and strict regulation. In the post-crisis period, the increasingly open and complicated market environment made more strenuous demands on the ability of financial policy-makers to achieve this. Singapore's concentrated party structure allowed the government to be decisive and agile, and it was promptly delivering the institutional and regulatory changes for which the new market conditions were calling. No sooner had market liberalisation plans been announced in early 1998 than the MAS, under the direction of top PAP leaders, revamped its organisational structure and established new planning and inspection units, in support of its expanding functions and in line with its new regulatory approach that prioritised risk-based supervision. The MAS also synergised securities and derivative businesses by merging the SES and the Singapore International Monetary Exchange into an integrated Singapore Exchange (SGX) in late 1999. This aimed to enhance market transparency, reduce transaction costs and generate more funds from the capital market (Hew 2005; MAS *Annual Report* 1998/99: 55–56).

Changes to the legislative framework of capital market regulation were more politically painful and controversial but no less expeditious. The government's efforts to enhance the regulatory authority of the MAS and consolidate securities and futures regulations through extensive legislation met with strong resistance from private market agents who tried to cling to the old hierarchy of self-regulation. However, with only one veto player, government decisions prevailed over private interests and were translated into practice and law swiftly. At the heels of the organisational revamping of the MAS noted earlier, the government amended the MAS act to centralise a wide range of new regulatory powers in the hands of the quasi central bank.[14] This was followed by a quick move to craft extensive amendments to the Securities Industry Act and Futures Trading Act and get them passed by parliament in late 2000. The amendments integrated the securities and futures legislation, closed regulatory loopholes and enabled MAS technocrats to act even more forcefully against rule violators.

In sum, the centralised decision-making apparatus of the Singapore government that derived from the concentrated party system equipped financial policy elites with very effective instruments to decisively respond to external market shocks and pressures. The political significance of this institutional framework was fully illustrated in the rapid but carefully managed formulation and unleashing of strong market reform measures in the thick of the post-Asian crisis economic turmoil that deterred such policy changes in many neighbouring countries.

Market reform successes

In Singapore, successful market reforms were contingent not only on the ability of PAP policy elites to initiate reform programmes decisively but also on their ability to commit to sustaining the programmes over time. In the post-Asian crisis period, as in the 1990s, the centrally and coherently organised PAP and its systemic dominance combined to work powerfully for the resolute and credible implementation of given reform policies. There are specific causal pathways through which the PAP's internal organisational strength bore strongly upon the ability of financial policy-makers to carry capital market reforms through to the end.

In the first place, the highly centralised decision-making structure within the ruling party meant that key decisions about major financial policy changes were made by party leaders and were strictly enforce-able on party office holders and economic technocrats. In late 1997 and early 1998, for instance, top PAP leaders sidelined and demoted a couple of key MAS technocrats who had demurred at the rapid liber-alisation of the capital market and even tried to slow the process down (*EUICR*-Singapore 4th Quarter 1997: 13 and 1st Quarter 1998: 24). In late 2002, the Temasek (the investment holding company of many GLCs) chairman, a senior and veteran PAP politician, came out against the institution of a quarterly reporting regime, a core corporate reform mea-sure designed to enhance information disclosure and bring Singapore's securities regulations in line with best practices. However, the party lead-ership pushed him aside and stood firmly by agreed-on policy decisions (Ho 2005: 284–285). On these and many other occasions, organisational centralisation that limited the number of actors in the financial policy process and allowed party leaders to screen out mavericks nipped in the bud intra-party disputes over reform implementation, maintained the convergence of policy positions among key party officials and increased market reform resoluteness.

Furthermore, a stable core of financial policy-makers dominating the MAS, the finance ministry and other policy-relevant state agencies contributed to coherent inter-bureaucratic operations and thus reform policy consistency. The solidarity of the financial policy elite, which rested upon the inter-party and intra-party organisational strength of the PAP strengthened in the post-Asian crisis period. In his triple capac-ity of the deputy prime minister, MAS chairman and finance minister, Lee Hsien Loong was well positioned to consolidate close working ties among key decision-makers in the economic bureaucracy. When taking over the prime ministership in 2004, he relinquished the MAS chair-manship but stayed on the finance portfolio. Goh Chok Tong, who retired into the position of senior minister previously occupied by Lee Kuan Yew, took the helm of the MAS. Lee Hsien Loong and Goh main-tained their close relationship that had been formed over the previous 14 years. A remarkable stability thus continued in the top personnel who occupied the most important economic and financial posts, as shown in Table 4.1. This stability provided the Singapore government with a durable and solid core of policy-makers who were able to develop the experience and expertise needed to carry out new reform initiatives consistently.

The effects of personnel stability in the key state economic agencies on the credibility of reform policies were reinforced by the close and long-standing ties between these agencies, particularly the MAS and the finance ministry. As argued in the previous section, the strong organ-isational structure of the PAP hardened the ability of its leaders to contain intra-agency disputes, orchestrated the exchange of top per-sonnel between the agencies and maintained the unified and cohesive leadership in them. In the late 1990s and early 2000s, the scope of cap-ital market reforms significantly expanded into a wider range of policy and regulatory issue areas. While the MAS saw its policy-making power broaden during the continued process of market reforms, it shared authority with the finance ministry, the ROC and other state agencies over the enactment of an array of reform measures. Well-established working relationships enabled these agencies to overcome the difficul-ties of horizontal communication and co-ordination, and effectively co-operate with each other in the reform process. Such co-operation created an institutional environment that strongly favoured the smooth and coherent implementation of reforms related to securities legislation and corporate governance for which these agencies had shared regula-tory responsibilities (*BT*-Singapore 17 December 1999: 6; MAS *Annual Report* 1999/2000: 44–45, *Annual Report* 2000/2001: 16).

Finally, in the centrally and cohesively structured PAP, national lead-ers possessed the forceful institutional leverage to compel party offi-cials and legislators to support public-regarding financial reforms that advanced aggregate national interests. Together with the centralising pressures brought about by the concentrated party system upon the PAP to maintain a broad electoral coalition, these intra-party organi-sational features shifted financial policy to the national level, virtually eliminating the influence of particularistic interests on the market reform process. In the late 1990s and early 2000s, as in the past, the MAS actively engaged with the private financial community in the formation of reform programmes. But party centralisation and coher-ence prevented financial technocrats and politicians from being closely linked or beholden to narrow and specific economic interests. This had the effect of diffusing opposition to the consistent implementa-tion of politically painful liberalisation measures and facilitating the maintenance of support for given reform decisions.

A good example in point lies in the determined efforts of financial policy elites to liberalise commission rates. While private market agents had made futile attempts to block the initiation of this reform measure in 1998, they did not throw in the sponge. No sooner had the measure been introduced than they resorted to all possible political means to temper with its enactment. Stockbrokers and securities firms demanded that the MAS slow down the liberalisation process on the ground that cut-throat competition for commissions and customers would reduce profit margins and undermine systemic stability (*BT*-Singapore 26 October 1999: 10 and 2 December 1999: 2). They applied collective pressure on MAS technocrats through their interest-representing associations and even by establishing new lobby organisations (*BT*-Singapore 29 August 2000: 5 and 31 August 2000: 5). When these efforts failed to achieve their desired goal, big stockbrokers colluded in setting minimum rates and re-establishing the commission cartel. While the MAS tried to ease the pains of reforms by allowing securities firms to broaden their business scope, it had little tolerance of their efforts to restore the oligopolistic market structure and pushed through, ahead of schedule, the liberalisation plan that lowered the costs of stock transactions and benefited a wide range of investors, including poorer Singaporeans.

Another important illustration of the impact of PAP organisational strength on reform resoluteness is the strict enforcement of securities laws. Not only did MAS officials constantly revise and upgrade the legal frameworks of securities market and corporate governance in line with the rapidly liberalised capital market, as mentioned above, they also had a demonstrated ability to force compliance with laws and rules. Such ability derived as much from their technical expertise as from the strongly organised ruling party and the authoritative executive. These institutional structures oriented politicians towards PAP-determined reform objectives, shaved off intense demands for supervisory laxity and vested MAS regulators with the power to effectively check fraudulent activities. As in the past, the MAS showed little forbearance towards the violators of securities rules and never hesitated to impose severe fines and penalties upon them, often in defiance of political pressure. These violators ranged from well-connected domestic private financiers to powerful foreign stockbrokers and from transnational merchant banks to giant Chinese SOEs.[15] As a result, Singapore was rated much stronger than most East Asian economies in terms of the effectiveness of securities market and corporate governance, as illustrated in Table 4.2. Cross-national studies (La Porta et al. 2006) put Singapore ahead of not only most emerging markets but also many OECD countries on the key indicators of securities rule enforcement.

The consistent and resolute implementation of reform measures across the key policy and regulatory areas contributed towards the steady growth of a robust and well-built capital market. As a consequence, the overall financial market structure of Singapore had become more market-oriented and balanced by the late 2000s, with banks and equity markets playing differential yet equally important roles in

Table 4.2   Enforcement of securities and corporate governance rules[a]

	2000	2001	2002	2003	2004	2005	2006	All years
Malaysia	4.3	2.5	3.5	5.0	5.2	4.9	3.6	4.1
Singapore	7.0	7.0	7.5	6.5	6.6	5.6	5.0	6.5
Thailand	2.0	2.0	3.0	3.8	4.1	4.0	3.6	3.2
Group average[b]	3.5	3.7	4.3	4.7	4.8	4.4	3.8	4.2

Source: CLSA (various issues).
[a]The rules cover financial reporting standards, government efforts to improve securities laws, information disclosure, compliance with international best practices, independent board committees and minority shareholder protection. The score ranges from 1 to 10, with 10 indicating the best. The score trended downwards across all the countries from 2005, primarily as a result of adopting a more rigorous ranking methodology.
[b]This is the average score for 10 Asian economies—China, Hong Kong, India, Indonesia, South Korea, Malaysia, the Philippines, Singapore, Taiwan and Thailand.

financial intermediation and economic development. The annual average ratio of stock market capitalisation to deposit money bank assets, a commonly used measure of the size of capital markets relative to that of banks, increased from 1.21 in 1989–1993 to 1.82 in 2003–2007. By the same token, the annual average ratio of stock market trading to private credit by deposit money banks, usually applied to measure the relative importance of market trading activity vis-à-vis bank lending, jumped from 0.62 to 1.36 over the same period.[16] With the capital market and the banking sector strongly complementing each other's roles, the financial system was more efficient in meeting different financing needs and providing long-term capital for industrial growth. The real economy benefited from the well-functioning equity markets that acted as an indispensable source of risk capital to enhance entrepreneurship and provided the corporate sector with a crucial alternative to bank finance (MAS *Annual Report* 2006/2007 and 2007/2008). During 2004–2007, the economy grew at the annual average rate of nearly 8 per cent, an unusually high growth rate for such an economically mature country as Singapore.

More significantly, the sound capital market reduced the vulnerability of Singapore to stresses in the financial industry, particularly those caused by external economic shocks. The unprecedented global financial crisis and the resultant recession of 2008–2009 weighed heavily on Singapore, which experienced the sharpest export decline and economic contraction for many decades. Like everywhere else, credit conditions tightened in Singapore, as foreign capital inflows dwindled and domestic banks became more cautious amidst credit risk concerns and weakening corporate performances (MAS 2009: 53–55). This disrupted credit flows to industrial firms and exacerbated the externally induced economic slump. However, the capital market quickly picked up the slack in the banking system and became a more important source of industrial financing. Funds raised by the corporate sector from the SGX amounted to S$9.6 billion in the first half of 2009, as compared to only S$4 billion provided by government-backed loan schemes (Heng 2009). As a result, more credit flew to the corporate sector, stimulating investment activities and facilitating recovery. By mid-2009, the Singapore economy rebounded by a dramatic 22 per cent and was among the few East Asian countries to show the strongest sign of recovery (*Economist* 15 August 2009: 57–59; *WSJ* 14 July 2009: A8). While it remains to be seen whether the recovery is sustainable, the well-developed and well-regulated capital market has played a critical role in helping Singapore ride the global crisis.

Conclusions

This chapter has endeavoured to show that the concentrated party system and the centrally and coherently organised PAP interacted to heavily influence the orientation and process of capital market reforms in Singapore over the past two decades. Party systemic concentration and PAP organisational strength combined to create incentives for political elites to harness market reform programmes to such public-regarding policy objectives as financial development and economic growth. Equally importantly, the inter-party and intra-PAP organisational configurations institutionalised the strong ability of financial policy-makers both to initiate decisive capital market reforms, often in response to market and political pressures, and to follow these reforms through to the end, frequently in defiance of political and institutional obstacles. The case material presented in this chapter thus lends robust support to the proposed causal explanation that market reform successes derived primarily from the strong party structure in Singapore.

5
Thailand: Reform Failures amidst Political Changes

This chapter provides a chronological narrative and analysis of capital market reforms in Thailand since the late 1980s. The central proposition is that the highly fragmented party system interacted with decentralised and incohesive parties to create strong incentives for politicians to pursue private-regarding interests through market reforms for much of the period under question. Equally importantly, these inter-party and intra-party configurations weakened the ability of policy-makers to initiate and implement reform policies decisively and resolutely, even in response to significant external market pressures and economic shocks, particularly the Asian financial crisis of 1997–1998. In the early and mid-2000s, more decisive and programmatic market reforms were introduced, primarily because of the increasingly concentrated party and political structure dominated by the Thai Rak Thai. However, the ruling TRT, while more centralised and cohesive than most other Thai political parties, was plagued by critical organisational weaknesses. As a result, reform policies continued to suffer from considerable instability and poor credibility. The overall process of capital market reforms was thus less successful in Thailand than in Singapore.

The chapter is divided into five sections. The first section discusses the evolution of the Thai capital market prior to the late 1980s, and major policy and regulatory obstacles to capital market development. The second section examines initial efforts to reform capital market structures and regulatory frameworks through the mid-1990s and provides a detailed account of market reform failures. The following two sections focus on the changing patterns of capital market reforms in the aftermath of the Asian financial crisis and, more importantly, under the TRT government in the early and mid-2000s. The fifth and final section summarises and concludes the chapter.

Capital market development: Pre-reform obstacles

By the late 1980s, Thailand had established a financial system that was both broader and deeper than the financial systems of many other developing countries with similar development levels. It boasted a wide array of bank and non-bank institutions and maintained a relatively high ratio of financial assets to GDP (Fry 1995; Zahid 1995). Dominating the domestic financial market was a handful of commercial banks that controlled the lion's share of the country's financial assets. However, this well-established bank-based financial structure set off the under-development of the capital market by contrast. The Stock Exchange of Thailand (SET) was formally set up in 1975 on the basis of the Bangkok Stock Exchange, which had been in existence since the early 1960s. The SET remained small in size and inactive in trading during much of the first decade of its establishment. Over the period 1976–1987, the annual average market capitalisation and trading value of the SET accounted for merely 4.42 and 3.16 per cent of GDP respectively.[1] By the same token, the government securities market remained largely dormant and the corporate bond market was virtually non-existent.

There were various impediments to the development of the Thai capital market, but structural obstacles and regulatory weaknesses constituted the most crucial ones. The securities industry in general and the stock market in particular was hierarchically organised, stifling competition, increasing transaction costs and depressing market growth. The securities industry in which both pure securities firms and hybrid finance and securities companies operated developed in a rapid yet haphazard manner in the 1960s and 1970s. The lack of effective government controls, particularly with regard to licensing requirements and supervision, saw a rapid expansion of the industry. More crucially, the desire of foreign banks to gain direct access to an otherwise closed market and of local banks to expand their business scope by establishing finance and securities companies encouraged a further influx of new entrants (Pakorn 1994: 37–41; TSBI 1994: 72–74). As a result, there had been more than 80 securities and finance companies by the late 1970s.

This seemingly pluralist structure of the securities sector belied the fact that it remained concentrated in a relatively small number of companies. By late 1980, the top 20 finance and securities companies controlled more than 50 per cent of total assets in the sector. Given that the sector's business was largely fee rather than fund-based and was thus only partially reflected in balance sheet size (Skully 1984: 330–333), this percentage understated the dominance of the leading companies. For instance, the largest 20 companies typically accounted for over 90 per cent of the total net income of all finance and securities companies in the late 1980s (Wellons and Horikoshi 1996: 278). As a result, the market concentration of pure securities companies was higher than that of commercial banks, which was itself among the highest in the world (Mori and Tsutsui 1993: 76). Extensive ownership controls of major finance and securities companies by a few large banks, and close inter-firm linkages, further contributed to the oligopolistic structure of the securities industry. Lead finance and securities companies shunned the Thai Finance and Securities Association (TFSA) that mainly represented the interests of smaller firms; they constituted a de facto cartel that wielded great influence over businesses, market structures and even regulatory policies (*BP* 19 April 1985: 6; *BT* September 1983: 35–37).

Equally importantly, most of the top 20 financial and securities companies held seats on the SET. They were licensed to engage in full securities business—brokering (buying and selling securities), dealing (trading in securities), underwriting (managing the sale of securities) and investment advisory services. SET members operated in a dual-capacity system in which they, dealing for their own accounts and also representing the accounts of their clients, acted as both stockbrokers and market makers. Prior to the late 1980s, the total number of SET members had been limited for many years to no more than 30 finance and securities companies. As in the broader securities sector, the large SET member firms, by dint of their bank affiliations, strong asset structures and solid client bases, tended to monopolise securities transactions. They formed a small club of powerful stockbrokers and played a key role in shaping business practices and market rules, often through the co-ordination of the Association of Members of the Stock Exchange of Thailand (AMSET).

It is clear from the preceding analysis that the major Thai finance and securities companies constituted the core of a hierarchical securities market. They strongly preferred the status quo, which created entry barriers, limited the number of competitors and resisted regulatory changes in membership restrictions, particularly in the stock market. SET membership rights were not transferable; occasionally non-member securities firms obtained membership but only by purchasing an existing member. Limited market access constrained price competition and resulted in a rigid and high brokerage structure. Commission fees charged by SET members were non-negotiable and remained fixed at 0.1 per cent for government bonds and at 0.5 per cent for all other securities. This guaranteed high profits for simple services. As SET members earned large and growing incomes for brokering trades over the 1980s, they developed a vested interest in defending the oligopolistic market. But high commissions deterred individual investors, suppressed the demand for tradable shares and posed a crucial stumbling block to stock market growth (*BT Annual Review* 1975: 25–26; Somjai 1988: 73–77).

The concentrated structure of the stock market also resulted from the fact that foreign firms seeking entry and membership were kept largely at bay. In the 1980s, proposals made by financial technocrats that foreign firms be allowed in to improve market efficiency met with strong and persistent resistance from large SET members and AMSET leaders (*BP* 25 September 1987: 5). While foreign banks obtained direct access to the Thai financial market through their operations in finance and securities companies, they had been limited to a maximum of 25 per cent ownership of these companies prior to the late 1980s. Moreover, not only could foreigners only invest in the SET through special funds, their ownership of listed Thai firms was restricted to less than 50 per cent. Coupled with high withholding taxes on capital gains, the ownership restrictions hindered the entry of foreign investors, particularly institutional investors, who might have been able to provide more investible funds, stabilise stock trading and broaden the Thai capital market (Bailey and Jagtiani 1994; *BBMR* September 1985: 411–418).

Government regulations abetted the emergence of an oligopolistic stock market. The rapid expansion of finance and securities companies concerned financial authorities, who moved to control entry by first requiring incumbent and new firms to obtain licenses in the early 1970s and then suspending the granting of licences in the late 1970s. The number of companies declined considerably in the 1980s when many were closed down in the aftermath of the massive failures of finance firms. Furthermore, from the inception of the SET the government deliberately kept the number of stockbrokers small, worrying that too many players would lead to cut-throat competition and market instability (BOT *Annual Economic Report* 1974: 45). Potential entrants had to buy into SET membership by paying 200,000 baht for a seat on the stock market and a monthly fee of 4000 baht in the late 1970s; the membership and monthly fees increased to 2 million baht and 18,000 baht respectively in 1987 (*Nation* 20 April 1987: 5). The high cost of obtaining SET membership put off small and medium-sized finance and securities firms and helped to maintain the clubby structure of the stock market.

Structural obstacles aside, there were also regulatory and institutional weaknesses that impeded the development of the Thai capital market. Such weaknesses were manifest, first and foremost, in the fragmentation of securities market regulation (Pakorn 1994; Somjai 1988: 11–13).

Prior to 1992, several agencies had been responsible for regulating different aspects of the securities industry: the finance ministry granted licences, oversaw securities trading and authorised listings; the Bank of Thailand (BOT, the central bank) supervised finance and securities companies; the SET board of governors regulated stockbrokers and managed the day-to-day operations of the stock market; and the commerce ministry acted as the registrar of public companies that made initial public offerings. Furthermore, these agencies operated under a plethora of laws, commercial codes and regulatory rules that were not completely compatible and even contravened each other (Ekamol 1993: 122–123). This dispersed institutional framework in which the different agencies regulated and represented the various segments of the securities sector generated competing interests among regulators.

The negative impact of dispersed regulatory powers over capital market development was clearly visible in the ad hoc manner in which fiscal policy that purported to promote the securities industry was enacted. The BOT and the SET, which were keener to see a robust capital market and had more symbiotic ties with the securities sector, supported strong tax incentives for more investors to buy shares and for more firms to go public. They pressed for reducing dividend and capital-gains taxes and increasing differences in the corporate taxes of listed and non-listed firms, particularly when adverse economic conditions dampened stock trading and eroded the profits of securities firms. On the other hand, revenue-conscious officials from the finance ministry were more concerned with the impact of tax incentives on the fiscal status of the government. They were inclined to reduce securities-related taxes when state coffers were strong but increase them when government revenues ran low or fiscal deficits were high. Policy incentives provided to promote capital market growth thus remained thin, piecemeal and inconsistent (*FEER* 25 September 1986: 92; *Nation* 13 February 1986: 7).

The fragmented institutional structure also weakened the ability of regulators to co-ordinate their efforts to develop strong securities rules in a timely manner and to enforce these rules strictly. Shared yet dispersed regulatory authority blurred the division of labour among the agencies, made it difficult to ascertain where the ultimate responsibility lay and created incentives to neglect duties. This generated significant loopholes in market regulation and allowed unscrupulous traders and firms to engage in questionable and even illegal activities in the capital market. Over the first decade of the SET's operation, over-speculation, market-rigging, insider trading and many other malfeasant practices were both prevalent and persistent. These practices implicated SET members and other securities firms, many of which eventually found themselves in deep financial trouble and collapsed under the weight of mounting bad debts, triggering successive bouts of crises in the late 1970s and the early and mid-1980s (Johnston 1989). In the aftermath of these crises, investors shied away from the securities market and the SET fell into a protracted atrophy.

Botched market reforms through mid-1990s

In the late 1980s, the Thai government made an initial effort to remove the structural and regulatory obstacles that had impeded capital market growth. In Thailand, as in Singapore, the mid-1980s global recession and the resultant balance-of-payments crisis precipitated the introduction of capital market reforms as a crucial part of the overall financial liberalisation programme. Pressures leading to reform initiatives also emanated from international financial institutions, particularly the World Bank and the IMF, and Western governments and financial firms that advocated capital market liberalisation either for improving the prospect for economic development or for ensuring market access (*BP* 8 November 1993: 8, 26 December 1994: 6; *EIUCR*-Thailand No. 2 1990: 23). Equally significantly, the end of the decade-long hostility in Indochina in the late 1980s and early 1990s provided Thailand with a good opportunity to improve diplomatic and commercial links with its neighbouring countries. The Thai government pushed for economic co-operation that would focus on Thailand and span the international boundary lines of the region, and actively promoted Bangkok as a regional financial centre. It thus saw a stronger and more efficient capital market as a key linchpin of this strategic plan. While these factors might not operate equally throughout the reform process, a secular trend towards financial globalisation appears to have been a constant impetus. Policy-makers intended to nurture the growth of the capital market in the hope that it would help the national economy to take advantage of opportunities presented by global market integration (Aroonsri and Pongpanu 1993).

Despite strong external political and market pressures, capital market reforms were largely a failure for much of the period under review in this section. Reform measures were harnessed mainly to private-regarding rather than broad national policy objectives. Indecisive action and inordinate postponement invariably plagued the enactment of market reforms; even when systemic pressures thrust reform policies onto the government agenda, most of these policies were considerably diluted or abandoned in midstream. The botched reforms resulted from the fragmented party system and weakly organised parties in the ruling coalition that combined to undermine the ability of financial policy-makers to promote financial and economic development through capital market reforms.

Private-regarding reform policies

In Thailand, the initiation of capital market reforms coincided with important changes in the political regime. In the July 1988 general election, Chatichai Choonhavan, a retired army general and a prominent politician with business experience, was swept into office as the country's first fully elected prime minister in 12 years. The election of Chatichai ushered in a crucial transition from the semi-democratic system that had existed under the tutelage of an unelected prime minister, Prem Tinsulanonda, during 1980–1988 to a more democratic polity in which the power of elected politicians increased at the expense of that of bureaucratic and military elites. More competitive elections, together with the growing assertiveness of diverse social groups operating in an increasingly open political milieu, subjected politicians more intensely to the electorate's demands and preferences.

While electoral pressures intensified, they did not translate into incentives for government politicians to provide public-regarding policies that would enhance the welfare of the general public. In the financial policy arena, as in many other public policy areas, Thai politicians were strongly inclined to favour narrow and particularistic constituencies over the broad citizenry. Inter-party structural fragmentation and intra-party organisational malaises combined to institutionalise the proclivity of political elites, more specifically party leaders, government ministers and legislators, to be more concerned with pursuing private-regarding policies than with achieving collective national goals in the process of capital market reforms.

As detailed in Chapter 3, the highly fragmented party system often resulted in more than 15 parties running in any given election and as many as ten parties winning seats in parliament. With such a large number of small parties competing in elections, the proportion of votes that each party needed to secure in order to win seats and participate in government was small. For general elections held between 1988 and 1997, the average winning party garnered only 10 per cent of the popular vote; the largest winning on average obtained 23 per cent of the vote but seldom secured more than 30 per cent (Nelson 2001: 286–288). The ability to win elections with such low percentages in this multi-party environment considerably reduced the incentive for politicians to appeal to a broad range of voters. They were strongly motivated to mobilise particular segments of society for electoral support and formed narrow coalitions that were often based on geographic characteristics. Thai parties and their corresponding electoral coalitions were each so small that politicians were keen to channel specific benefits to their particularised supporters.

The period under review also witnessed the growing strength in the political process of provincial politicians whose supporting factions and vote-canvassing structures were heavily regionally based. These politicians, who were backed by and beholden to local business interests, exerted significant influence over public policy in the 1980s and 1990s (Ockey 1994; Pasuk and Baker 2002: 351–356). They largely dominated the successive governments, particularly under the premiership of Chatichai Choonhavan (1988–1991), Banharn Silapa-archa (1995–1996) and Chavalit Yongchaiyudh (1996–1997). While the first Chuan Leekpai government (1992–1995) featured more economic technocrats, provincial politicians still occupied a weighty position in the many parties of the ruling coalition. With their electoral and support bases strongly localised and regionalised, party and factional leaders lacked both incentives and capabilities to aggregate a wide range of interests into national policy programmes. The ascendancy and dominance of provincial politicians enhanced the tendency of political particularism in the financial policy process.

The private-regarding orientation of politicians derived from party system fragmentation was further reinforced by the organisational weaknesses of the Thai political parties themselves. As was made clear in Chapter 3, weak party controls over candidate selection and financial resources rendered politicians more loyal to their local financial and electoral networks than to their own parties. Furthermore, the lack of strong and distinct party labels and platforms placed a premium on the ability of individual politicians to resort to candidate-focused campaigns by developing narrow bases of support and depending upon localised electoral coalitions. Rampant factional activities and persistent intra-party rivalries further encouraged politicians to link their career prospects closely to the welfare of their particularised constituencies and seek private-regarding policies for which they could claim personal credit. Consequently, parochial constituent interests rather than aggregated party policies dictated the behaviour of politicians and prevailed in the decision-making process of Thai parties.

The preferences of Thai politicians towards capital market reforms directly reflected the private-regarding incentives of the political party framework in which they operated. The fragmented party structure interacted with organisationally decentralised and incohesive parties to strongly encourage political elites to generate divisible political goods that could be used to build and maintain their localised financial and electoral networks. During the democratic transition of the late 1980s and 1990s, perennial desires to deliver particularistic policies targeted to their specific supporters for such purposes rendered politicians uninterested in such collective national policies as capital market reforms, which would spur financial development and sustain economic growth. This was not only because market reforms threatened to harm the interests of politicians' cronies, particularly in the securities sector, as will be shown below, but also because their narrow constituencies did not enjoy the full benefits of these reforms, which were to be dispersed across society.

While politicians had few incentives to initiate policy reforms to develop a more balanced and efficient financial system and provide general benefits to Thai society at large, they were eager to dispense regulatory favours to banks and promote them as an important source of political patronage. Unlike the capital market in which the decision calculus of vast numbers of individual investors was not easily controlled, a handful of banks permitted politicians to deliver targeted benefits to their specific constituents. They appropriated resources from banking institutions and used these resources to reward key supporters, promote pork-barrel-style projects in provinces or finance electoral campaigns (Pasuk and Baker 2000; Traisorat 2000). Politicians heading economic ministries (and members of parliament more generally) who regarded banks as a crucial asset from which to extract particularistic goods and services actively championed policy changes that bolstered the dominant position of banks in the 1980s and 1990s. They pushed for regulatory reforms that significantly enhanced the income and asset bases of private banks but did not weaken the oligopolistic structure of the financial sector controlled by a few banking families (Zhang 2002: 105–133). The pursuit of pro-bank policies for private-regarding purposes by politicians led to a systematic under-attention to the formulation of coherent and consistent capital market reforms.

Thai politicians were not completely uninterested in capital market reforms; to the extent that they were interested, however, they intended to capture such reforms as a vehicle for seeking rents for themselves or for their constituents. Prominent politicians, with large holdings of listed stocks or direct stakes in securities firms, had highly private pursuits in relation to stock market liberalisation. They were not so much concerned with long-term market development as with short-term measures to bolster share prices and rake in quick profits (*Asiamoney* September 1996: 10–13; *BP* 3 October 1996: 5; *Nation* 2 September 1990: 1). Some politicians, eager to keep the securities industry closed to competition and preserve regulatory favours for their cronies, resisted efforts to deregulate barriers to new entrants, but others pressed financial authorities to allow well-connected securities firms to obtain seats on the SET. Privatisation, partly designed to broaden and increase the supply of tradable shares on the stock market, was also opposed and manipulated by politicians for private-regarding purposes. Politicians in charge of the ministries that supervised the public sector kept SOEs under their control as a source of political patronage and used board and management positions in SOEs to allocate rents to strategic constituents (Handley 1997: 109–113; Hicken 2002: 234–246). The need to accommodate political constituencies and patron–client networks constantly pushed politicians to harness reform policies to rent-seeking activities.

Within the national government, public-regarding capital market reforms thus lacked political champions willing to marshal the necessary political support for consistent and coherent efforts. The strongest advocates of such reforms were technocrats in the BOT, the National Economic and Social Development Board (NESDB) and the Securities and Exchange Commission (SEC). They were eager to reform the capital market with a view to mobilise more investment funds for industrial development and foster a more robust financial sector.[2] These policy objectives took on added importance in the 1980s and 1990s when the gap between savings and investment in Thailand widened and the Thai financial market was forced to adapt to an increasingly competitive regional and global environment (Aroonsri and Pongpanu 1993; Ekamol 1993). However, technocrats had difficulty translating their preferences into actual policy reforms, primarily because their authority and autonomy were radically devalued in the 1990s (Zhang 2005). While prime ministers frequently appointed technocrats to take up the economic portfolios, they were still accountable to their political masters who lacked strong incentives to provide reform programmes that were attuned to the priorities of national development.

Indecisive and irresolute reform processes

Not only did Thai politicians lack strong incentives to pursue public-regarding policies through capital market reforms, they were unable to initiate decisive reform policies in response to domestic and

international challenges. As noted earlier in this section, external economic shocks, systemic political pressures and national development
imperatives congregated to press for capital market reforms in Thailand.
But the Thai government constantly failed to formulate and enact such
reforms during much of the period under review here. This primarily
resulted from the fragmented party system that invariably produced
multi-party coalition governments in the 1980s and 1990s. While veto
authority formally rested with the lower house of parliament, the coalition governments that typically comprised six or more different parties
or veto players produced highly decentralised policy-making structures
(Hicken 2002; MacIntyre 2003: 43). Equally crucially, virtually all the
parties in the ruling coalitions featured multiple and long-standing factions, as made clear in the analysis of the organisational profiles of Thai
parties provided in Chapter 3.

The large number of parties and their competing factions in the
cabinet, which represented different constituent interests and specific
economic groups, brought diverse and conflicting particularistic interests to bear upon the process of capital market reforms. This made
it difficult for prime ministers, as coalition leaders, to accommodate
these interests and satisfy every party and faction when formulating
reform policies. While some parties in the ruling coalitions supported
certain reform measures, others were in a position to block or slow the
enactment of these measures if they threatened to harm the interests
of their constituents. Prime ministers were restrained from introducing
politically painful reforms unless they wanted to risk the defection of
key coalition partners and the collapse of coalition governments. The
results were stalemates or gridlocks, with sporadic regulatory changes
and protracted negotiations, and extensive policy logrolls required to
initiate policy reforms. While successive governments announced plans
to reform the capital market, fragmented party institutions blunted the
translation of these plans into decisive policy action.

These institutional problems worked against the efforts of technocrats
to put an end to the oligopolistic practices that had long prevailed in the
stock market. As discussed in the preceding section, commission fees
charged by SET members remained fixed at 0.5 per cent for most securities. While generating fat profit margins for stockbrokers, fixed and
high commissions increased transaction costs, harmed the interests of
investors and dampened the demand for shares. In the late 1980s and
early 1990s, financial policy-makers tried in vain to make the commission structure more negotiable and flexible; this failed primarily because
of the fierce opposition from large SET members and their supporters

in the government. In the mid-1990s, reform-minded technocrats in the Chuan cabinet pushed for more competitive commission rates as an important part of their master financial plan (*FEER* 9 March 1995: 62–63; *WSJ* 28 February 1995: 1, 12). However, they were also frustrated in their liberalisation attempts by influential politicians who had close ties with securities firms or controlling interests in stockbroking companies (*BP* 7 May 1996: 15; *BPER* 30 June 1994: 27).

Efforts to remove obstacles to entry in the securities industry were also bogged down by opposition. While financial technocrats were eager to liberalise the investment markets for new domestic and foreign participants, they often found their hands tied by their political masters who had different and even opposing preferences. Powerful SET members had political allies in the ruling coalitions that maintained symbiotic ties with the stockbroking community and were hostile to entry deregulation. In the late 1980s and early 1990s, proposals to introduce more competition to the stock market were rejected by dominant parties in the Chatichai government (*Nation* 2 September 1990: B1, B2). Likewise, technocratic elites in the Chuan cabinet formulated plans to reduce entry barriers, particularly to foreign access, only to see them get lost in the quagmires of political squabbles. While Chuan's Democratic Party were supportive of entry deregulation, leaders of major coalitional parties stood against it; one of them even threatened to leave the coalition if foreign firms were given full access to the domestic equity markets (*BP* 28 August 1995: 8). Unwilling to see his shaky multi-party government founder over the disputes, Chuan halted the liberalisation of entry barriers.

The same organisational logic of Thailand's political party structure also asserted itself in the privatisation of state-owned enterprises. Apart from their efforts to strengthen state coffers, financial policy-makers intended privatisation to broaden the supply of shares and stabilise stock trading. This was deemed important, particularly given the fact that large Thai firms were reluctant to go public and the resultant scarcity of tradable shares often led to market volatilities. However, SOEs under the supervision of most line ministries were considered crucial assets from which politicians heading these ministries could derive particularistic benefits. Privatisation essentially meant the loss of a valuable source of patronage and it thus ran into strong opposition from politicians who led the supervising ministries (*EIUCR*-Thailand 1st Quarter 1995: 11–12; Kraiyudht 1992). As a result, the Thai government failed to enact coherent divestment programmes, although plans to privatise specific SOEs were announced piecemeal.

Dispersed veto authority most manifestly weakened the ability of the Thai government to reform the fragmented regulatory framework and introduce decisive institutional changes. From the late 1980s when the reform of securities market regulation arrived on the agenda the process was plagued by repeated delays. The initial bills for regulatory reforms were submitted to the cabinet for consideration in 1986 but languished in the finance ministry for nearly six years. They were met with strong resistance from private bankers and their political patrons in the government, who feared for greater competitive pressures brought about by market reforms; senior members of large parties in the coalition, who had direct stakes in securities firms, attempted to delay and water down the bills that would subject these firms to tighter supervision; local politicians, worried about the prospect of funds being attracted away from provinces by a stronger and larger stock market, dug their toes in against regulatory reforms (*BBMR* September 1987: 361–369; *BP* 25 October 1988: 5, 29 January 1990: 3; *FEER* 18 April 1991: 69–70).

The foregoing analysis does not suggest that the Thai government was unable to initiate any capital market reforms at all. At critical junctures during the early and mid-1990s, financial policy-makers rode on propitious political and external forces to press for market reforms. Nowhere was the impact of these forces more manifest than in the instalment of Anand Panyarachun, a former diplomat and widely respected businessman, as an interim prime minister by the military in the wake of the early 1991 coup that toppled the Chatichai government and in the aftermath of the May 1992 demonstration and massacre. Top military leaders who worried about the impact of their putsch on economic growth and had a direct stake in sustaining prosperity gave technocrats a free hand to manage the economy. They saw sound economic policy and market-oriented reforms as crucial in boosting confidence among investors, particularly foreign investors, and in encouraging capital inflows that played a key role in driving Thailand's economic boom (*AF* 15 September 1991: 73–74; *FEER* 18 July 1991: 31–34). The interim Anand governments reinstated the technocratic apparatus and its leading personalities and deflected the tendency to subvert economic policy to the whims of politicians that had been so prevalent under Chatichai. Financial technocrats regained their leverage vis-à-vis politicians and took the opportunity to introduce reform measures, including stock market liberalisation and the establishment of the SEC in 1992 (*BP* 15 April 1992: 28; *FEER* 12 March 1992: 52).

Like their counterparts elsewhere in the developing world, Thai technocrats, particularly those in the BOT, the NESDB and the SEC, perceived a well-developed capital market as the totem of Thailand's financial strength and economic modernisation. More than just institutional trappings, the capital market and its performance were regarded as a barometer of investor confidence in economic and financial policies. The interest, both materialistic and ideational, of financial policymakers in capital market growth hardened their resolve to push through key reform policies. Their ability to do so was sometimes enhanced by systemic political and market pressures that helped to weaken resistance to capital market reforms. This was particularly true of the Chuan economic team, who used forceful demands from the US and international financial institutions for stock market liberalisation to legitimatise and initiate crucial reforms amidst vociferous opposition (*BP* 8 November 1993: 8, 26 December 1994: 6).

While domestic political changes and external pressures occasionally thrust capital market reforms onto the policy agenda of the Thai government, these reforms, which were neither as deep nor as broad as reforms in Singapore, faced the constant danger of reversal. Political pressures often mounted for the change and relaxation of policy and regulatory reforms that were designed to promote the capital market. Institutional obstacles, mainly derived from intra-party organisational weaknesses, contributed to policy instability and irresoluteness in several important ways.

In the first place, decentralised and incohesive parties that fostered candidate-focused strategies and appealed to specialised constituents had the effect both of facilitating the play of particularistic interests and of impeding reform implementation. Unsuccessful efforts at capital market reforms certainly reflected the preferences and organisational resources of powerful financial and corporate actors in Thailand. As implied above, private financiers constantly lobbied for the protection of their regulatory privileges and resisted competitive pressures associated with market liberalisation; the strong opposition of SOE managers and employees frustrated government plans to divest state assets. However, this is not a simple story of reform policies being captured. Private market agents were able to assert themselves, primarily because internally weak parties interacted with fragmented party systems to encourage politicians to build and operate within narrow coalitions of supporters. Politicians and parties that represented such coalitions were beholden to a few influential private pressure groups and were prone to change, dilute or even abandon given reform policies that harmed these groups. As a result of policy-makers becoming obligated to particularised interests, various private actors gained enhanced access to financial policy processes. The political obstacles to which private capture gave rise yielded erratic and irresolute capital market reforms.

Furthermore, factionalised parties made party leaders vulnerable to policy blackmail by powerful factions threatening to switch parties. With multiple factions rife in the large parties that led the successive coalition governments, there was little prospect of the cabinet following through on reform plans that might hurt the interests of factional leaders and their key supporters. To keep their parties together and maintain their dominant position within the coalition, prime ministers were often compelled to put on hold or scrap altogether agreed-on reform measures. This was manifest in the largely futile attempts of the Chatichai and Chuan governments to open up the securities market to new entry, deregulate commission rates and implement tighter securities rules.

Intra-party organisational weaknesses also contributed towards unstable government that in turn undermined the maintenance of given reform policies. Recent studies (Anusorn 1998; Chambers 2005) have shown that the frequent collapse of Thai governments and the instability of cabinets in the democratic era rested as much with intra-party rivalries as with intra-coalition conflicts. High degrees of instability denied party leaders in the cabinet the power to set up coherently planned mechanisms and procedures to ensure satisfactory enactment of market reform programmes. Government and cabinet volatility was mirrored in a much higher turnover of financial policy-making elites in Thailand than in Singapore, as shown in Table 4.1. The low tenure inhibited the ability of key financial and regulatory officials to develop the policy expertise and market information necessary to formulate and maintain a consistent set of reform priorities. This resulted in ill-considered and frequent policy changes, undermining the effective and stable implementation of capital market reforms.

Highly fractionalised and disorganised parties in government enervated the authority of the executive and rendered prime ministers vulnerable to the problem of the lame duck. This severely weakened the ability of political leaders to control the behaviour of the economic bureaucracy and left them powerless to resolve conflicts between the BOT, the finance ministry, the SEC and other line ministries, which intensified and persisted against a backdrop of the growing politicisation of economic policy processes in the 1990s (Unger 1998: 99; Zhang 2005). Given that these agencies shared the responsibility for the overall management of financial and regulatory policies, the conflicts made it difficult for the government to develop the institutional cohesion with which to pursue market reform measures. Many of these measures were poorly designed and haphazardly enacted, partly due to the lack of co-operation and open rivalries between politicians or technocrats who headed the key regulatory agencies. In 1989 and 1990, for instance, plans to privatise a number of large SOEs were aborted by disputes between the BOT and the finance and transport ministries (*BP* 21 June 1989: 14 and 27 June 1989: 8; *EIUCR-Thailand* No 3 1990: 15–16); the SET's attempts to ease listing requirements and seek fiscal incentives for listed firms ran on the rocks in 1990, due to conflicts between the SET and the BOT behind it on the one side and the finance ministry on the other (*Nation* 19 October 1990: B1, B12); and the enforcement of financial and securities laws was severely compromised by personality clashes and power struggles between leading officials in the BOT, the finance ministry and the SEC that intensified in the mid-1990s (Zhang 2002: 160–167).

As a direct result of indecisive and irresolute reform processes, the Thai government had made little progress in the major areas of capital market liberalisation by the mid-1990s. Commission rates remained fixed and determined through large securities firms that dominated the hierarchically organised stock market. While the total number of SET members increased to more than 40, this reflected not so much the attempts of technocrats to liberalise entry barriers as the private-regarding efforts of politicians to secure the sought-after SET seats for their cronies, as mentioned earlier. More significantly, powerful SET/AMSET firms lobbied to increase the membership fee from 2 million baht to more than 3 million in 1994—making SET seats perhaps the world's priciest and putting off potential entrants (*FEER* 26 May 1994: 80)—and re-impose a ban on further entry in 1996 when stock trading slumped (*BP* 14 October 1996: 18).

The Thai government also faced grave difficulties in its privatisation efforts. Not only did the successive coalition governments fail to put in place coherent legal and institutional frameworks for enacting privatisation, they were unable to establish centralised organisations to carry out divestment programmes. Prior to the mid-1990s, only two pieces of privatisation legislation had been adopted by the interim Anand governments in which elected politicians were brushed aside and their influence over economic policy considerably diminished. To the extent that ad hoc plans to privatise specific SOEs were pressed through various political obstacles, they were seldom implemented completely as planned. In those cases of successful, if limited, privatisation, the government retained ownership with concessions and contracts to private firms rather than selling their assets on the stock market. As a result, the total number of privatised SOEs was small and the assets generated from privatisation remained minuscule (Hicken 2002: 256–258; Mithani and Pairat 2000: 243–244). While rapid and successful privatisation efforts in Singapore helped to expand the securities market, the halting and piecemeal process in Thailand hampered capital market growth.

Political barriers to decisive and consistent capital market reforms, derived from the underlying maladies of inter-party and intra-party structures, also contributed to a failure to establish an effective and efficient legal structure necessary to improve securities market operations. Laws promoting the sound and sustainable development of the equity markets were a low priority for party politicians and thus the necessary legislation was undersupplied. Bills inaugurating the SEC and strengthening securities market governance were on the back burner for many years, as noted above. Even existing laws were subject to political interference. Politicians who had personal and particularistic interests in the reform and development of the securities market, had strong incentives to undermine the efforts of regulatory agencies and officials to strictly enforce market rules and regulations. From its inception in 1992, the SEC was constantly susceptible to intense lobbying to limit its oversight of insider dealing and other fraudulent activities on the capital market. This was crucially manifest in the inability of the SEC to press charges against the prominent stock traders and financiers of major political parties who were implicated in price manipulation and to move against politically well-connected securities firms that engaged in over-speculation and market-rigging.[3] The result was that the Thai legal framework regulating the securities market was limited in scope and weak in enforcement (Handley 1997; Pakorn 1994).

During the late 1980s and much of the 1990s, the capital market grew much more slowly in Thailand than in Singapore. While the equity market became larger and more active, it remained relatively underdeveloped, and the financial market structure was essentially bank-based. Over 1989–1996, for instance, the annual average stock market capitalisation only accounted for 55 per cent of GDP in Thailand, as opposed to 133 per cent in Singapore.[4] Thai industrial firms continued to rely upon banks rather than securities markets as the major source of corporate financing. As a result, corporate leveraging remained high and even increased in Thailand during the period, making firms vulnerable to money market volatilities, particularly rapid increases in interest rates. Furthermore, the inability of the lacklustre capital market to mobilise long-term capital contributed towards the widening investment–saving gap. This led the government to encourage foreign capital inflows, much of which took the form of overseas borrowings and had short maturities. Finally, inadequately regulated securities firms and the poorly governed stock market fuelled speculative investments and aggravated the misallocation of financial resources. These micro-economic problems weakened the financial and corporate sectors and became the key precursors of the financial crisis of 1997–1998 that produced an unprecedented economic reversal in Thailand's post-war history of development.[5]

Post-crisis reforms: New challenges, old patterns

In the wake of the financial crisis, the Chavalit government, wracked by party and factional divisions and the resultant inability to respond to the crisis, resigned in ignominy (MacIntyre 2003: 58–69). This brought to office a new coalition government led by Chuan's Democratic Party. The economic turmoil revealed financial and corporate weaknesses and laid bare the political causes of these weaknesses. It galvanised broad public support not only for economic reforms and but also for political changes, which culminated in a new constitution. The new government moved swiftly to close down several dozen insolvent finance and securities companies and significantly tightened fiscal and monetary policies. More crucially, it saw the crisis as an opportunity to push through much-needed and long-delayed structural reforms in the financial and corporate sectors. Political economy analyses of post-crisis policy changes are now legion,[6] so there is little need for a detailed review of these changes. It is only important to note that many structural reforms constituted renewed and new efforts to reform the securities industry. These reforms are the analytical focus of this section.

In the face of mounting economic problems and external political pressures, particularly from the IMF, the initial stance of the Chuan government towards post-crisis reforms appeared quite decisive. However, this proved to be the exception rather than the rule; as the worst of the crisis waned, the government found itself subject to familiar political pressures and barriers. While the new constitution that promised to make the Thai political party structure more cohesive was adopted at the wake of the crisis, the full impact of its major provisions were not felt until the first post-reform election in 2001.[7] As a result, the Chuan government operated under many of the political constraints of the old system, which were manifest in a multi-party and inherently unstable coalition and, equally importantly, decentralised and fractionalised parties in the coalition. In combination, these factors oriented many reform policies towards private-regarding interests, generated gradual and halting processes, and yielded irresolute and modest outcomes.

As made clear in the preceding section, the fragmented party system interacted with weakly organised parties to render Thai politicians more concerned with directing benefits to their particularised supporters than with pursing national collective policies. In the post-crisis period, as during much of the pre-crisis era, politicians in coalition parties, including Chuan's party, had strong incentives to promote the welfare of their narrow constituencies in the process of financial and capital market reforms. Such incentives allowed private interests to permeate the formulation of major post-crisis policy changes and deflected the public-regarding purposes of the overall reform programme. While leading technocrats in the Chuan government were keen to develop a more robust and efficient capital market through various reform measures, they saw their policy objectives constantly undermined by the efforts of party politicians to capture the reform process as a vehicle for seeking rents for themselves and for their key supporters.

The private-regarding interests of politicians thus weakened the ability of the Chuan government to deliver the types of nationally oriented reform policies conducive to long-term growth. This was amply evidenced in the financial restructuring process. The initial strategy of the Chuan government was to take a tough stance with insolvent financial firms, recapitalise viable institutions and prioritise capital market growth, with the view to crafting a more balanced and robust financial architecture (Kawai and Takayasu 1999). However, this strategy quickly gave way to an uneven-handed approach that largely favoured banks. While the government shut down ailing securities firms, it backed away from closing insolvent banks and absorbed very large losses as a result. It made a large sum of money available for recapitalising banks, although it sought to limit public expense by forcing private banks to bear the costs. Eventually the burden of bank recapitalisation was born not so much by bank owners, whose losses were limited by government forbearance, as by taxpayers (*FEER* 3 September 1998: 49–50; June and Pornkamol 2002; *Nation* 28 October 1998: B2). In the meantime, the government paid scant systematic attention to the reform and revival of the capital market, although short-term measures to boost share prices were adopted in an ad hoc manner.

This bank-oriented approach to financial restructuring was not untypical in crises of this magnitude, as the massive failure of banks would have devastated the real economy. The government also saw the revitalisation of banks as instrumental in improving credit lines to business firms and pulling the economy quickly out of the post-crisis recession. However, the policy biases reflected not so much the exigencies of the crisis and recovery imperatives as the parochial interests of politicians. On the one hand, the long-established and highly personalised linkages between banks, politicians and bureaucrats, particularly in the finance ministry, not only made the government susceptible to the demands of private bankers but also enhanced their ability to project their preferences into the reform process (*FEER* 4 November 1999: 10–13; Imai 2006). On the other hand, politicians saw banks as a more controllable and manipulatable policy tool than the capital market to bail out financially strapped firms with which they maintained symbiotic ties. They were the major driving force behind the granting of six banking licenses in the aftermath of the crisis. They also pressed for large capital injections into specialised banking institutions, such as the Export-Import Bank of Thailand, and for the establishment of similar institutions, such as banks for rural development and for small and medium-sized enterprises, which they could use to allocate resources to their narrowly targeted constituents (*BP* 5 February 1998: 16).

Closely related to financial restructuring was corporate restructuring, the nature of which was also shaped by the rent-seeking inclinations of politicians. In Thailand, as in many other crisis-stricken East Asian countries, the resolution of corporate debts was crucial to the reduction of massive non-performing loans in the banking sector and effective financial transformation. Through corporate restructuring, technocratic reformers also sought to reduce the heavy debts of listed firms and improve their performance, thus restoring investor confidence and resuscitating the crisis-battered equity market (Kawai and Takayasu 1999). More importantly, academics and policy-makers both within Thailand and without opined that governance practices in Thai firms, particularly bank-based financing and family ownership, had generated severe weaknesses in the corporate and financial sectors and had directly contributed to the capital market crisis in 1997–1998 (*Asiamoney* May 2000: 11–15; Dollar and Hallward-Driemeier 2000). The government thus saw corporate restructuring as providing the key to reforming corporate governance in listed firms (*Asiamoney* March 1999: 20–23).

While the government created a Corporate Debt Restructuring Advisory Committee (CDRAC) in mid-1998, its restructuring plans clashed with vested interests. These interests, mainly represented by industrial debtors, made persistent efforts to align the reform of laws, particularly those governing bankruptcy and foreclosure that were central to corporate restructuring, with their private-regarding goals. Not only did they strategically manoeuvre their cash flows to avoid debt repayments (June and Pornkamol 2002), they mobilised political resources to press for regulatory favours in the process of legislative reforms. Their demands found sympathetic ears in the Senate, many members of which were well connected with specific industrial sectors or were themselves owners of heavily indebted groups. While the Senate only had the power to review rather than veto legislation, the review process gave politicians an opportunity to secure concessions favourable to industrial debtors (*BP* 23 January 1999: 11; Haggard 2000a: 160). Particularistic interests thus diluted much of the corporate reform legislation and produced a weak legal and administrative regime for bankruptcy and foreclosure that benefited debtors at the cost of the government's objective to strengthen the financial position of listed firms and revitalise the capital market.

Not only did the fragmented and incohesive party structure subvert the public-regarding goals of market reforms, it also constituted formidable obstacles to the decisive enactment of reform programmes. In the second Chuan government, as in the first, economic policy demonstrated a strong technocratic and reformist bent. But the six-party coalition faced the same institutional barriers to the initiation of politically painful market reforms. While Chuan's Democracy Party, as the largest in the coalition, occupied many top economic positions, it was forced to share economic management power with other parties and to accommodate different claimants on economic policy. Equally crucially, coalition parties, including Chuan's party, were invariably torn between rival factions that represented diverse constituent interests. Multi-party government, incohesive coalition parties and influential private business combined to create a recipe for dilatory and indecisive reform processes. Decision-making on a range of capital market-related issues, particularly stock market liberalisation, privatisation and corporate governance reform, stalled.

As mentioned earlier, the government moved with unusual dispatch to close down many ailing securities companies at the wake of the crisis. As a result, the total number of SET member firms declined sharply from 50 to 27. In late 1997, regulatory authorities announced a freeze on new entry into the stockbroking industry, at the urging of the surviving SET members whose asset structure had been wrecked by the stock market crash and depressed trading activity (*BP* 23 December 1997: 16). The government was acutely aware of the need for recapitalising the crisis-stricken securities firms but, faced with the massive bill of bank bailouts and constrained by the depleted state coffers, was not in a position to do so. It had no choice but to turn to cash-rich foreign securities companies and allowed them majority ownerships in Thai securities brokers. On the other hand, the standby agreement signed with the IMF also committed the Chuan government to open up the securities industry to greater foreign participation. However, no sooner had foreign firms bought into the stockbroking industry than they formed a tacit alliance with their local partners to restore and consolidate a hierarchical and clubby structure and press regulatory authorities to maintain the freeze on new entry into the investment and equity markets.[8]

The increased oligopolistic power of securities firms enhanced their ability to set commission rates in line with their preferences but frustrated the efforts of regulators to allow the rates to be guided by market conditions. When stock trading was on the rise, leading SET members tried to fix brokerage fees at high levels in order to take advantage of eager investors; when trading declined, large securities firms pushed for lower and more flexible rate structures as an important way to force small SET members out of the market (*BP* 20 March 1998: 16, 1 July 2000: 20). While the SEC had planned to fashion a freer commission regime two years after the crisis, this was resisted by powerful SET and AMSET members who demanded a lengthy transition period and mobilised senior politicians in both the ruling coalition and opposition to back their demands. As a result, brokerage liberalisation became bogged down in protracted negotiations between SEC officials and a powerful anti-liberalisation alliance of private financiers and their allies in government (*BP* 23 December 1999: 15; SEC 2002: 76–79).

The existence of multiple veto players and the influence of interested parties also served to delay the process of privatisation. In the aftermath of the crisis, the Chuan government was under heavy pressure from the IMF to reduce state presence in the national economy; privatisation had been a condition of the third Letter of Intent with the IMF that stipulated a timetable to speed up the reform pace (*BP* 5 April 1998: 7). Thai policy-makers were also keen to divest state assets as a crucial strategy to replenish the depleted state coffers and reduce the fiscal burden of subsidising loss-making enterprises. In early 1998, the government formulated a master plan for state enterprise sector reform and set up more centralised organisations to ensure satisfactory implementation. While privatisation was designed more to address discrete policy concerns than to spur capital market growth, the effective enactment of the plan would have supplied more tradable shares and facilitated the reform and revival of the capital market.

However, the privatisation plan quickly ran into formidable political obstacles. The political problems were primarily manifest in the strong desire of politicians to retain SOEs as the key mechanism by which to dispense patronage and seek rents. While labour resistance and bureaucratic bottlenecks retarded progress in developing specific privatisation frameworks, opposition from rent-seeking politicians delayed the passing of enabling legislation. The politics of privatisation came to centre on the corporatisation act that would allow SOEs to be corporatised ready for divestment and facilitate public share offerings. When the cabinet tabled the act for deliberation in parliament in mid-1998, it provoked strong resistance from the Senate, which used its constitutional power to review and thereby delay the privatisation legislation. Many senators who benefited from SOE directorships or had cronies as SOE managers used growing public hostility to foreign purchases of Thai assets to protect their own interests under a cloak of nationalist rhetoric (*BP* 1 December 1998: 15, 29 December 1998: 11). In the ruling coalition, senior politicians who headed the line ministries supervising SOEs were antagonistic towards the corporatisation act. Given that Chuan needed his major coalition partners to maintain his razor-thin majority in parliament, he was forced to cave into their pressures (*BP* 21 April 1999: 14). In the end, the privatisation act had not been passed until late 1999.

The delaying effects of party fragmentation were similarly salient in the reform of corporate governance, which was crucial to securities market regulation and capital market growth. The initiation of corporate governance reform was contingent upon successful corporate restructuring. However, not only were the overall objectives of corporate restructuring subverted by particularistic interests, as discussed above, but government efforts to reform the bankruptcy and foreclosure laws governing the restructuring process were repeatedly foiled by the Senate (Haggard 2000a: 159–162). This made it difficult for reformers to link corporate restructuring to their plans to enforce stricter accounting standards, greater information disclosure and better investor protection in the corporate sector, all of which stood to facilitate the development of the capital market. Acutely aware that these reform measures were most likely to be opposed by those who had influential business interests and their allies in government, financial policy-makers could not muster their courage to introduce amendments to such existing laws as the Securities and Exchange Act and the Public Companies Act that were expected to strengthen corporate governance. As a result, none of these laws had been revised by early 2001 when the Chuan government collapsed amidst mounting corruption scandals.

It should be made clear that the Chuan government did manage to pass more than 40 economic reform bills, many of which boded well for capital market growth, in the parliamentary session that ended in December 1999. This was more than the combined achievements of the two preceding coalitions headed by Banharn and Chavalit respectively. An acute sense of national emergency, particularly in the immediate post-crisis period, external political pressures and the strong reformist propensity of Chuan's party all helped harden the resolve of the government to push the reform bills through political obstacles. While important economic reforms were initiated, they were not resolutely implemented as planned. By the time the coalition government came to grief in early 2001, few of the initiated capital market reforms had been followed through. The primary factors that undermined the maintenance of given reform policies were inter-party and intra-party organisational weaknesses.

As was made clear in the foregoing analysis, virtually every coalition party in the Chuan government featured decentralised and incoherent decision-making structures, weak party controls over backbenchers or rampant factional infighting. Atomised party leaders and different factions within the coalition parties constantly found themselves embroiled in internal squabbles and jostling for cabinet positions. They often threatened to and did bolt from their parties and the coalition if their demands were not met. These intra-party struggles ran parallel to intra-coalition conflicts over executive and legislative posts and greater roles in policy-making processes. In order to keep major coalition parties together and thus prevent the disintegration of the coalition, Chuan was forced to change ministerial allocations through frequent cabinet reshuffles. Furthermore, persistent inter-party and intra-party conflicts caused the frequent resignations of party and factional leaders who often headed important line ministries (*BP* 1 October 1998: 13; *EIUCR*-Thailand 2nd Quarter 1999: 15, 1st Quarter 2000: 14).

These organisational problems led to unstable capital market reforms in two different yet interrelated ways. First, they contributed to the quick turnover of key economic officials responsible for implementing reform policies. While the finance minister, Tarrin Nimmanahaeminda, managed to cling onto the fiscal portfolio, the BOT governor, the SEC secretary-general and other economic ministers were replaced, sometimes more than once, within the short tenure of the Chuan government. Frequent changes in top economic personnel impeded the policy-makers' efforts to develop expertise and experience with which to implement institutionally complicated reform measures (SEC 2002: 152). On the other hand, securities firms acted as an important channel through which specific regulatory changes could be effectively made; new rules concerning corporate governance and securities market regulation were unlikely to be implemented and sustained unless they were firmly embedded in the operations of private firms. However, the instability of financial policy elites and the resultant inconsistent and even conflicting policy directions made it difficult for private market agents to incorporate regulatory reforms and rules in their behaviour.[9]

Second, Chuan, who was weighed down by his constant attempts to appease rebellious politicians in his own and other parties and hold intra-coalition rivalries in check, had weakened executive controls over the economic bureaucracy. This was mainly reflected in his inability to resolve persistent inter-agency conflicts. These conflicts, particularly those between state agencies responsible for financial and regulatory policies, seriously compromised the implementation of capital market reforms. The plan of privatising the state railways of Thailand was abandoned midway, primarily due to the disputes and poor co-ordination between the finance and transport ministries, for instance (*BP* 11 May 1998: 15); long-running power struggles between the SEC and the SET frustrated government efforts to amend the SEC act and improve market governance (*BP* 30 October 1998: 15, 5 November 1998: 11); and policy differences between the finance minister and the BOT governor interrupted the plans to improve the corporate governance of listed companies (*BT* April 2000: 9; *Nation* 9 April 2000: B2).

Both intra-party and intra-coalition conflicts encouraged politicians who traditionally had close links with particularised constituent interests to be responsive to these groups as an important strategy to enhance their positions in their competition with other rival factions or parties. This had the effect both of making policy-makers inclined to change or even abandon given reform programmes that threatened to harm the interests of specialised economic groups and of providing these groups with enhanced access to policy processes. These problems subjected capital market reforms to the whims of private market agents, compromising the resoluteness of reform policies.

The problems were clearly manifest in the implementation of commission liberalisation. Following the SEC announcement of a more flexible fee structure in September 2000, fierce competition for customers ate sharply into the profit margins of securities firms. SET members and politicians who had constituent interests in the stock-broking community pressed for easing fee liberalisation. SEC officials, who were also worried about the positions of small firms, caved into political pressure and returned to the fixed structure several months later (*BP* 9 September 2000: 17; SEC 2002: 76–79). By the same token, the Chuan government experienced chronic difficulty following through the specific plans of corporatising and privatising major SOEs, despite the passing of the key privatisation legislation in late 1999. The splits within the coalition facilitated the penetration of the privatisation pro-cess by a range of private actors who had vested interests in continued state ownership (EAAU 2000: 180–189; Praipol 2003). As a result, the divestment of key SOEs in the energy, transport, water and telecommu-nication sectors was either implemented partially, shelved indefinitely or scrapped altogether.

Nowhere was the destabilising impact of private capture enabled by factionalised party structures more salient than in the reform of corpo-rate governance. Deterred by strong political opposition from reforming corporate governance-related laws, regulatory authorities, more specifi-cally the SEC and the SET, introduced an array of administrative rules to strengthen board independence, investor protection and financial dis-closure in 1998 and 1999. They saw the new rules as crucial in improving corporate practices, particularly in listed firms, and providing a sound foundation for long-term capital market growth (*Asiamoney* March 1999: 20–23, May 2000: 11–15; EAAU 2000: 169–171). However, key empiri-cal studies (Deunden 2005; Walter 2008: 78–98) have shown that most of these rules existed on paper only and were ineffectively enforced. They have attributed low levels of rule enforcement to the resistance of controlling shareholders, who perceived corporate reforms as a direct threat to their own interests. This is certainly true but the problem had a deeper institutional cause: senior politicians in the ruling coalition who were closely linked or beholden to specific corporate interests con-stantly pressed the SEC to exercise forbearance towards rule violators (Imai 2006; White 2004).

Reforms under Thaksin: More decisive but less credible

In the early and mid-2000s, Thailand's capital market reforms departed in a way from their previous patterns, as a result of crucial changes in both inter-party and intra-party structures. As made clear in Chapter 3, the 1997 constitution ushered in a more concentrated party system that enabled the TRT under Thaksin Shinawatra to win more than 40 per cent of the popular vote in the 2001 election and 60 per cent of the vote in the 2005 election. Thailand had a de facto dominant-party system in 2001–2005, despite the existence of a coalition government, and had a single-party government in 2005–2006. Equally significantly, the TRT was more centrally and cohesively organised than all of the counterparts that had operated during the democratic transition of the late 1980s and 1990s. This resulted from the TRT having a more centralised decision-making structure, more independent financial resources and more effective controls over candidate selection.

Unlike the previous fragmented party structure that had enabled a large number of small parties to win parliamentary seats with low vote percentages, the more concentrated system dictated that the TRT generate majoritarian support and secure votes nationwide in order to win elections. This began to institutionalise incentives for TRT politicians to appeal to a wider range of constituencies and build broader electoral coalitions. The TRT had to reach across social groups to a greater degree than political parties who were operating in multi-party environments. Furthermore, as the TRT was organisationally stronger, its leaders were better positioned to make key decisions about party platforms and enforce them on party office-holders. TRT leaders acquired the enhanced institutional leverage to compel party members, legislators and even factional leaders to support party-determined principles. The greater centralisation and cohesiveness of the ruling party weakened the influence of particularised interests on party decision-making processes and shifted party policies and priorities more to the national level.

Growing centripetal forces created by greater party concentration and organisational strength increased the incentive for TRT leaders and politicians to provide public goods policies. This was particularly true in those policy areas in which the interests of top party leaderships were engaged. Empirical studies (Hicken 2006; Kuhonta and Mutebi 2006) have clearly shown that the TRT not only campaigned on programmatic platforms but also enacted national-level social policies contained in those platforms.[10] The same holds true for the orientation of financial and regulatory policies. On entering office, the Thaksin government formulated a long-term master plan to reform the Thai capital market, with the explicit objectives of overcoming the structural hazards of the bank-based financial system and developing a more balanced and efficient market structure. These objectives were prioritised in the second master plan for capital market development that was initiated shortly after the TRT had been re-elected in a landslide victory in 2005 (*BPER* year end 2005: 23; *EIUCR*-Thailand November 2005: 32). Specific regulatory reforms that encouraged a wider array of firms, particularly medium-sized and small firms, to get listed on the SET and broaden share-holding across different segments of the population were given priority on the agenda of the government.

However, changes in inter-party and intra-party organisations did not eliminate particularism in the process of capital market reforms; private-regarding strategies were still commonplace in the formulation of reform policies. The incentives of the more cohesive party structure that might have more strongly predisposed politicians towards a national policy orientation were counteracted by three old institutional patterns that were manifest in the TRT. First, the TRT remained heavily imbued with internal conflicts. A dozen factions were pitted against each other over party executive positions, cabinet portfolios and legislative posts; such conflicts persisted through the first Thaksin government and intensified in the second. Second, Thaksin failed to build his own party-oriented bases of support and depended upon political factions and provincial politicians with existing local electoral networks for canvassing and securing votes. As detailed in Chapter 3, provincial barons, who comprised most faction leaders, went to great lengths to reinforce their personal networks in order to boost their power position vis-à-vis that of rival factions within the TRT and enhance their chances in local and general elections. And third, the electoral triumph of the TRT represented the direct entry of private business into politics (*FEER* 11 December 2003: 16–18; Hewison 2005) and made the Thaksin government particularly beholden to special economic interests in the policy-making process.

These institutional patterns continued to create strong incentives for politicians to cultivate narrow bases of support and pursue particularised interests, despite the fact that the TRT was now using more programmatic policy appeals as a crucial vote-getting strategy. Intra-TRT rivalries in the government, legislative and electoral processes encouraged politicians to develop personalised strategies that centred on the delivery of benefits to factional supporters. Such strategies were important in strengthening the weight of competing factions against each other within the party. Factional leaders, driven by the desire to boost their positions in constant intra-party struggles over political resources, were under intense pressure to direct particularistic goods to their key constituents. As they controlled electoral networks and influenced election outcomes, they continued to hold considerable sway over party decisions and manipulated public policies for private-regarding purposes. More importantly, the enhanced penetration of government processes by big business obligated politicians to align economic policy with private preferences. Even many of the party-list members of parliament who were supposed to concentrate their energies on issues of national importance were inclined to capture financial and regulatory reforms as a vehicle for seeking rents for themselves and for their strategic constituents (Hewison 2005; Kitti 2007).

In the formation of capital market reforms, strong incentives to pursue particularistic interests on the part of TRT politicians existed alongside and often prevailed over more nationally oriented policy intentions. These interests, which worked against programmatic efforts at orienting the bank-based financial system towards a more balanced and efficient structure, were amply evidenced in the process of bank restructuring, privatisation and stock market development.

While setting out to boost capital market growth in the master plans, Thaksin and his close associates were more concerned with revitalising and using banks as an effective means to deliver rents to their clienteles. A Thailand Asset Management Corporation, established to take bad loans away from banks shortly after Thaksin had come to power, quickly became a major source of crony capital and was used by TRT leaders for bailing out well-connected companies and businesspeople (*FT* 26 September 2001: 31; Pasuk and Baker 2004: 112). During the first Thaksin government, new banks were licensed, public financial institutions were upgraded to commercial banks and existing banks received massive capital injections. All of this was designed not only to support Thaksin's populist socio-economic policies but, more crucially, to favour specific businesses. While TRT leaders directed banks to shower money on large corporate groups in the TRT inner circle, factional and provincial heavyweights channelled bank credit to local businesses that helped to strengthen personal electoral networks (*BPER* year end 2004: 25; *EUICR*-Thailand February 2002: 33; *FT* 3 February 2005: 15; Pasuk and Baker 2004: 109–112). Under the Thaksin government, as under its predecessors, policy reforms that favoured banks for private-regarding purposes were enacted at the cost of the overall development of the capital market.

The divestment of state assets, which was purported to raise the market capitalisation of the SET and deepen and broaden the capital market, was also subjected to political manipulation. The pursuit of privatisation through stock-market listings actually acted as an important instrument for TRT politicians to seek and distribute rents. For example, when a number of large SOEs, especially the state petroleum agency, were partly privatised and their shares were sold on the exchange, the relatives of line economic ministers and business cronies of the ruling TRT acquired large holdings while retail investors were not given equal opportunities to receive shares (*BPER* 28 December 2001: 13; *EUICR*-Thailand February 2002: 32–33; *FEER* 18 March 2004: 21; *Nation* 20 April 2004: B1). Privatisation, like bank restructuring, became a vehicle for turning state assets into private capital and for subsuming public-regarding reform policies under narrow and particularistic pursuits.

Incentives to supplement nationally oriented policies with private-regarding interests were particularly strong in the formulation of specific strategies to boost stock market growth. In early 2002 and again in early 2004 when the SET was mired in the doldrums, the government introduced tax incentives, mobilised state pension resources and created investment funds, such as the Thailand Opportunity Fund and the Vayupak Fund, in order to strengthen the investor base, animate stock trading and encourage new listings (*Nation* 6 January 2002: B1, 19 April 2004: B3). While these measures stood to foster the development of the capital market, they were also intended to promote particularistic interests. Prominent members of the cabinet who had large holdings of listed stocks were keen to use public funds to shore up stock prices; factional leaders and senior politicians in the TRT who had direct stakes in securities firms or who wanted to use bloated asset values to leverage their bank credit pressed for similar measures (*BPER* Mid-Year 2004: 18; Thanee and Pasuk 2008).

The combination of party structural changes with old institutional patterns not only generated mixed reform incentives but also mixed outcomes in the process of implementing reform policies. The concentrated party system dramatically reduced the number of veto players in the policy-making process, and centralised policy authority in the hands of TRT leaders and Thaksin in particular. Equally importantly, TRT politicians occupied almost all the ministerial portfolios in the first Thaksin government, although two small parties were invited to partner with the TRT. Single-party controls over the bureaucracy enabled the TRT government to contain inter-agency rivalries, co-ordinate various reform programmes and increase policy-making decisiveness. The two comprehensive and multi-stage master plans for reforming and developing the capital market were formulated relatively decisively, for instance; a well-designed long-term strategy for further liberalising the securities industry was initiated without a hitch; when Thaksin and his close associates decided to divest state assets to stimulate stock market growth and strengthen state coffers, they were able to revive the privatisation programme fairly quickly.

However, given that intra-party organisational structures still strongly oriented politicians towards private-regarding pursuits, the decisiveness of capital market reforms under the TRT was issue-specific. The government moved swiftly to enact those reform policies that promised to provide both public and particularistic goods but procrastinated if reforms threatened to harm the interests of TRT politicians and their key constituents. Legislative amendments to the BOT and SEC acts that stood to enhance the independence of financial technocrats and weakened the ability of politicians to seek rents through political interventions were made by fits and starts (*FT* 4 October 2004: 16). By the same token, key reforms of corporate governance that were to dilute ownership concentration, protect minority investors and subject corporate decision-making to market disciplines slowed to a crawl (Deunden 2005). While the privatisation effort was quickly revived, regulatory reforms that would minimise regressive redistributive effects and limit the ability of politicians to use asset divestment as a source of pork and patronage lacked a political champion and took a backseat (Praipol 2003: 24).

Even those capital market reforms that were decisively initiated were unlikely to be effectively implemented as planned. In the Thaksin government, as in its predecessors, organisational weaknesses in the ruling party constituted the most crucial political barriers to the resoluteness of reform policies. More specifically, the strengthening of symbiotic ties between TRT politicians and businesses provided private market agents with enhanced access to the centre of financial policy and buttressed their ability to undermine the enactment of politically painful measures.

While the first master plan set the clear goals of increasing competition in the securities sector and deregulating commission rates, stock market liberalisation was halting, meandering and ultimately ineffective. Efforts to allow banks to offer brokering and underwriting services were repeatedly foiled by powerful AMSET members and politicians who had controlling interests in securities firms (*BP* 7 January 2002: 17). Following the futile attempt to liberalise the fixed commission structure in early 2002, the SEC moved to turn the structure into a more flexible modus operandi in early 2004. However, brokers staged a forceful campaign to maintain oligopolistic practices under the co-ordination of the AMSET. More crucially, senior TRT politicians pressed regulatory authorities to time fee changes in such a manner that the interests of private firms could be protected. The SEC caved into political pressures and held fee liberalisation in abeyance (*BP* 17 March 2004: 13). In late 2005, market regulators managed to thrust the issue back onto the agenda of capital market development, only to see their efforts go to the wall again (*BP* 30 November 2005: 13). The second master plan did not seek to fully liberalise commission fees until 2010.

The play of particularistic interests in reform processes also undercut the enforcement of securities market rules. The two master plans emphasised the importance of establishing a well-regulated and robust capital market; the SEC followed this up with specific rules to strengthen the governance of listed firms and securities companies. However, new rules, particularly those concerning bankruptcies, accounting standards and board independence, were progressively relaxed by the TRT government as it sought to promote the interests of debtors, business families and corporate directors, many of whom were senior TRT politicians themselves (*EIUCR*-Thailand November 2001: 22–23; *FEER* 1 August 2002: 38; White 2004). More importantly, while the SEC imposed more fines for breaches of regulations and blacklisted more listed forms, its ability to strictly enforce existing securities rules remained weak and limited. Not only did market regulators lack legal teeth to force corporate groups to comply with new governance standards that threatened family controls, but they were politically constrained from acting harshly towards the violators of securities market rules (Deunden 2005; Walter 2008: 80–91; White 2004).

The failure of the government to amend the SEC and other relevant acts, as made clear above, certainly contributed to the problem. However, securities market governance would have been improved if the existing rules that the SEC had painstakingly developed since the Asian financial crisis had been effectively enacted. Weak enactment resulted as much from inadequate legal capacities as from political obstacles associated with party organisational weaknesses. It was essentially the strong desire of TRT politicians to protect and promote the interests of corporate families as their key constituents that compromised compliance with corporate governance rules (Dixon 2004; Imai 2006). By the same token, opposition from prominent figures in the ruling party overwhelmed SEC officials' resolve to move in on well-connected securities executives and corporate directors who flouted market rules.[11] As a result, few rule violators were indicted and prosecuted in the Thaksin era, despite rampant insider trading, price manipulation and fraudulent transactions (Barton et al. 2004; Karuntarat et al. 2005).

The irresoluteness of capital market reforms in Thailand also derived from another intra-party organisational problem—the heavily factionalised TRT and resultant cabinet instability. While increased party system concentration and the enhanced leverage of Thaksin over coalition partners combined to make the government more stable, persistent and fierce factional rivalries within the TRT led to cabinet volatility. Between early 2001 and late 2004, Thaksin reshuffled the cabinet 12 times; frequent cabinet reshuffles gave rise to a high turnover in economic policy-making elites. This was especially clear in the case of the low tenure of top personnel in the finance ministry and associated erratic policy changes. Barely two years into the first Thaksin administration, the finance minister, Somkid Jatusripitak, was kicked upstairs to become a deputy prime minister and his deputy, Suchart Jaovisidha, took the helm at the treasury in a cabinet reshuffle designed to patch up differences between line ministers and buttress the position of Thaksin vis-à-vis that of factional leaders (*BP* 14 February 2003: 3; *Nation* 10 February 2003: 2). In order to brush aside widespread doubts about his capacity and prove his mantle, Suchart pushed for new and renewed reform measures that were intended to liberalise commission rates, tackle share speculations and divest a few key SOEs. However, these measures were either delayed or reversed by Somkid, who was more beholden to particularistic interests in March 2004, when he made a surprise comeback to the financial portfolio in another reshuffle (*EIUCR*-Thailand May 2004: 39; *Nation* 16 March 2004: B2). Capital market policies were returned to a more reformist track in August 2005 when Somkid was replaced by Thanong Bidaya, a veteran technocrat, in yet another cabinet reshuffle.

In sum, the more concentrated party system interacted with old institutional patterns within the TRT to create conflicting incentive structures and mixed policy outcomes. While TRT politicians aligned some reform policies with public-regarding purposes, they were simultaneously motivated to pursue particularistic interests in the reform process. The centralisation of veto power contributed to decisive reform initiatives but intra-party organisational weaknesses subjected initiated reform measures to the shifting and erratic preferences of powerful actors and undermined policy resoluteness. As a result, progress in major reform areas was partial, inconsistent and mediocre. The oligopolistic structure of the securities sector lingered on, as entry barriers remained and commission rates stayed largely fixed. During its first term in office, the Thaksin administration oversaw the listing of only three out of more than 20 key SOEs slated for privatisation (*EIUCR*-Thailand May 2005: 20). Efforts to improve securities market and corporate governance suffered as private fraud and malfeasance remained rampant. Thailand under Thaksin was rated weaker than not only Singapore but also many other East Asian economies on the key indicators of securities rule enforcement (see Table 4.2).

Ineffective market reforms did not facilitate and indeed impeded the growth of the securities industry. During the post-Asian crisis period, the capital market in Thailand developed more slowly than that in Singapore. Over 1997–2007, the annual average stock market capitalisation accounted for 49 per cent of GDP in Thailand, as opposed to 181 per cent in Singapore.[12] While the Thai capital market, particularly the bond market, became larger and more active in the early and mid-2000s than in the 1990s, this was mainly attributable to structural and contingent factors. Sustained economic growth and increased income levels generated differentiated needs for financial products that banks were unable to meet and strengthened the role of the capital market in the Thai economy. More directly, the capacity of major private banks to lend was severely constrained by their weak asset structures and stricter capital adequacy requirements. This forced many large industrial firms to resort to direct financing. Equally importantly, the dire need of the government to finance corporate and financial restructuring through bond issues greatly facilitated capital market growth. However, as the lending capacity of banks strengthened and the government eased its efforts to support financial and corporate sectors, the growth of the capital market slowed down sharply in the mid-2000s (Chalongphob and Pakorn 2007). Without effective policy and institutional reforms, the Thai securities industry was unlikely to develop in a robust and sustained manner.

Conclusions

This chapter demonstrates that the pattern of capital market reforms in Thailand was an important function of the changing configuration of political parties. From the late 1980s to the late 1990s, the fragmented party system and weakly organised parties in the ruling coalition combined to encourage politicians to seek particularised interests in the process of market reforms. Equally significantly, these institutional maladies weakened the ability of policy-makers to formulate and implement reform policies effectively. While external market and political pressures thrust major reform measures onto the government agenda at critical junctures during the 1990s, the overall approach to capital market reforms remained indecisive and irresolute. In the early and mid-2000s, the increasingly concentrated party system rendered the Thaksin government more decisive than its elected predecessors; it was able to pursue important reform initiatives, particularly those that engaged the interests of TRT leaders. However, intra-party organisational weaknesses within the TRT not only oriented financial policies towards private-regarding objectives but also undermined the resolute and consistent implementation of market reform programmes. The foregoing analytical account clearly illustrates the policy impact of temporal changes in Thailand's political party structures. Policy failures and regulatory changes hypothesised under the theoretical model advanced in Chapters 2 and 3 were indeed the ones exhibited in the overall process of capital market reforms.

Following the coup of September 2006 that ousted Thaksin, the military-backed interim government set constitutional reform as one of its top priorities. Seeing the 1997 constitution as crucially instrumental in having concentrated power in the hands of TRT leaders, the government went all out to prevent the re-emergence of powerful political parties that were wont to threaten the authority of conservative forces, including the military, in Thailand. The new constitution that was approved via a close-fought referendum in August 2007 replaced single-seat with multi-seat districts, weakened the ability of party leaders to rein in factions and removed barriers to party switching. These changes signified a huge step backwards in party institutionalisation (*EIUCR*-Thailand October 2007: 13–16, January 2008: 10–12; Hicken 2009: 136–143). The party system became increasingly fragmented over the ensuing years and major parties, both old and new, continued to have decentralised and incohesive structures. As a result, the two successive governments led respectively by the People Power Party (PPP), a reincarnation of the dissolved TRT, and the Democratic Party featured shaky and unstable multi-party coalitions, a hallmark of Thailand's political scene in the 1990s.

Economic management in general and financial policy-making in particular seemed in many respects like a return to the old days of the pre-2000s governments. As politicians spent their time and resources pursuing particularised interests, long-term and nationally oriented reforms designed to boost capital market growth were undersupplied. The weak, unwieldy and short-lived governments undermined not only decisive and effective reform planning but also policy continuity. Subjected to particularised pressures and hamstrung by intra-agency conflicts, financial technocrats were unable to make any significant progress in the improvement of market institutions and regulatory oversight (*FT* 13 August 2007: 7; *WSJ* 25 August 2008: C6). While the SEC formulated a new capital market development plan in 2009, its implementation remained sporadic and largely ineffective. The negative impact of institutional weaknesses on capital market reforms was aggravated by protracted and convoluted conflicts between the pro- and anti-Thaksin alliances throughout 2008 and 2009.[13] The resultant government instabilities also enervated the ability of economic officials to initiate needed market reforms and carry through given policy changes.

The failure to enact effective market reforms and promote capital market growth took its toll on the economic resilience of Thailand in the global financial crisis of 2008–09. Thailand suffered more in terms of reduced GDP growth and recovered less strongly than not only Singapore but also many other East Asian economies (Son and Andres 2009; World Bank 2010a). Obviously, the relatively poor performance of the Thai economy was contingent upon an array of external and domestic factors but a detailed analysis of these factors cannot be accommodated here. However, the weaker role of the capital market as the backup source of industrial financing was causally important. This is particularly the case when Thailand is put in comparative perspective. As in Singapore, the crisis reduced the provision of bank credit, dampened private investment and exacerbated the externally induced economic recession in Thailand. But unlike in Singapore where the well-developed capital market was able to pick up the slack in banking, provide an alternative source of industrial financing and facilitate recovery, as mentioned in the preceding chapter, in Thailand the relatively poorly developed capital market failed to do so (Ito et al. 2009; Son and Andres 2009). The differential ability of Singapore and Thailand to withstand the crisis thus reflects the cross-country variation in the development of capital markets and, more crucially, its political underpinnings.

6
Malaysia: Mixed Record on Reforms

In Malaysia, as in Singapore and Thailand, initial efforts to reform the capital market were made in the aftermath of the global recession of the mid-1980s and associated domestic economic woes. While the timing of market reforms and external stimuli to these reforms were comparable, the pattern of regulatory changes in Malaysia displayed striking differences. Political elites were generally able to align reform programmes with public policy purposes but simultaneously used reforms as a vehicle for pursuing particularised interests. Equally importantly, while the Malaysian government had a demonstrated ability to enact largely decisive reform policies, they were less capable of sustaining these policies. The central argument is that the public-regarding incentive of policy-makers that stemmed from party system concentration was significantly undercut by intra-party conflicts and rampant factionalism within the UMNO, which spawned particularism in the reform process. Similarly, party concentration facilitated policy decisiveness but intra-party organisational weaknesses compromised reform resoluteness. The upshot is that capital market reforms were more successful in Malaysia than in Thailand but less so than in Singapore.

This chapter, like the preceding ones on Singapore and Thailand, proceeds chronologically through the case study of capital market reforms in Malaysia since the late 1980s. The first section describes, in broad strokes, the key defining features of capital market structure and regulation in the 1980s. This provides the backdrop for the political analysis of market changes that unfolded throughout the ensuing two decades. The second section examines the process of policy and regulatory reforms during much of the 1990s and the third section focuses on further reform efforts following the Asian crisis of the late 1990s. The fourth and final section concludes by exploring how Malaysia's mixed record regarding capital market reforms impacted its economic performance in the global financial crisis of the late 2000s.

Pre-reform market structure and regulation

In Malaysia, while stock exchanges began to emerge as early as in the late nineteenth century, they evolved in a rather haphazard manner and remained inchoate throughout the first half of the twentieth century.[1] It was not until 1960 that a formal joint stock market was established in Singapore and Kuala Lumpur and shares were traded publicly in line with a relatively rudimentary regulatory framework. The joint market came to an end and the Kuala Lumpur Stock Exchange (KLSE) was incorporated as a separate market in 1973, but cross listings on the KLSE and the SES continued through the late 1980s. While the capital market was long in existence, it remained on the periphery of the financial system. The equity market, the more developed component of the capital market, was smaller and much less active than the banking sector. For instance, equity market capitalisation and trading value as ratios of GDP hovered around 0.35 and 0.07 respectively in 1978–1982; by contrast, bank assets and private credit by banks as ratios of GDP averaged 0.70 and 0.48 respectively in the same period.[2]

In Malaysia, the urgency of achieving rapid industrialisation, particularly in the 1970s and 1980s, dictated that banks rather than the poorly developed capital market provided most investment capital and thus should be given top priority in the financial policy agenda. While reflecting the development imperative, the slow growth of securities markets also had important political underpinnings. The Malaysian government prioritised the development of banks over securities markets, in part because the banking sector proffered an easily manipulatable and effective tool for pursuing the political strategy of promoting *bumiputera* interests that constituted the core of the New Economic Policy (NEP).[3] While Malaysia never had an industrial finance system that approached activist systems such as Korea's, policy-makers deliberately used the banking sector to foster specific industries. Favoured borrowers, mainly *bumiputera* firms and state-owned enterprises, developed a vested interest in debt financing. The political calculus of state elites interacted with private interests to reinforce the bank-centred structure of the Malaysian financial system.

Associated with the bank-centred system was an array of regulatory and structural barriers that hampered capital market growth. In the first place, equities and corporate bonds had been subject to not only hefty stamp duties but also various dividend, capital-gains or interest-income taxes prior to the late 1980s. By contrast, interest incomes earned on deposits of 12-month and longer maturities with commercial banks had been exempt from any tax. Together with high fixed commissions on securities trading, these taxes increased transactions costs and dampened demand for equities and corporate bonds. While tax structures were generally biased against the capital market, policy-makers were keener to nourish the public bond market, reflecting the increased debt-financing needs of the government, particularly in the late 1970s and early 1980s. Interest incomes earned on government bonds were exempt from income tax and transactions on such bonds were subject to a very low brokerage fee of 0.015 per cent. More importantly, large institutional investors, such as the Employees Provident Fund (EPF) and insurance companies, were required to invest a substantial proportion of their funds in public bonds. This buttressed demand for government securities but severely restrained the investments of these financial institutions in equities and corporate bonds (*AF* 15 June 1986: 52–57; Aziz 1989).

Furthermore, high transaction costs in general and fixed commission rates in particular also derived from the exclusive and oligopolistic nature of the securities industry. Operating as a self-regulatory body, the KLSE had long jealously guarded its decision-making autonomy and resisted government intervention in its business until the 1980s. While the KLSE had more than 50 member firms in 1988, the securities industry remained more concentrated and less competitive than this relatively large number of brokerage firms suggested. Roughly ten large and well-capitalised stockbrokers, many of which were affiliates of banks, dominated the industry. The others were either poorly capitalised, had a narrow customer base or operated outside the Kuala Lumpur area; they were unable to compete with large firms across the full spectrum of securities business (*AF* 15 June 1985: 64–65, 15 September 1987: 100–101). Government regulation further abetted market concentration by prohibiting other segments of the financial industry from fully participating in equity broking and dealing (Harwood 1996). Large firms thus constituted the core of the KLSE and exerted a shaping influence over capital market development. Not only did they grab the lion's share of stockbroking business, their preferences carried considerable weight with professional standards, entry restrictions and regulatory policies.

For years, a small and closely knit club of influential KLSE firms kept aspiring members at bay by resorting to exorbitant entry fees, high professional qualifications and regulatory barriers (*MB* February 1977: 3–4; *NST* 28 November 1983: 4). They resisted policy changes in price and entry restrictions, fearing that market liberalisation would eliminate fat profit margins from fixed commissions. For instance, the government tried in vain to press existing brokerage firms to take in partners, both domestic and foreign, through corporatisation, and to fully liberalise access to the securities sector in the mid-1980s (*AF* 15 June 1985: 3; *BT*-Kuala Lumpur 22 April 1987: 8, 24 August 1987: 2). To the extent that a few stockbroking licences were issued, they invariably went to well-connected *bumiputera* firms or state-owned banks. Anticipating increased pressures for market liberalisation against the backdrop of globalisation, stockbroking firms set up, in 1986, the Malaysian Stock Brokers Association (MSBA) that served as a crucial channel to organise interest articulation and credibly exercise voice.

A final institutional obstacle to the development of the capital market in Malaysia in the pre-reform period was the highly unstructured and fragmented regulatory regime (Chooi 1991). As many as six agencies were established and operated under different legal and administrative frameworks. While they were mandated to regulate different segments of the securities industry and the investment banking sector, their roles and functions correlated and even overlapped. At the centre of the regulatory regime was the Capital Issues Committee (CIC) that had existed as a consultative body from 1968 and only become a statutory agency in 1983. However, the CIC had to consult with the Registrar of Companies for the regulation of securities listing and quotation. Moreover, the Foreign Investments Committee (FIC), established in 1974, oversaw the acquisition of assets by foreign interests and, together with the CIC, set the prices of shares issued by local Chinese and foreign firms in the interest of Malays. Added to this array of bodies in 1986 was the Panel on Takeovers and Mergers. These agencies came under the oversight of various government departments—the Bank Negara Malaysia (BNM, the central bank), the Ministry of Finance, the Ministry of Trade and Industry or the Prime Minister's Office.

The fragmentation of regulatory authority posed a serious problem to horizontal communication and co-operation between the various agencies. The resulting administrative inefficiencies often complicated the overall planning and development of the capital market (Isa 1997: 184; Lin 1994: 120–121). Furthermore, individual agencies that were created at different times and in different circumstances had different organisational cultures and institutional interests. This spawned and sometimes intensified inter-agency disputes and conflicts arising out of battles for regulatory jurisdiction and bureaucratic turfs, perverting the management of financial and regulatory policies. More significantly, inter-agency rivalries prompted market regulators to seek alliances with different political actors, creating the opportunity for powerful private interests to penetrate and capture regulatory processes and for politicians to infringe upon the authority of financial technocrats. As a result, regulatory integrity and efficiency declined and market irregularities and frauds were on the rise (Chooi 1991; *BT*-Kuala-Lumpur 25 November 1991: 16; *MB* 1 June 1986: 5–11).

Reform approaches and outcomes in 1990s

As noted above, capital market reforms in Malaysia began to gather momentum in the wake of economic shocks in the 1980s. The prolonged global recession of the early 1980s landed Malaysia in an unprecedented bank-of-payment and fiscal crisis. No sooner had the government formulated initial policy responses to the crisis and the overall economic situation begun to improve than the country was engulfed in another recession of the mid-1980s that saw the external and government budgetary positions deteriorate sharply. The external shocks laid bare the serious structural problems of the race-based NEP and the dirigiste heavy industrialisation drive launched by Mahathir in 1981. They significantly dented the capacity of the government to continue sustaining these costly social engineering and industrial programmes and brought mounting pressure to bear on UMNO elites to change the tack of development strategy. Between the two recessions and particularly in the aftermath of the second recession, crucial policy reforms that were designed to reduce state involvement in the economy, relax foreign investment controls and increase trade openness were thrust onto the agenda of the government (Jomo 1987; Robison 1989). These changes rendered the overall policy environment increasingly market-oriented and set the stage for financial liberalisation in general and capital market reforms in particular.

The real economy crisis ran parallel to and indeed exasperated the financial market turmoil. Malaysia had a massive banking crisis in the mid-1980s involving three banks, a number of deposit-taking co-operatives and illegal credit institutions. Equally crucially, the collapse of a major company in late 1985 that was jointly listed on the KLSE and the SES sent several stockbrokers reeling from sharply decreased transactions and severe liquidity problems and led to the stock market crisis (*MB* 16 December 1985: 5–11; *NST* 5 December 1985: 7).

The banking and stock market crises had reverberations throughout the financial system and proved to be one forceful spur to financial reform efforts. As part of these efforts, capital market reforms were initiated to strengthen the competitiveness and efficiency of the stock-broking industry, streamline and improve the supervisory framework and promote the sustained growth of the securities market through both deregulatory and re-regulatory measures (Aziz 1989).

While market pressures that stemmed from the financial sector crises and the broader balance-of-payments and fiscal difficulties provided initial stimuli to capital market reforms, one more enduring causal mechanism was UMNO elites' perception that market reforms would reassure foreign investors and thus ultimately induce capital inflows (Mahathir et al. 1991). They were constantly pushed by competitive pressures to liberalise and foster the capital market as a strategic plan to attract long-term investment funds from abroad. Throughout the 1990s, top political leaders actively promoted Kuala Lumpur as an important financial centre in the Asia-Pacific region in their jockeying for foreign capital and regional economic influence (*Asiamoney* September 1995: 10–14; *FEER* 11 November 1993: 67; *NST* 6 July 1996: 5). Promoting equity markets and a financial market economy, which were the primary institutions of a regional financial centre, became the linchpin of this strategy.

Economic crises and market pressures were certainly at play in the process of Malaysia's capital market reforms during the period under review here. But their effects on financial and regulatory policy changes that influenced the nature and direction of market development were mediated by domestic political institutions. Central to these institutions was the configuration of political party structures that shaped the incentives of UMNO politicians towards capital market reforms and their strategies for achieving desired political and economic objectives through the reforms.

Mixed incentives towards market reforms

The institutional framework in which Malaysian politicians functioned strongly structured their incentives to seek public-regarding policy objectives through capital market reforms. Several authors (Case 1996a, 2002; Crouch 1996b) have argued that elections in Malaysia that were more than a ritual providing a cloak of legitimacy played an important role in forcing politicians to take into account popular interests. While the substantial authoritarian powers of the UMNO often allowed it to ignore or even repress popular demands, the ever-present need to attract sufficient electoral support to win most of the Malay-majority seats pressed ruling politicians to be significantly responsive to Malay voters. At the same time the ruling party also had to be attentive, albeit to a lesser degree, to the interests of non-Malays, whose support was necessary for electoral victory. This was particularly the case when intra-party rivalries within the UMNO weaken the Malay base of its political support. While elections did make a difference, they did not determine ex ante whether they would force UMNO politicians to promote the interests of the broad voting public or those of particularised constituencies in electoral and policy processes. How electoral pressures shaped the policy orientation of politicians was contingent upon the institutional structure of political parties in Malaysia.

The institutional profile of political parties provided in Chapter 3 clearly shows that the party system structure in Malaysia remained concentrated in the 1980s and 1990s. A hegemonic party system in which political power was centralised in the hands of the UMNO was the essential defining feature of the Malaysian polity. This invariably resulted in relatively few parties running in any given elections and even fewer winning seats in parliament. With a small number of large parties competing in elections, the proportion of votes that the UMNO-dominated BN needed to secure in order to garner the majority of seats and thus control the government was large. In general elections held between 1986 and 1999, the BN won on average 58 per cent of the popular vote. The need to win elections with such high percentages in this concentrated party system considerably reduced the incentive of UMNO politicians to make appeals to narrow and localised constituencies. They were disposed to mobilise large swathes of the population for electoral support and form a broad coalition that was based on national characteristics. The electoral coalition of the UMNO was so encompassing that political leaders were inclined to pursue nationally oriented policies.

Centripetal forces associated with the concentrated party system thus motivated UMNO leaders to claim credit for capital market reforms that promised to advance the interests of their broad constituencies. While politicians were keen to generate local support with which to capture branch and divisional leadership positions in order to win BN candidacies for elections, party system concentration and centralised party controls within the UMNO placed a relatively low premium on the ability of party leaders to excessively use market reforms as the vehicle for delivering targeted benefits to specific interests. They saw capital market growth as crucial to mobilise long-term funds to support national development programmes and industrial investments. In the key policy statements of the 1990s, UMNO leaders repeatedly expressed a strong desire to promote a more market-oriented and balanced financial structure as a fulcrum of sustained economic growth (*Asiamoney* May 1996: 34–35; Mahathir et al. 1991; *MB* 16 July 1995: 34; *NST* 23 June 1995: 1). These policy interests were embodied and incorporated in the successive five-year Malaysia plans from the mid-1980s (EPU, various issues).

The policy statements advocating public-regarding market reforms were more than rhetoric. In relative terms, the centralised and coherent party structure was institutionally disposed to make Malaysian political leaders more concerned than their Thai counterparts with pursuing a national-level agenda through policy and regulatory changes. This was manifest in how the strong interests of UMNO policy-makers in capital market growth rendered them more willing to resist political opposition to pro-market reform measures. In the early and mid-1990s, for instance, private bankers, many of whom were influential *bumiputera* financiers and had close ties with state elites, felt the pinch of growing competition from the securities markets and clamoured for protective measures. But UMNO leaders and financial technocrats were able to shrug off the intense preferences from private bankers and continued pushing for market-oriented changes (Chin and Jomo 2001; *MB* 16–30 April 1991: 46–48, 16 February 1994: 20, 40). The combination of party system concentration and the centralised policy-making structure of the UMNO created disincentives against seeking unlimited divisible rents on the part of politicians.

More importantly, top UMNO leaderships were willing to marshal political support for nurturing the capital market and building a more efficient financial architecture. While technocrats in the BNM and the Malaysian Securities Commission (MSC) were strong advocates of pro-market reforms,[4] they were able to win the continued backing of UMNO elites who headed the finance ministry that oversaw the BNM and the MSC. Public-regarding incentives deriving from the desire of political leaders to maintain the broad electoral coalition oriented them to align their policy interests with growth-enhancing reforms. Such policy interests manifested themselves clearly in the sustained efforts of the government to deepen and broaden the equity and bond markets as an important way to mobilise funds for capital formation and industrial development in the 1990s (Lin 1994; Wilson 1999). As a result, the capital market became an increasingly important source of industrial financing, rivalling and even overtaking the intermediating role of the banking sector. Funds raised by the private sector from the equity market steadily rose from a mere 0.9 billion ringgit in 1988 to 18.4 billion ringgit in 1997 (BNM 1999: 303). The rapid growth of the capital market that benefited from programmatic reform policies played a key role in sustaining economic growth (Singh and Yusof 2005).

However, while capital market reforms were generally oriented towards public policy objectives, specific liberalisation measures were frequently captured by politicians as the means by which to pursue particularistic interests. The public-regarding orientation of reforms that stemmed from party system concentration was significantly diluted by the rent-seeking behaviour of politicians, which derived mainly from intra-UMNO organisational attributes. As noted earlier, centralised decision-making structures, effective controls over candidate selection and strong party reputations within the UMNO encouraged politicians to follow party-oriented policies. But increasingly decentralised party financing patterns and intra-party rivalries simultaneously spawned policy particularism in the process of capital market reforms.

As detailed in Chapter 3, while single-member districts with plurality voting geared politicians towards co-operating with co-partisans in general elections, competition within the UMNO for leadership positions across all levels of the party remained fierce in the 1980s and 1990s. Intra-party rivalries that were concerned more with control over political power and patronage resources than with ideological and policy differences gave rise to the emergence and persistence of factions in the UMNO. The party remained severely factionalised, with factional leaders jostling to develop their power bases and move up the party hierarchy. As a result, factional conflicts became so open and untoward that they often erupted into party splits. Furthermore, in parallel with the ability of the UMNO to achieve financial self-sufficiency through direct and extensive business involvements, individual politicians, local party organs and various factions also owned or controlled business concerns and established patron–client ties with both Malay and non-Malay corporate interests. This gave them considerable latitude in not only collecting but also using funds in ways that were more attuned to their preferences and priorities rather than those of the party.

These intra-UMNO organisational weaknesses generated centrifugal pressures upon politicians to supplant party-centred policies with personal pursuits in policy processes. Persistent and intensive factional conflicts encouraged politicians and factional leaders to build and maintain narrow bases of political support. Such strategies were instrumental in strengthening the power position of their own factions vis-à-vis other rival factions within the UMNO. They thus created significant incentives for politicians and factional leaders to seek particularistic regulatory and policy changes that were expected to promote the interests of their strategic supporters. Moreover, in intra-UMNO rivalries, politicians and factions lavished money to secure the party positions that would provide them with enhanced access to state resources and economic rents (Gomez and Jomo 1997; Lim and Ong 2006). The prevalence of money politics abetted politicians to explore and develop their autonomous sources of finance. These politicians and their factions, with their own business interests and corporate backers and their own mechanisms of collecting funds, seldom depended upon centralised party leaderships for funding support and operated increasingly independently of national party organs. As particularism dominated the party apparatuses, politicians became indifferent and even opposed to the collective policy goals of the UMNO.

The desire to promote particularised interests and dispense patronage among factional supporters thus predisposed UMNO politicians to temper the public policy objectives of capital market reforms with their private-regarding interests. The literature on the Malaysian political economy is replete with accounts of rent-seeking activities in the process of financial development, including stock market growth (Chin and Jomo 2000; Gomez and Jomo 1997). Such activities were also prevalent in the formulation of capital market reforms in the late 1980s and 1990s.

One key objective of capital market reforms, as stipulated in the fifth and sixth Malaysia plans, was to improve the competitiveness and efficiency of the securities industry. The achievement of this policy goal was predicated upon an array of important measures—the removal of entry barriers, the decontrol of commission rates and the improvement of KLSE members' capital adequacy. Technocrats in the BNM and the finance ministry pushed for these measures right after the stock market crisis of the mid-1980s and formulated, together with MSC officials, liberalisation programmes in the ensuing years. But the strong interest of their political masters in protecting the privileges of securities companies that were controlled by the ruling party, connected to political elites or affiliated with state banks compromised these programmes. UMNO policy-makers were keen to adopt an incremental approach to market liberalisation, with a view to ensuring the profitability of many of KLSE members (*BT*-Kuala Lumpur 24 August 1987: 2; *FEER* 22 February 1990: 45–47; *MB* 16 July 1995: 34–35). The approach reflected as much the prudential considerations of financial regulators and the active resistance of private financiers as the desire of UMNO politicians to seek rents for their key constituents in the financial community.

Similar particularistic influences also diluted the public-regarding purposes of re-regulatory efforts. Following the stock market debacle of the mid-1980s, a set of revised securities market rules were issued to vest financial technocrats with enhanced regulatory authority, and the MSC was set up in late 1992 to streamline and strengthen the fragmented regulatory framework. These institutional reforms were designed to put stock market growth on a sound footing and reflected the intention of UMNO leaders to promote the capital market as a key provider of finance for economic development (Aziz 1989; BNM 1999: 314–320; *NST* 23 October 1992: 6). However, the play of particularistic interests remained unconstrained when it came to the enforcement of market rules. The interest of UMNO politicians in supporting favoured private market agents complicated re-regulatory reforms and created incentives for lax market regulation. While financial regulators were often able to press charges against violators of market rules, they found their hands tied when the violators were powerful corporate backers of UMNO factions or private interests close to party elites. In mid-1991, for instance, several well-connected businessmen who had been implicated in insider dealings were cleared after investigation (*EIUCR*-Malaysia No. 3 1991: 25).[5]

Nowhere is the impact of mixed incentives on capital market reforms more manifest than in the process of privatising SOEs. Privatisation, which was initiated in the early 1980s amidst the global recession, began to gather momentum in the late 1980s and early 1990s. The major objectives and implementation specifics of privatisation were laid out in the fifth Malaysia plan and finalised in the privatisation master plan of 1991. Privatisation was purported to strengthen the state coffers, improve efficiency, promote private-sector investment and foster *bumiputera* entrepreneurship. While evidence on the achievement of these objectives was mixed at best (Jomo 1995), privatisation did facilitate capital market reforms (Chin and Jomo 2001; Jomo 2003). The desire of UMNO policy-makers to use the stock market as a vehicle for divesting state assets reinforced their interest in nourishing a favourable regulatory environment for capital market development.

However, the public policy objectives of privatisation were overlaid with particularistic efforts to seek rents for strategic constituencies on the part of UMNO politicians. Extant literature (Gomez and Jomo 1997: 75–116; Jomo 1995) that has emphasised privatisation as a new tool for achieving the objective of ethnic redistribution has perceived inter-ethnic politics as the powerful factor that made politicians favour *bumiputera* investors and businesses when corporate shares were allocated and state assets sold. While true, this account is incomplete and fails to consider the impact of intra-party organisation. Perennial rivalries within the UMNO strongly motivated different party leaders to capture the privatisation programme as the political mechanism with which to control resources and thus to strengthen the bases of their factional support. In other words, privatisation was in part driven by the process of intra-UMNO struggles over party and state positions and associated economic rents. In his detailed analysis of the politics of privatisation, Tan (2008) emphasises the changing balance of power between the 'pro-distribution' and 'pro-growth' factions in the UMNO as a major driving force behind extensive privatisation in the 1990s and as a primary determinant of the particularistic agenda for divesting state assets.

Decisive yet unstable reform policies

Capital market growth required not only strong incentives to provide pro-market reforms but also sustained political consensus on the reform agenda. In Malaysia, the centralised system of government made it relatively easy for policy-makers to take strong and decisive action on market-oriented regulatory changes. The concentrated party system combined with the centrally controlled UMNO apparatuses to provide political leaders with the institutional resources with which to enhance their policy autonomy and to rally the support of party members and followers behind their policies. This is not just a function of authoritarianism that began to creep into the Malaysian political scene in the early 1980s (Case 2002; Slater 2003). The centralisation of political and policy-making authority that stemmed from the party organisational structures was so heavy that there were virtually no significant institutional constraints on the ability of UMNO elites to pursue their policy interests.

With policy-making power highly concentrated in the executive, translating pro-market preferences into market reform programmes was a relatively straightforward process. The UMNO leadership and Mahathir in particular exerted political will with robust force in those policy areas that directly engaged their interests, both public and private regarding, and were of crucial importance to financial development. In response to the growing weaknesses of the securities industry in the aftermath of the stock market crisis of the mid-1980s and to increased global market volatilities in the 1990s, the government took decisive action on several policy and institutional fronts, most notably by making extensive amendments to the banking and securities acts that were designed to strengthen the domestic financial sector and enacting regulatory reforms that culminated in the establishment of the MSC. By the same token, top financial policy-makers moved with considerable alacrity and efficacy to formulate a comprehensive package of stock market liberalisation measures in the aftermath of the Mexican peso crisis of 1994 and associated financial market instabilities in East Asia. Not only did the package have clear objectives, it set the specific schedule for implementing the liberalisation measures (*Asiamoney* September 1995: 10–14; *EIUCR*-Malaysia 3rd Quarter 1995: 30–31). To the extent that there were delays and hitches in the formation of these regulatory reforms and liberalisation plans, they mainly reflected the desire of UMNO politicians to protect powerful private interests, as mentioned above.

The same logic that was seen in Malaysia's concentrated party system also asserted itself in the initiation and formation of the privatisation programme, which UMNO leaders saw as an important way to foster the capital market (*NST* 21 March 1991: 20) as well as to improve economic efficiency, as noted above. This logic has two key institutional dimensions. The first dimension rests with the fact that the foundation of the privatisation programme was a cabinet-level body—the Economic Planning Unit (EPU) in the Prime Minister's Department. The EPU was given significant powers to recommend final decisions and oversee the divestment process. While line ministries drew up specific plans to privatise SOEs under their oversight, these plans had to be approved by the EPU. The second dimension was related to the power of the prime minister to appoint and remove all members of the cabinet at any time. This greatly limited attempts by different line ministries to resist privatisation and vested the EPU with overall planning authority. As a result, all privatisations followed the same top-down pattern of centralised decision-making (Milne 1991; *NST* 25 May 1993: 14). The Malaysian government was thus able to overcome obstacles and set up well co-ordinated procedures to ensure decisive and swift enactment.

The systemic political dominance and party-controlled policy processes within the UMNO helped make the executive powerful and authoritative enough to formulate legal and regulatory changes as it saw fit. This was particularly crucial when market crises and external economic shocks demanded swift and effective changes to the existing legal and institutional framework. In Malaysia, laws that authorised pro-market reforms and gave the process legitimacy were often high priorities for UMNO leaders. Legislation mandating new regulations, improving market infrastructures and strengthening the powers of the BNM and MSC was carried out in a decisive manner, sometimes over the vociferous opposition from state and societal actors who stood to lose out from these legal and regulatory changes. This was most clearly demonstrated in the well-planned revision of the Banking and Securities Acts in the early 1990s (*MB* 16–30 April 1991: 46–48, 16 February 1994: 20).

The concentrated veto authority that enabled the government to initiate capital market reforms does not appear to have considerably compromised its capacity to sustain some key reforms over time. In comparison to Thailand, Malaysia was more successful in carrying out largely consistent reform plans that significantly deepened and broadened the capital market. The stronger organisational structure of the UMNO was a major contributing factor. On the one hand, the intra-party organisational strength underpinned the ability of party leaders to centralise decision-making processes and align the behaviour of party members and supporters with the overall policy objectives of the party. On the other hand, the strong need of UMNO leaders to rely upon party unity for commanding majority support in parliament encouraged them to stick to given financial policies. This was particularly true when these policies had a consequential bearing upon the interests of a wide range of party members and followers. In the early and mid-1990s, financial authorities made sustained efforts to nurture the development of trust funds that helped ordinary *bumiputera* investors, many of whom were UMNO members and followers. This signified the attempts of party elites to maintain a stable and broad cohort of supporters that was crucial to buttressing the hegemonic position of the UMNO.

The implementation of capital market reforms in general, and re-regulatory changes in particular, also benefited from the relative durability of policy-makers in the BNM, the MSC and the finance ministry. Both politicians and technocrats who headed these agencies in the 1980s and 1990s had longer tenures than their Thai counterparts, as shown in Table 4.1. As a consequence, they had more time to obtain market information and develop policy resources to design and implement market reform programmes. The greater stability of financial policy elites provided the higher organisational cohesion needed to follow through on reform policies. This effect was amplified by the fact that the three agencies maintained largely close ties with each other in policy and regulatory processes (*MB* 1 November 1994: 32–34, 16 March 1995: 8–12; *NST* 19 February 1997: 12, 4). Such inter-agency relations helped overcome the difficulties of horizontal communication and strengthen the institutional basis for enacting a relatively coherent reform strategy through effective co-operation.

These features of the financial bureaucracy conformed with and indeed derived from the structure of the party system. The systemic political dominance and centralised party controls within the ruling party enabled UMNO leaders to influence the career paths of economic bureaucrats and exercise leverage over their behaviour. Political elites thus had institutional resources with which to align the policy interests of the bureaucracy with party-determined strategies and priorities. UMNO leaders did not unfailingly commit to policy efficiency and technocrat management, as evidenced in the sacking of prominent financial technocrats. For the most part, however, they delegated considerable powers to the BNM and the MSC and played a crucial role in maintaining a smooth working relationship between the key state economic agencies. To the extent that inter-agency conflicts occasionally arose and threatened to derail the implementation of given financial policy changes, UMNO leaders often moved quickly to sort them out. In 1991, for instance, Mahathir intervened forcefully to nip in the bud inter-agency disputes over the formulation of the new securities act, shepherding the process to successful enactment (*MB* 1–15 July 1995: 31–32; *NST* 4 August 1998: 22).

This analysis does not suggest that there were not serious problems of irresolute implementation of given market reform policies. While the organisational strength of the party and the financial bureaucracy tended to generate stabilising effects on capital market reforms, they were often counteracted by intra-party conflicts, particularly at the national level. Such factional conflicts undermined the organisational and policy effectiveness of the government and weakened the ability of financial technocrats to carry through agreed-on policy programmes, rendering capital market reforms in Malaysia less resolute and coherent than those in Singapore. Good cases in point include the breakaway of an UMNO faction in 1987 led by the then trade and industry minister, Razaleigh Hamzah, and the successful challenge to the UMNO deputy presidency and deputy prime ministership of Ghafar Baba in 1993, mounted by Anwar Ibrahim, one of the three UMNO vice-presidents. In the former case, the factional infighting disrupted and stalled the enactment of the financial reform programme formulated in the wake of the economic recession (Crouch 1992). In the latter, the scramble for the number two post in the party and government delayed the planning of stock market liberalisation (*BT*-Singapore 18 May 1993: 24; *FEER* 30 September 1993: 18–21). While not directly related to capital market reforms, these power struggles within the UMNO dislodged the reforms, if only temporarily, from their intended trajectory.

Intra-party rivalries had another and more durable constraint on the ability of the government to maintain financial policy stability and credibility, specifically with regard to privatisation. As made clear above, the divestment of state assets was in part driven by the efforts of UMNO politicians to dispense patronage among strategic followers and bolster their personal bases of support. This turned out well, as long as the process brought about relatively equal benefits to all factions involved. However, when privatisations favoured some factions at the expense of the others, factional conflicts erupted and the process of divestment stalled. The problem was aggravated in the mid-1990s when the most lucrative assets had been sold and there were not enough state rents generated through privatisation to go around (Gomez 1996a: 11–14). Factional conflicts over the division of privatisation spoils bogged down the divestment of many key SOEs, particularly those that had large transaction values and would thus generate substantial rents (Jomo 2003; Tan 2008). Between 1991 and 1995, merely 37 per cent of planned privatisations went ahead; privatisations with a transaction value above US$20 million only accounted for 12 per cent of all the SOEs privatised over the same period.[6]

Persistent intra-party competitions and the resultant patronage-based party–society linkages rendered UMNO politicians beholden to special interest groups and provided private market agents with enhanced entrée to financial policy processes. This often subjected capital market reforms to the erratic preferences of particularistic interests and created implementation difficulties. Nowhere was this impact more clearly illustrated than in stock market liberalisation. Financial authorities moved to liberalise commission rates and lower entry restrictions as part of the overall financial reform plan enacted in the aftermath of the economic crisis of the mid-1980s. These measures stood to benefit the investing public, but they threatened to undermine the profit margins of KLSE members. Private financiers and their political patrons in the government went to every length to resist and delay stock market liberalisation (*BT*-Kuala Lumpur 15 August 1987: 6; *FEER* 28 January 1988: 78–79). As a result, broking fees remained high. While a new system of graduated commissions was introduced and fees for share transactions of large values were reduced, the overall commission structure remained rigid. Equally importantly, the handful of brokerage licences that were issued went to well-connected bankers. The removal of regulatory barriers had been held in abeyance until 1995 when the government was prompted by intense market pressures to improve the efficiency of the equity market. Entry barriers were lowered, but potential entrants faced high membership fees, performance standards or ownership restrictions. The upshot was that the KLSE stayed largely impenetrable, particularly to foreign firms seeking membership.

Finally, the same underlying political dynamics were also at work in the enforcement of securities market regulations and rules. The organisational strength of the party system that gave UMNO leaders effective control over the behaviour of the economic bureaucracy also enabled them to submit state regulatory agencies to particularistic interests. Such interests again derived from the persistent internal rivalry of the UMNO that strongly encouraged politicians to maintain their narrow bases of support and thus rendered them obligated to powerful corporate actors. While financial technocrats upgraded the legal and regulatory framework in response to market crises and changes in the late 1980s and 1990s, they were not immune from particularistic pressures for regulatory forbearance. The MSC and the BNM, widely respected for their technical competence and professional integrity, helped keep the manipulation of market rules for private ends from reaching the same level as in Thailand (Hamilton-Hart 2002: 114–128). But political elites never refrained from interfering with securities market governance and were reluctant to underpin supervisory standards with the greater enforcement capacity of financial regulators. Political intervention for such purposes prevented financial technocrats from enforcing otherwise strict rules effectively and consistently and taking tough disciplinary action against rule violators. There were thus repeated instances of rent-seeking by UMNO politicians and their cronies through the MSC and the BNM and of feeble implementation of existing rules (see, for example, *EIUCR*-Malaysia No. 3 1991: 25, No. 3 1992: 29–30, 1st Quarter 1995: 12; *FEER* 18 July 1991: 66). As a result, market irregularities remained rampant and insider trading became the norm (*AMF* July/August 1992: 31–33; *ID* April 1994: 21; Mooi and Lim 2006). This shows that Malaysian financial technocrats, who were less effective in rule enforcement than their Singaporean counterparts, were only able to impose what Hamilton-Hart (2002) aptly dubs 'partial discipline' in the process of regulating the securities market.

It is clear from the preceding analysis that Malaysia's political party structure exerted a shaping influence over the direction and outcomes of capital market reforms in the late 1980s and 1990s. While external market and political pressures acted as forceful stimuli to the reforms, the systemic attributes of the party structure and intra-party organisational configuration of the UMNO combined to determine how market reforms were oriented and implemented. Party system concentration created incentives for policy-makers to align market reforms with national-level policy objectives, but factional rivalries within the ruling party predisposed politicians to capture the reform process as a vehicle for seeking rents. Similarly, while the dominant position of the UMNO in the Malaysian polity provided the government with institutional resources with which to formulate decisive reform policies, intra-party organisational weaknesses often plagued the resolute implementation of the agreed-upon reform policies. As a result, the whole programme of market reforms veered between public-regarding and particularistic pursuits and between decisive initiatives and irresolute outcomes.

Market reforms since the Asian crisis

Like other countries in East Asia, Malaysia was engulfed in the financial crisis of 1997–1998. While the country withstood the crisis better than many of its neighbours on the back of its stronger economic fundamentals, it experienced a severe economic slump and was weighed down by associated structural weaknesses in the financial and corporate sectors.[7] The government was somewhat slow in devising a policy response for reasons that will become clear below, but it was prompted by the crisis to push for market-oriented policy changes, including capital market reforms. While the worst of the crisis waned over 1999, a secular trend towards greater financial integration appears to have provided a more durable impetus behind continued market reforms during the post-crisis period. Malaysian policy-makers were under constant external pressures to promote the growth of the capital market as a key strategy to nurture Kuala Lumpur into becoming a regional financial centre and to attract foreign capital (*EIUCR*-Malaysia June 2007: 15–16; *FEER* 17 May 2001: 56).

Following the Asian crisis, Malaysia's capital market reforms thus carried forward the content and direction of the reform programme of the 1990s. The government continued with both deregulatory and re-regulatory reform policies. On the one hand, it made further efforts to remove regulatory restrictions, deregulate the commission rate structure and lower entry barriers, particularly to foreign financiers and stockbrokers. On the other hand, the NBM and MSC formulated a wide range of revisions to the existing financial and securities regulation legislations. More importantly, new reform measures were introduced to the policy agenda, with corporate governance, securities investment liberalisation and debt market development occupying central stage. While the government often pursued a zigzagging reform course in the post-crisis period, as in the 1990s, it had a sustained commitment to developing a robust and efficient capital market.

Like Singapore but unlike Thailand, Malaysia demonstrated a high degree of continuity in the character of its political regime and the political economy supportive of that regime. To be sure, there were crucial UMNO leadership changes, evidenced in the purge of Anwar Ibrahim in 1998 and the succession of Mahathir by his deputy, Abdullah Badawi, in 2003. Equally importantly, the opposition made unprecedented electoral gains in the 1999 and 2008 general elections and was at times poised to shake the hegemonic position of the UMNO. However, over the decade that followed the Asian crisis of 1997–1998, the political landscape of Malaysia remained largely intact. If there were any discernible political changes in the country, they appeared to be in the direction of increasing authority in the executive that derived from party system concentration. While the UMNO leadership maintained effective controls over intra-party decision-making, electoral procedures and policy platforms, the ruling party remained imbued with political and factional rivalries across all the levels of the party apparatus. Basic institutional continuities in the external and internal organisational structures of Malaysia's political party system suggest that post-crisis capital market reforms followed a similar trajectory, despite changing policy environments and new reform measures.

Public versus private-regarding reform policies

As in the 1990s, the post-crisis process of capital market reforms saw the intermingling of public-regarding policy objectives with particularistic interests. This mixed reform orientation continued to be an important function of Malaysia's unique political party structure in which systemic concentration ran parallel to rampant intra-party competition and factionalism. In the post-crisis period, the party system remained centrally structured, with the UMNO dominating the electoral and legislative processes. While the opposition saw their electoral grounds strengthen, the ruling party still managed to garner more than 50 per cent of the popular votes in all three general elections through to late 2008. Party system concentration and growing electoral competitiveness combined to create even greater incentives for UMNO politicians to maintain the broad electoral coalition and obtain the majority of Malay and non-Malay support. They thus continued to be strongly disposed to pursue public-regarding reform policies that stood to benefit large swathes of the general population.

At the same time, however, intra-party conflicts within the UMNO remained as prevalent and intense as ever. The most serious of these conflicts was that between Mahathir and Anwar in the wake of the Asian financial crisis and the arrest and imprisonment of the latter. Intra-party rivalries were not subdued after Mahathir had stepped down. While the ruling party under Abdullah was spared major fissures, factional infighting raged on among up-and-comers within the UMNO. This was reflected not only in the ever-lasting jostling among factional leaders and party regulars for different party positions and associated opportunities for seeking rents but also in the emergent clashes between Abdullah and Mahathir and their respective followers (*FEER* July/August 2008: 30–34; *NST* 21 June 2004: 1, 28 June 2006: 6, 10 March 2008: 19; *WSJ* 3 July 2006: A4). Persistent intra-party rivalries continued to push UMNO politicians to develop their narrow bases of political support and to be beholden to special interest groups. They thus saw financial and regulatory policy processes as the politically expedient instrument with which to reward their particularised supporters and constituents and enhance their power positions in factional conflicts.

The result was that while the concentrated party system generated centripetal incentives for policy-makers to seek public policy objectives through market reforms, intra-party competition and factionalism brought centrifugal and particularistic pressures to bear upon politicians in the making of reform policies. The public-regarding and private-regarding policy incentives continued to assert themselves simultaneously throughout the post-crisis process of capital market reforms. For example, while capital controls imposed in the wake of the Asian crisis renewed export competitiveness and enlivened the stock market (Kaplan and Rodrik 2002),[8] they also greatly benefited local business elites (*ID* September 1998: 6–8; Johnson and Mitton 2003). Furthermore, the government sought to reorient the broking commission structure towards a more flexible regime in the early 2000s but large and well-connected stockbrokers were allowed, if only implicitly, to collude in setting and influencing commission rates through oligopolistic practices (*FT* 16 April 2003: 25; *NST* 27 June 2002: 1). While policy elites followed through with privatisation in the post-crisis period, with a view to promoting equity market growth as well as to replenishing the state coffers, they continued to give lucrative projects to companies with strong political links (*FEER* 25 January 2001: 53–54; Tan 2008). The formulation and enactment of virtually every key post-crisis reform policy was overlain with private interests that were associated with prominent UMNO politicians and their factions. This was particularly discernible in the new and renewed efforts to restructure the corporate sector and reform corporate governance, consolidate the securities industry and nourish the development of institutional investors.

In the wake of the Asian crisis, the growing depth of domestic corporate and financial distress was one of the most severe challenges facing the Malaysian government. The distress was primarily manifest in high debt levels and declining returns on capital across the manufacturing industry. These corporate weaknesses weighed the banking sector down with mounting non-performing loans, as many industrial firms that floundered in ever graver financial difficulties were unable to honour their debt obligations. In response to the corporate woes, the government established new institutions for dealing with the non-performing loans (NPL) problem, recapitalising banks and restructuring the corporate sector.[9] While different in their respective roles in the financial and corporate restructuring process, these institutions, which mirrored best practice and had clear mandates, were designed to restore the crisis-stricken economy to its rapid-growth trajectory. Equally importantly, given that banks tied up much of their assets in the equity market and many large ailing firms were listed on the KLSE, the effective management of corporate restructuring by the new institutions would be the most likely way to nurture the crisis-battered capital market back to healthy and robust growth.

However, the operation of the formal institutions did not constitute the full scope of the official approach towards restructuring the corporate and financial sectors. The Malaysian government resorted to an array of corporate bailouts, the most conspicuous beneficiaries of which ranged from large state-owned enterprises to the indebted corporate interests of UMNO elites and from newly privatised companies to Malay-controlled banking institutions (*EIUCR*-Malaysia 1st Quarter 1998: 24–25, 2nd Quarter 1999: 24–25; *FEER* 30 April 1998: 62–62; Haggard 2000a: 162–171). The beneficiaries were invariably closely associated with and were strategic supporters of prominent UMNO leaders. The bailouts thus went beyond close state–business relationships and reflected the desire of Mahathir and his associates to reward their factional supporters and followers. This was crucial to their efforts to strengthen the base of their political support, given that the UMNO had just experienced a severe clash among its leadership and that the government was confronted by an increasingly strong reform movement that was galvanised by popular outrage over the purge of Anwar.

As the government bailed out UMNO-linked business interests and relied heavily upon an interventionist approach to reforming the corporate sector, it ran the risk of shifting real and potential losses onto the corporate restructuring institutions and undermining their mandates and policy objectives. As a result, the overall process of financial and corporate restructuring slowed down and even stalled at one time in late 1999 and early 2000 (*FT* 16 August 2000: 11). The halting pace of corporate reforms and the selective bailouts of public and private firms dampened the confidence of investors, particularly foreign investors, as they felt insecure about the future of their investments in such a climate. While capital controls were eased in 2000, foreign investors, who had bolstered the earlier vigour of the Malaysian bourse, now shied away from it (*FEER* 29 June 2000: 51). The stock market, which staged a short-lived recovery in early and mid-1999, began to dip again in late 1999 and remained bearish through 2000, despite an impressive economic growth figure of more than 8 per cent for that year.

The political costs of the dismal capital market were looming large in the minds of top UMNO politicians. Millions of *bumiputera* investors in unit trusts, many of whom were poor villagers, saw their investments and even life savings being eroded by the swelling losses of these trusts. The bailouts of well-connected business interests, contrasting with the anxieties and hardships endured by unit investors, fuelled widespread discontent. This could not have come at a worse moment, as the opposition rode on the surging social and political ferment to make surprisingly large gains in the 1999 general election. For Mahathir and his associates, a key to placating disgruntled *bumiputera* investors, stemming the opposition's electoral gains and maintaining the hegemonic position of the UMNO rested with restoring and promoting capital market growth. This, in turn, required the resurrection of investor confidence. For all his ranting about the iniquities of the global financial system, Mahathir worked to lure back foreign portfolio investors by accelerating corporate and market reforms.

In early 2001, there was a flurry of policy developments pertaining to the speedy reform of corporate governance practices. The government introduced stronger regularised procedures in the corporate sector that emphasised information disclosure, investment protection and international accounting standards. To implement corporate governance

reforms, Mahathir appointed young technocrats to the major regulatory and corporate restructuring agencies while edging out the finance
minister Daim Zainuddin, who had been closely involved in unpopular bailout deals (*Asiamoney* April 2001: 52–53; *FEER* 14 June 2001:
24–28). However, the government did not unfailingly commit to the
public policy objective of corporate governance reforms and the technocratic management of the reform process. The reforms were also used
as a political weapon in the intra-party rivalry of the UMNO. This is
evidenced by the fact that several prominent supporters of Anwar were
charged with corporate malfeasance and that cases were brought against
industrial owners and managers in order to punish party defectors or
cut off financial backers in the bitterly contested divisional and, more
importantly, general assembly elections of the UMNO (Gourevitch and
Shinn 2005: 236).

The similar, Janus-faced mingling of public-regarding objectives and
particularistic interests also prevailed in the post-crisis process of restructuring the securities industry. Capital market intermediaries that had
overextended themselves during the prolonged bull market of the early
and mid-1990s suffered the consequences when this came to an abrupt
end in the Asian crisis of the late 1990s. Many of them saw their capital
bases severely weakened and their performance wrecked by the tum-
bling equity market. In contrast to Thailand and other countries in
East Asia, the Malaysian regulatory authorities did not move to close
distressed stockbroking companies; rather, it sought to consolidate the
securities sector through a merger plan. Mergers would cut the number of stockbrokers from 64 to 15 or fewer. The plan also envisioned
the establishment of universal brokers that would eventually be permitted to provide a complete line of capital market services (*MB* 16 May
2000: 28–30; *NST* 17 February 2000: 10). In the short run, the merger
plan was expected to stabilise the increasingly fragile securities industry and make stockbrokers strong enough to pull the capital market
out of its post-crisis doldrums. In the longer term, policy-makers saw
the plan as crucial to building securities firms big and robust enough
to withstand the more significant market liberalisation and associated
competitive pressures that would become inevitable in the years ahead
(*EIUCR*-Malaysia June 2000: 32; *NST* 19 May 2000: 24).

However, the merger plan soon became politically contentious and
controversial, as stockbrokers scrambled to be the lead firms that would
have the priority to select the merger targets and the right to establish
universal brokers on their own terms. The lead brokers would not only
be able to retain their ownership controls but would run the merged

firms in line with their own managerial styles and professional standards (*BT*-Kuala Lumpur 12 June 2001: 1). The most contentious political issue was that many of the stockbrokers who successfully lobbied to be designated one of the lead firms were neither financially strong nor professionally managed. It transpired that they had close links to UMNO elites, were financial backers of the dominant factions in the ruling party or had prominent politicians as major shareholders (*MB* 1 April 2003: 34–35). This raised serious doubts over the soundness and viability of many of the would-be universal brokers and, more significantly, compromised the policy objectives to be achieved through such mergers.

Finally, government efforts to develop institutional investors, particularly public funds, vacillated between broad, national and narrow, particularistic orientations. The KLSE had traditionally been plagued by the dominance of small, poorly informed investors who tended to be highly subject to crazes and panics. To develop a broad and stable equity market, financial authorities had made worthwhile attempts to strengthen institutional investors of various kinds prior to the Asian crisis. The dramatic manner in which the stock market tumbled amidst the massive unloading of shares by panicky individual investors prompted the government to make further efforts to promote institutional investment in the post-crisis period. They liberalised the rules governing the operations of institutional investors and removed entry barriers into the asset-management industry; they also established new public investment funds and strengthened the capital bases of existing public funds, such as the EPF, Khazanah Nasional, the government investment agency, and Kumpulan Wang Amanah Pencen, the civil service pension fund.

As a result, these public funds, which rapidly became large financial institutions and institutional investors, shaped the development of the asset-management industry in Malaysia. By 2002, for example, the EPF had accumulated total assets of about RM 250 billion, accounted for 17 per cent of national savings and held two-thirds of fixed-income instruments in the public bond market; with shareholders' funds amounting to RM 14.3 billion, Khazanah often had at its disposal billions of ringgit to invest in a wide range of businesses. More importantly, these public funds played a key role in influencing equity market conditions and transactions. The EPF held more than 20 per cent of its assets in equities, making it the biggest investor in the stock market. By the same token, Khazanah made equity investments in several dozens of listed companies that accounted for a large chunk of market capitalisation in the KLSE (*MB* 16 January 2004: 26–32). By deploying massive funds in stock transactions, these public funds, which on the whole maintained a reputation for reasonably competent investment management, contributed towards the growth of a broad and stable capital market.

The market-enhancing roles of public funds were not completely immune from the play of particularistic interests. The EPF and Khazanah were periodically tainted by scandals surrounding subsidies to well-connected *bumiputera* firms and other dubious transactions. While it is difficult to ascertain whether the firms were selected on the basis of political criteria alone, it is safe to argue that the discretionary and non-transparent means of rescuing the UMNO's private partners by tapping the funds of the EPF and Khazanah undermined their roles in promoting capital market growth. The most visible case involved these two public funds taking up, in 1999, the bonds issued by Projek Lebuhraya Utara-Selatan, the operator of the lucrative North–South Expressway, to support its troubled parent, Renong, the main corporate instrument of the UMNO's holding company, Fleet Holdings (*EIUCR*-Malaysia 2nd Quarter 1999: 24–25). The next controversy was the government's decision to arm-twist the EPF and Khazanah into absorbing unwanted shares issued by TIME dotCom, a politically connected mobile phone operator, when it listed in 2002. A final scandal implicated the EPF in the rescue of Malaysia's fourth-largest bank, which was owned by the family of the pro-government chief minister of Sarawak, in early 2007 (*FT* 12 March 2007: 18). In these and many other cases, the private firms that were shielded by public funds from losses were either strategic constituents or financial backers of the dominant faction of the ruling party.

The public funds were also used by the government to boost share prices, particularly when the KLSE was depressed. Given widespread equity ownership, the efforts to support share prices served broader political and policy purposes. However, institutional investors were often directed to support the shares of listed firms in a highly selective manner, raising concerns that these efforts were not completely public-regarding. In mid-1998, for instance, the government mobilised public pension fund money to bail out politically connected firms while allowing those closely associated with Anwar to wither. In early 2003 and again in late 2008, the government channelled billions of ringgit to prop up the low share prices of the 'fundamentally strong companies' that had close ties to UMNO elites (*EIUCR*-Malaysia March 2003: 20; *FT* 10 March 2003: 22; *WSJ* 21 October 2008: A12). Not only did the price-boosting operations of institutional investors often land them with heavy losses, the selective support of favoured firms' shares also undermined official efforts to improve professional standards in the field of public fund management and reform corporate governance practices in the securities industry. As a result, the use of public funds by UMNO politicians for private-regarding purposes threatened to weaken the role of these funds in promoting institutional investment, as they were intended to broaden and stabilise the equity market.

The Malaysian approach towards capital market reforms in the post-crisis period appears to have two faces. On the one hand, the government oriented reform programmes towards collective national-level policy objectives and established administrative and institutional mechanisms for delivering these objectives. On the other hand, the public-regarding orientation of market reforms was diluted and the policy mandates of the reform institutions were emasculated by the efforts of UMNO politicians to seek rents for themselves or for their narrow constituents. This was manifest in the process of liberalising the stock market, improving corporate governance practices, consolidating the securities industry and promoting institutional investment. It should be noted that the play of particularistic interests in the formation of reform programmes did not show any sign of lessoning under the Abdullah government, which avowed to combat patronage and corrupt practices. Operating within the same institutional constraints as his predecessor, Abdullah and his associates were under equally strong particularistic pressures to temper capital market reforms with private-regarding pursuits, as was made clear above.

New reform programmes, old implementation patterns

In the post-crisis period, as in the 1990s, Malaysia's political party structure not only generated the mixed orientations of market reform policies but also shaped the patterns of reform formulation and implementation. While the concentrated party system enabled the government to initiate generally decisive reform measures, often in response to external shocks and market pressures, the long-running intra-party organisational weaknesses of the UMNO undercut the ability of policy-makers to commit to sustaining the given reform programme.

As noted in the preceding section, the Malaysian government was somewhat slower in coming up with a coherent policy response to the Asian crisis of the late 1990s. This was not only because the depth of the problem in the financial and corporate sectors was substantially less but, more importantly, because the intra-elite conflict between Mahathir and Anwar intensified in the wake of the crisis. The two top leaders clashed over a range of economic and political issues, tearing government policy in opposing directions and paralysing decision-making processes (MacIntyre 2003: 79–90). The political conflicts and stalemate were short-circuited in mid-1998 when Anwar was ousted and Mahathir centralised policy-making power in his own hands by occupying the finance and home portfolios concurrently with the prime ministership. Abdullah followed suit for much of his tenure through late 2008.

With the policy authority of the executive recentralised and indeed increased, the government deployed its political resources and institutional capacities to introduce a wide range of capital market reforms through a three-pronged strategy. In the first place, the government moved swiftly to establish new administrative and regulatory agencies with clear mandates and professional staff to design long-term plans for market development, improve standards for securities governance and make revisions to existing corporate and capital market acts. In early 1998, the High Level Finance Committee (HLFC) was established to reform and enhance corporate governance in Malaysia; in late 2001, the government merged the ROC and the Registrar of Business to form the Companies Commission of Malaysia (CCM) that was mandated to ensure compliance with business registration and corporate legislation. In close interaction with the existing regulatory agencies—the MSC and the KLSE—these new institutions provided the government with well-planned and co-ordinated organisational mechanisms by which to formulate effective reform programmes.

Furthermore, with the regulatory institutions and procedures renewed and enhanced, financial authorities proceeded to develop strategic plans and governance codes for further boosting capital market growth. These converged on two different yet interrelated policy and regulatory areas. In its Report on Corporate Governance of 1999, the HLFC made an array of recommendations for improving corporate governance practices, which were approved by the government with alacrity. The resulting Malaysian code of corporate governance that was endorsed by the MSC and incorporated by the KLSE into its listing rules elaborated voluntary best-practice principles (*ID* May 1999: 13–16). On the other hand, a capital market master plan (CMMP), drafted by the MSC in consultation with other regulatory agencies and private-sector actors, was quickly approved by the finance ministry in late 2000 and unveiled in early 2001. The master plan, which set six key policy objectives to be achieved through 24 strategic initiatives and 152 recommendations, was primarily designed to lower the cost of fundraising, accelerate the development of the bond market and encourage the greater presence of foreign firms as well as to strengthen corporate governance derived from the HLFC's 1999 report. The document, in conjunction with the companion financial sector master plan announced in March 2001, charted the strategic directions for placing capital market growth in a sustained footing for the next decade (BNM *Annual Report 2001*; *EIUCR*-Malaysia March 2001: 19–21; *ID* May 2001: 4–6).

The third and final prong of the post-crisis reform strategy rested with timely efforts to revise and strengthen existing regulatory and legal frameworks. In marked contrast to the halting process of legislation in Thailand prior to the early 2000s, laws mandating new regulations and improving securities market governance were often made decisively in Malaysia. Between late 1998 and early 2001, parliament passed extensive amendments and changes to the securities and corporate acts, usually at special and expedient sittings, paving the way for the establishment of the new regulatory agencies and the development of the master plans discussed above (*FEER* 12 November 1998: 74; *MB* 16 November 1998: 6–10). In line with rapid changes and an increasingly liberalised environment in the capital market, the government followed this up with important revisions to legislation in early and mid-2000s. These culminated in the overhaul of the Companies and Securities Commission Acts and the transformation of the fragmented securities and futures industry laws into a more streamlined and efficient Capital Market Services Act in 2007. Decisive and swift revisions to these laws not only vested financial technocrats with enhanced regulatory powers but also endorsed the new market institutions and development plans in formal legal frameworks.

This discussion by no means suggests that institutional, policy and legal reforms in the post-crisis period were not without problems and difficulties. As a matter of fact, official efforts to build regulatory agencies, design liberalisation programmes and revise securities laws sometimes slackened and even stalled, as particularistic interests had to be assuaged and side payments made to soften the resistance from powerful political actors (Case 2005; Rodan 2004b: 119–139). Overall, however, institutional building, policy formation and regulatory improvements were largely immune from serious political and legislative gridlock, thanks primarily to the concentration of veto authority in the top UMNO leadership. As a result, the Malaysian government was able to strengthen and invigorate the institutional structure of financial policy-making and market governance. This ensured the effective initiation and formulation of the various strategic plans for liberalising and promoting the capital market. More importantly, the centralised policy structure and the resultant decisive and programmatic reform of financial laws put Malaysia not only ahead of most of its peers in developing Asia but also on a par with many developed countries in terms of the overall legal framework governing the securities industry and the corporate sector (CLSA, various issues; Walter 2008).

These various institutional, policy and legal developments in post-crisis Malaysia indicated the UMNO government's eagerness to project itself as committed to market-oriented reforms in the face of external market and political pressures, and certainly some crucial changes were under way. But just how deep and resolute were these reforms, and what was the likelihood of the decisive and programmatic policy and institutional changes being sustained over time? In the 2000s, as in the 1990s, the ability of the Malaysian government to translate the reform plans to concrete market outcomes was stronger than its Thai counterpart, largely due to the UMNO's tight controls over party decision-making processes and the economic bureaucracy and the relatively stable core of financial policy elites. By the end of 2006, for instance, more than 50 per cent of the HLFC's recommendations on corporate governance had been implemented (CLSA 2007: 25); nearly 70 per cent of the CMMP's policy objectives had been achieved towards late 2008 (BNM *Annual Report 2009*: 106). As will be demonstrated below, however, these reform achievements were qualified ones and were largely technical in nature. Many of the key policy and institutional changes that were politically contentious and painful were invariably subject to delays, dilution and even abandonment. The implementation difficulties were particularly visible in the process of liberalising the stock market, consolidating the securities industry and enforcing existing market and corporate governance rules.

These difficulties primarily resulted from internal organisational weaknesses in the UMNO. The preceding analysis shows that the factional clashes at the very top of UMNO leadership generated delays and reversals in the formation of economic policy responses to the Asian crisis in general and to financial market reforms in particular. But intra-party competition and factionalism had a more durable destabilising impact on the implementation of specific reform measures, as will be illustrated below. While the systemic logic of party concentration dictated that the UMNO pursue a coherent and programmatic reform approach, factional rivalries disposed politicians to capture reform policies to obtain individualised political resources and maintain bases of particularised support. They were thus inclined to delay, dilute or change given reform measures that threatened the interests of narrow constituents who provided such resources and support. Furthermore, the inclination of politicians to be beholden to particularistic interests magnified the influence of specialised economic groups and private market actors, subjected reform policies to their erratic and volatile demands and compromised reform resoluteness.

As mentioned in the preceding section, financial technocrats tried in vain to break through the clubby structure of the domestic stockbroking community in the 1990s. The Asian crisis of the late 1990s and the resultant urgency of eliminating the oligopolistic practices that spawned various inefficiencies in the securities industry opened a crucial window of opportunity to liberalise the stock market. Central to the market liberalisation was the deregulation of fixed and rigid brokerage fees that had remained the highest in the world for many years and harmed the interests of the investing public. In early 2000, the MSC announced a two-stage plan to make the brokerage commission structure more flexible and market-oriented. From September 2000, brokerage fees on trades above RM 100,000 were to be liberalised while transactions below that threshold would carry a fixed rate of 0.75 per cent. From July 2001, fees on all trades would be fully negotiable, subject to a cap of 0.7 per cent, in line with the main thrust of the CMMP to reduce the costs of fundraising. The plan was seen by many observers as an overdue yet positive step to develop a more competitive and transparent stockbroking sector in Malaysia (*FT* 2 May 2000: 44).

It should be clear that this staged and controlled liberalisation of commission rates was highly incremental, reflecting the concerns of financial policy-makers that a more drastic deregulation would compromise their regulatory responsibility and, more significantly, provoke strong political resistance. Their concerns were certainly not misplaced. No sooner had the first stage of commission liberalisation been implemented than private financiers put up a vigorous opposition. Powerful members of the MSBA and the KLSE, who were key constituents or financial backers of prominent UMNO politicians, mobilised political resources to temper and delay the liberalisation process (*BT*-Kuala Lumpur 29 September 2000: 1). In early 2001, senior finance ministry officials signalled that the deregulation of commission rates should take into account the ability of stockbrokers to adapt themselves to new market conditions (*BT*-Kuala Lumpur 23 March 2001: 17). During the first half of the year, MSC technocrats were under growing political pressure to cave in to particularistic demands. Under the circumstances, it did not come as a surprise that the MSC decided to put on hold the deregulation of commission rates just before the second stage was due to start in July 2001.

Even the partial liberalisation of brokerage fees was subject to weak enactment in the ensuing years. Financial technocrats often found the effectiveness of their liberalisation efforts dented by the tenacious attempts of private financiers to control price competition among themselves and maintain fat profit margins from fixed commissions. In mid-2002, under the co-ordination of the MSBA, almost all stockbrokers agreed to fix the brokerage fees that they charged retail investors for small share transactions at the top of 0.7 per cent. While some smaller stockbrokers later breached the agreement by offering lower than the MSBA-sanctioned rates, the leading members stood firm and maintained the cartel (*BT*-Kuala Lumpur 27 June 2002: 1). Given that the leading stockbrokers held the bulk of assets in the sector and dominated share trading, their decision carried great weight in determining the direction of commission rates. Less than a year later, large MSBA members played the same old trick, on the pretext of low trading activities and poor market conditions (*FT* 16 April 2003: 25). As a consequence, individual investors who lacked organisational capabilities to credibly exercise voice and counterbalance the market influence of well-connected private financiers had to pay high fixed commissions to stockbrokers to process KLSE transactions.

A similar pattern of partial and irresolute implementation also manifested itself in the consolidation of the stockbroking industry. In parallel to their efforts to liberalise the securities sector, financial policy-makers planned to merge existing stockbrokers into larger and stronger universal brokers in anticipation of greater foreign entry and increased competitive pressures in the sector, as discussed above. The plan was highly directive: financial authorities determined the total number of universal brokerages emerging from the process, stipulated the fiscal incentives they would receive and set a minimum share capital of RM 250 million that they would be obliged to have. They unveiled the plan in April 2000 and set out to complete the mergers by the end of the year.

However, the consolidation was far from plain sailing. Smaller stockbrokers resisted the pressure for merger, fearing that they would lose ownership control; the larger stockbrokers who successfully lobbied to be designated the lead firms were reluctant to take on weaker partners. All of them were strongly opposed to the timeline for the mergers and the minimum share capital required of the enlarged and merged firms. Senior UMNO politicians who had controlling stakes in large stockbroking firms or saw private financers as strategic constituents in their efforts to strengthen their factional bases of support also dug their heels in against the plan (*EIUCR*-Malaysia September 2000: 29; *FT* 9 January 2001: 34). MSC officials backslid on their consolidation attempts and the mergers stalled. In early 2003, the merger plan made a comeback as part of the renewed government effort to prepare the Malaysian financial industry to tackle the challenges of liberalisation and globalisation. The plan was modified to allow for a larger number of the lead stockbrokers, the original timeline on the mergers slackened and the minimum share capital lowered. These changes signalled the government's frustration with the very limited success of its efforts to encourage tie-ups in the securities industry. But even this diluted merger plan failed to achieve its desired goals. By the end of 2008, the total number of firms operating in the stockbroking industry stood at 29, well above the original consolidation target.

Reform irresoluteness was also salient in the weak implementation of securities market and corporate governance rules. As noted earlier, the introduction of reform bills in these areas, following the Asian crisis, brought Malaysia closer to international best practices. Equally, legal and institutional reforms considerably strengthened the formal power of key regulatory agencies—the MSC and the KLSE—to adopt these practices. However, the enforcement of securities and corporate governance rules in Malaysia, while stronger than in Thailand, was much weaker than in Singapore, as illustrated in Table 4.2. When explaining the significant gaps between the formal adoption of internationally acceptable governance rules and the weak enforcement of these rules, several key studies (for example, Gourevitch and Shinn 2005: 232–237; Walter 2008: 120–125) have emphasised the political resistance of powerful corporate interests and the tendency of financial authorities to commit regulatory forbearance. While true, these accounts have failed to make more explicit the profound institutional sources of the problems. Consistent with the central proposition of this chapter, weak enforcement stemmed primarily from the intra-party organisational dynamics of the UMNO, which drove political elites to build and maintain particularised support and thus to be beholden to private corporate interests.

As detailed above, factional competition and rivalry created incentives for UMNO policy-makers to capture the financial and corporate restructuring process as a rent-seeking vehicle for bailing out well-connected firms. The same logic of intra-party weaknesses also asserted itself in the enforcement of market and corporate governance rules. There is no lack of examples in which these rules were used strategically and selectively to protect or persecute the corporate interests of different UMNO factions. In mid-1999, for instance, the MSC charged Ishak Ismail, head of FKC Holdings (Malaysia's largest fast-food chain) and Wan Muhamad Hasni Wan Sulaiman, chairman of Abrar Corp (an infrastructure and financial services company), both of whom were believed to be connected to Anwar, for allegedly breaching securities laws (*FEER* 5 August 1999: 48). On the other hand, nothing had transpired from investigations begun in late 1997 into alleged misappropriation of funds by government officials in connection with the Perwaja Steel project (*WSJ* 14 May 2002: A1). Similarly, charges brought by the MSC against two well-connected corporate high-fliers on unspecified violations of securities rules in early 1999 did not result in any arrests (*EIUCR*-Malaysia 3rd Quarter 1999: 28–29). Equally importantly, Daim, who arrogated financial policy authority to himself following the fall of Anwar, was believed to have interfered in the MSC investigations into the breaches of securities and corporate rules by his close business associates (*FEER* 27 June 2002: 40–41). The evidence of selective regulation, while anecdotal, raises serious doubts over the effectiveness of post-crisis corporate governance reforms in Malaysia. More systematic empirical analyses (Fraser et al 2006; Wahab et al. 2007) show that regulatory agencies tended to be more forbearing towards politically connected firms that had higher debt levels, poorer financial reporting quality and lower transparency.

The enforcement of market and corporate regulations did not improve with Daim edged out, however. Particularly troubling for Malaysian corporate governance was the inability or unwillingness of regulatory agencies to bring to account powerful government-linked or controlled business interests that were strategic supporters of the dominant faction of the UMNO, where shady deals or malfeasant practices were involved. In late 2000, the government bought 29 per cent of Malaysian Air System at a price roughly twice the market price, bailing out a major shareholder and shielding the airline from financial pressures. By the same token, the government was reluctant to subject Proton, the country's largest car-maker and Mahathir's pet project, to stricter governance standards and restructure the company through a foreign takeover (*EIUCR*-Malaysia March 2005: 15–16; *WSJ* 11 August 2005: A11). More generally, regulatory authorities had difficulty in getting government-controlled companies with close connections to influential UMNO figures to disclose more information and change opaque decision-making structures, primarily because these companies were keen to protect their political linkages. As a result, companies with significant government ownership tended to be more poorly governed (Ghazali and Weetman 2006; Tam and Tan 2007). Given that large government-controlled firms dominated the equity market, this posed an obstacle not only to corporate governance reform but to capital market development.

The impact of particularistic interests on the process of securities market and corporate governance also generated political constraints on the enforcement capacity of regulatory agencies. To be sure, the MSC and the BNM were generally recognised to be more meritocratic and competent than their counterparts in Thailand and other Southeast Asian countries (Hamilton-Hart and Jomo 2003; Zhang 2007). They were largely able to initiate crucial regulatory changes and implement these changes in those policy arenas that directly engaged the interests of the top political leadership. In the post-crisis period, legal and regulatory reforms increased the authority of the MSC and the BNM; UMNO leaders often allowed them considerable operational autonomy, particularly when they were eager to signal their commitment to market-oriented reforms and to attracting foreign capital. This strengthened the ability of financial technocrats to move towards violators of securities and corporate rules and press charges against them (*MB* 1 January 2003: 14–15, 16 July 2003: 26–40).

However, the commitment of UMNO leaders to rule-based regulation and the technocratic management of capital market development were not without limits. The ability of regulatory agencies to enforce rules and regulations appeared to be contingent upon the political priorities and particularised pursuits of UMNO elites. As mentioned above, when politicians wanted to protect their corporate constituents and accorded well-connected firms regulatory favours, MSC and BNM officials found their ability to bring rule violators to book considerably constrained. This demonstrates the reluctance of UMNO elites to underpin securities market rules and corporate governance standards with the effective regulatory autonomy of financial technocrats. While the formal power of market regulators strengthened through institutional reforms, their substantive capacity to check private malfeasance and fraud failed to improve significantly. As a result, the actual record of rule enforcement in the areas of securities and corporate governance has not shown any discernible upward trend in Malaysia over the decade since the Asian crisis (Table 4.2).

Conclusions

The pattern of capital market reforms and development in Malaysia during the 1990s and 2000s conforms to the theoretical expectations of this book about financial policy-making in a polity that couples the centralised political party structure with the factionalised ruling party. The combination of party system concentration and factional rivalry within the UMNO generated mixed policy orientations and reform outcomes. While the concentrated party system created centripetal incentives for political elites to deliver public-regarding policy objectives, institutionalised intra-UMNO conflicts brought pressures to bear upon politicians to pursue particularistic interests in the process of capital market reforms. Similarly, centralised veto authority that primarily derived from party system concentration enabled policy-makers to initiate decisive and swift policy and regulatory changes, while intra-party competition and factionalism disposed politicians to be beholden to private market agents and compromised reform resoluteness. The political party architecture of Malaysia thus provided crucial institutional underpinnings for its mixed record on capital market reforms.

Like Singapore, Thailand and other countries in East Asia, Malaysia was also hit hard by the global financial crisis of 2008–2009, just when the CMMP-guided market reform programme was about to draw to a close. While Malaysia, which was closely integrated with the global economic system, bore the brunt of the financial crisis in late 2008, it was most likely to benefit from the global rebound and foreign capital inflows in late 2009. But economic openness influenced the strength of Malaysia's recovery in interaction with domestic market institutions, particularly financial systems. As in Singapore and Thailand, two institutional features of financial markets were important in Malaysia: banking robustness and capital market development. While Malaysia had a well-capitalised banking sector, industrial firms still had difficulty isolating themselves from the impact of credit crunches that followed the global financial crisis. This was mainly because plunging growth rates, depressed business sentiments and market uncertainties forced banks to exercise extreme caution in their lending operations (Ito et al. 2009; Nambiar 2009). In the circumstances, whether private firms were able to obtain access to additional industrial financing and thus boost their investment and production quickly in response to increased demand was contingent upon the development of the capital market. In this sense, the mixed outcomes in capital market reforms inevitably had considerable impact on the ability of Malaysia to cope with the fallout of the crisis and to stage a forceful and sustained recovery. A detailed analysis of the causal linkage is far beyond the scope of this chapter, but a number of preliminary observations are in order here.

Despite its mixed record on reform approaches and outcomes, Malaysia on the whole carried out more successful market reforms and developed a more robust capital market than did Thailand. This mainly reflected the former's stronger political party structure and more decisive and programmatic reform policies, as made clear in this and preceding chapters. Over 1998–2008, the annual average ratio of stock market capitalisation to GDP was 1.447 in Malaysia but merely 0.517 in Thailand.[10] To the extent that the Malaysian capital market was able to pick up the slack in bank lending, it contributed more strongly to the country's recovery. The better developed capital market not only complemented banks in providing an alternative source of industrial financing but also played a key role in luring back foreign capital (BNM *Annual Report 2009*; Pomerleano 2009). As a result, Malaysia rebounded more forcefully from the financial crisis than did Thailand (World Bank 2010a: 66). However, intra-party organisational weaknesses in Malaysia rendered its capital market reforms less effective and growth-enhancing than reform policies in Singapore. Over the decade following the Asian crisis, the capital market became larger and more active in Singapore than in Malaysia: the annual average ratio of stock market capitalisation to GDP and of stock trading value to GDP in Singapore was 1.841 and 1.178 respectively.[11] The capital market in Singapore was thus able to play a more important role than its Malaysian counterpart in contributing to a stronger economic recovery, as explained in Chapter 4. Of course, national economic performance during the global financial meltdown was contingent upon a range of factors other than capital market development. But the varying degrees of economic resilience among the three countries brought to the fore the causal importance of different reform approaches and outcomes and their political underpinnings.

7
Conclusions and Implications

The central argument of this book is that inter-party and intra-party organisational dimensions interact to shape the orientation and pattern of financial policy-making in developing and emerging market countries. Drawing upon theoretical studies on the policy impact of political parties, this book has addressed cross-country differences in financial policy choices and capital market reforms in Malaysia, Singapore and Thailand over the past two decades. In the previous chapters, the explanatory approach that considers party system concentration in tandem with internal party organisational strength has shown that financial and regulatory policies varied significantly between the three cases in response to the national configurations of political parties. The different patterns of policy choices and regulatory changes in turn led to varied market reform patterns and development trajectories.

This final chapter summarises the major empirical findings that have emerged from the preceding analysis and reflects on the implications of these findings for theoretical and policy debates on financial market governance. It first compares the empirical evidence on the direction and outcomes of capital market reforms in the three countries and provides a more focused explanation of the policy differences between them. The purpose is not to recapitulate the analysis of the case chapters but to conduct a structured comparison of the dependent variables and to highlight the application of the explanatory variables to the case studies. The chapter then explores the theoretical implications of this book in light of the alternative explanations of reform patterns sketched out in Chapter 1, and examines the applicability of the party-based explanation to broader socio-economic policy arenas in Southeast Asia and beyond. Finally, the chapter discusses the implications of the empirical findings about the political underpinnings of financial market reforms and governance, particularly against the backdrop of increasingly frequent and severe financial crises, including the global financial meltdown of 2008–2009.

Focused, structured comparison

In Malaysia, Singapore and Thailand, capital market reforms were enacted as part of broader economic liberalisation programmes in the 1990s and 2000s. Major reform measures that were structured around stock market deregulation, SOE privatisation and regulatory improvement were initiated at critical junctures during the past two decades. While the timing and content of such market reforms were similar, the orientation, decisiveness and resoluteness of reform policies differed both across the three countries and over time, particularly within Thailand.

In the first place, there were salient cross-country variations in the extent to which capital market reforms were aligned with the public interest. In Singapore, policy-makers harnessed market reform programmes to such public-regarding policy objectives as financial development and economic growth. Thailand fell at the other extreme, at least prior to the late 1990s. Thai politicians were more concerned with capturing the reform process as a vehicle for seeking rents than with pursing public goods policies through market changes. While Thailand's financial policy demonstrated more public-regarding attributes in the early and mid-2000s, the overall reform programme remained oriented towards private-regarding purposes. Malaysia was in the middle, with political elites being generally able to align market reforms with public policy objectives but simultaneously pursuing reform policies in ways that were counter to public welfare.

Furthermore, the three countries displayed striking differences in the formulation and implementation of capital market reforms. The Singapore government was able to enact decisive and well-planned market reforms, often in response to external economic shocks, market pressures and financial crises. Equally importantly, a high degree of consistency and stability was manifest in the implementation of various reform measures. In Thailand, by contrast, indecisive action and inordinate postponement invariably plagued capital market reforms. Even when external market and political pressures thrust reform policies onto the government agenda, many of these policies were considerably diluted or abandoned in midstream. The Thai government under Thaksin formulated more decisive reforms in the early and mid-2000s, but the reform process continued to suffer from poor credibility. Malaysia was again arrayed in between, being more decisive and resolute than Thailand, particularly with regard to stock market liberalisation and privatisation, but less so than Singapore in the design and making of overall reform programmes.

The cross-country variation in the orientation, decisiveness and stability of market reform policies generated different reform outcomes across the three countries, as illustrated in Table 7.1. Singapore's public-regarding, decisive and resolute reform programmes contributed to the development of a larger and more active stock market. Largely private-regarding, indecisive and unstable reform policies in Thailand impeded the development of a sizable and efficient equity market. Malaysia's mixed record on capital market reforms appears to have produced middling outcomes: the KLSE was larger and more active than the SET but less so than the SES during much of the period under consideration in this book.

To account for cross-country variations in the direction, approaches and outcomes of capital market reforms in the three countries, this book has emphasised political party structures as the primary determinants. It has located the political sources of policy choices and market changes at the complex interplay of two key party variables—party system concentration and intra-party organisational strength. In Malaysia, Singapore and Thailand, politicians and their roles in the design of financial and regulatory policies occupied the central stage of capital market reforms. While they intervened in the policy process with the ultimate view to holding onto office, they differed in their incentives to deliver public-regarding reform policies and in their abilities to initiate reforms decisively and commit to maintaining them resolutely.

Table 7.1 Size and activity of stock markets

	1986–1990	1991–1995	1996–2000	2001–2005	2005–2008	All years
Stock market capitalisation to GDP, in percentage						
Malaysia	69.79	198.71	179.84	137.52	157.02	148.76
Singapore	88.31	141.21	197.35	189.29	196.21	162.47
Thailand	15.64	64.16	41.73	52.74	69.07	48.67
Stock market trading value to GDP, in percentage						
Malaysia	13.18	108.87	98.52	37.05	78.04	67.13
Singapore	29.51	79.39	78.35	81.29	190.46	91.80
Thailand	13.27	50.85	22.55	50.88	44.16	36.34

Source: Author calculations, based on data provided in Beck and Al-Hussainy (2010).

The central theoretical proposition of the book has posited that the integration of party system concentration and intra-party organisational strength offers a powerful perspective on the propensity of politicians to formulate nationally oriented reform policies, as opposed to particularistic ones, in the three countries. Equally importantly, party system configurations interacted with intra-party organisational structures to shape the ways in which politicians initiated and implemented capital market reforms.

More specifically, political party structures created incentives for politicians to be geared towards one reform orientation over the other via their effects on politicians' desire to maintain power. This held true in Malaysia and Singapore, two electoral authoritarian regimes, as well as in Thailand, an electoral democracy. While politicians in all the three countries were under comparable electoral pressures to respond to voter interests and build support bases, different party structures mediated these electoral pressures differently and thus created heterogeneous reform incentives. In Singapore, where the concentrated party system existed alongside the centrally and cohesively organised PAP, elections motivated political elites to be accountable to broader constituencies and have strong incentives to pursue party-focused strategies and policies. As a result, they were strongly disposed to promote public-regarding reform programmes for which they could claim partisan credit and that could deliver broad benefits to a large swathe of the general population. In Thailand, where the fragmented party system was married to poorly organised parties in the coalition government, elections pressed politicians to generate localised and particularised support as a strategically important way to enhance their political careers. Politicians were thus inclined to oppose capital market reforms that threatened to harm the welfare of their narrow constituencies or to capture the reform process to seek rents for particular private firms, discrete economic actors or special interest groups. In Malaysia, while the concentrated party system translated electoral pressures into the incentives to prioritise party-determined platforms and public goods policies in the reform process, perennial and prevalent intra-party conflicts and factional rivalries within the UMNO simultaneously motivated politicians to cultivate personalised bases of support and seek particularistic reform policies. This explains why Malaysian policy-makers had mixed incentives vis-à-vis the formation of market reforms and tempered public policy objectives with private-regarding pursuits.

Not only did political party structures influence the orientation of capital market reforms, they also bore crucially upon the formulation of such reforms. As clearly shown in the three country chapters, financial and regulatory changes were more likely to be programmatic and successful if they were initiated decisively and effectively. How decisive and effective policy-makers were in the initiation of policy reforms was primarily contingent upon the number of veto players or institutional or partisan actors whose consent was required for regulatory changes. In the process of capital market reforms in the three countries, the most important factor was the number of parties whose agreement was needed for existing market regulations to be altered and for new institutional frameworks to be established. Party system concentration determined the distribution of veto power exercised by partisan players in the formation of regulatory and financial policies.

In Singapore, the concentrated party system that minimised the number of partisan veto players and centralised financial policy authority strengthened the ability of the PAP government to initiate capital market reforms decisively. In Thailand, by contrast, the fragmented party structure that scattered veto authority among multiple actors representing heterogeneous interests impeded decisive and effective policy reforms. In the early and mid-2000s, the increasingly concentrated party system that stemmed from constitutional reforms produced swifter and more decisive reform initiatives in Thailand. But the military coup that toppled the Thaksin government in September 2006 made it difficult to observe how institutional changes in the Thai party system would impact the pattern of capital market reforms in the longer run. In Malaysia, so long as factional clashes among the top UMNO leadership could be contained, the concentrated party system facilitated the introduction of decisive reform programmes.

The strong ability of policy-makers to initiate swift and decisive policy and institutional changes might not lead to market reform success, however; public-regarding reform policies were unlikely to be implemented in a coherent and resolute manner if such policies were not sustained over time. One crucial empirical finding that has emerged from the country chapters is that the internal organisational configurations of political parties exerted a shaping influence on the ability of politicians to carry through policy reforms to the end. In Singapore, the centralised and cohesively structured PAP, which committed politicians to agreed-on decisions, isolated policy-makers from particularised interests and enhanced government stability, produced resolute and credible reform programmes. In Thailand, the incohesive, poorly organised and factionalised parties in the coalition government that encouraged private-regarding behaviour, subjected policy-makers to private pressures and undermined cabinet stability invariably generated irresolute and erratic market reforms. In Malaysia, the internal organisation of the UMNO, which was stronger than that of Thai political parties but less cohesive than that of the PAP, led to the middling progress of capital market reforms. When viewed in close interaction with the systemic structure of political parties, the varying degrees of intra-party organisational strength provide important insights into how the policy behaviour of the governments in the three countries differed between decisiveness and resoluteness.

Alternative explanations and theoretical implications

In Chapter 1, four categories of alternative explanations that emphasise policy resources, political regimes, technocratic capabilities and systemic forces were critically reviewed. For reasons already discussed and illustrated in the preceding chapters, each of these four categories is theoretically inferior to the party-based approach to understanding cross-country variations in the orientation and pattern of capital market reforms. In light of the major empirical findings summarised above, this chapter presents further critical analyses and teases out key theoretical implications.

As amply evidenced in the country chapters, policy and financial resources at the disposal of government politicians were not causally linked to the ways in which capital market reforms were oriented and implemented. Singapore, which had higher national wealth levels than Malaysia and Thailand, was theoretically better positioned to use policy resources to smooth the way for politically painful reform measures. But in the actual process of market and institutional changes, the PAP government made no concessions to political actors who stood to lose from various reform policies. It was the strong external and internal configurations of the political party structure that provided policy-makers with institutional resources with which to overcome political difficulties and ensure market reform success in Singapore. In Malaysia and Thailand, where the government did employ material incentives to get key social groups to fall in with their reform plans, capital market reforms were far less effective and successful. In Thailand and, to a lesser extent, in Malaysia, policy resources were so frequently misused to pay off the politically powerful that they only served to magnify the play of particularistic interests in the reform process. Equally crucially, there was little guarantee that compensatory schemes would facilitate the effective design and making of reform programmes. Both Malaysia and Thailand were less capable than Singapore of enacting and implementing decisive and resolute capital market reforms during the 1990s and 2000s.

Similarly, the impact of the causal variables suggested in the political regime explanation is much less determinate than that of the party-based variables developed in this book. The two electoral authoritarian countries, Malaysia and Singapore, differed in terms of the direction and trajectory of reform programmes. Singaporean politicians operating in a more centrally and cohesively organised party structure were both more strongly motivated to pursue public-regarding objectives through market reforms and more capable of following through on these reforms than their Malaysian counterparts. In the cross-national context of electoral democratic and authoritarian regimes, it was inter-party and intra-party organisational dimensions rather than macro-political structures that influenced the shape of financial policy reforms. Politicians in the electoral authoritarian country, Singapore, were much more disposed than their counterparts in the electoral democratic country, Thailand, to promote public goods provision and carry out decisive and resolute reform policies. This was primarily because the public-regarding orientation and policy-making capability of Singaporean politicians was underpinned by the much stronger political party structure. This lends robust support to one of the key claims of the book—that when elections generate comparable impacts on the strategic behaviour of politicians in electoral and policy processes regardless of regime type, countries with concentrated party systems and strongly organised parties would supply growth-enhancing financial policies and implement these policies effectively.

Furthermore, this book has placed less emphasis on the causal importance of administrative capacity and regulatory power. It is true that Singaporean technocrats were more competent and powerful than Malaysian market regulators who, in turn, enjoyed more policy-making authority than Thai financial officials during much of the period under review here. But these differences in the level of technocratic capabilities reflected more profound political and institutional variations. As clearly demonstrated in the country chapters, the ability of financial technocrats to formulate public-regarding and resolute reform policies was contingent upon the incentives of political leaders to grant technocrats policy capacity and enforcement powers. These incentives were in turn shaped by the external and internal organisational dimensions of political party structures. While Malaysian and Thai financial technocrats saw their regulatory authority increasingly strengthened throughout the 1999s and 2000s, particularly in the aftermath of major financial crises, their actual ability to enforce market rules and regulations independently of distributive pressures failed to demonstrate a significant increase. In Thailand and, to a lesser degree, in Malaysia, politicians remained reluctant to give full play to the newly gained policy powers of technocrats and enhance the status of regulatory agencies within the hierarchy of state economic institutions.

Finally, the empirical analysis of this book has not prioritised the impact of systemic factors on the approaches and outcomes of capital market reforms in the three countries. It has not denied that external market and political pressures were at play in the reform process. In the 1990s and 2000s, Malaysia, Singapore and Thailand, like many other emerging market countries, were under constant pressure from powerful Western governments and key international economic organisations to reform their capital markets along neo-liberal lines and adopt the market-oriented model of financial development. Equally importantly, these three countries were also prompted by competitive pressures to liberalise and foster capital markets as an important strategy for attracting foreign capital and enhancing the regional, even global, economic status of their respective capital cities. However, these comparable systemic forces did not translate into similar reform approaches and outcomes, as was made abundantly clear in the book. The impact of regional and global political and market forces was mediated through the different national configurations of political parties, who exerted varied shaping influences over the political incentives of politicians, the policy and regulatory capacities of financial technocrats, and the orientation and pattern of capital market reforms across the three countries.

This discussion of alternative explanations for cross-country variations in financial policy choice and capital market changes suggests that they are less plausible than the explanatory approach resting on the policy impact of political parties. But can the theoretical argument advanced in this book be sustained in other policy arenas across a wider range of cases? The research design of the book would not allow any generalisable conclusions to be made about the proposed causal linkage between capital market reforms and political parties. The case selection is neither broad enough nor comparatively matched in a sufficiently strategic way to apply the argument in broader national settings. Przeworski and Teune (1970) have suggested that random case selection is desirable as a way to improve the methodology for small-n case studies. The central proposition put forth here appears to hold across an array of public policy arenas in a number of randomly proposed cases in Northeast and Southeast Asia and beyond.

As mentioned in Chapter 1, there is a growing and rich literature concerned with the impact of political parties on economic governance. This literature has been primarily concerned with North America and Western Europe. Increasingly, however, it is expanding to embrace Northeast and Southeast Asian economies. Analytical attention has been paid to how national variations in party institutions have propelled divergent courses of authoritarian dominance and democratisation (Brownlee 2008; Cheng 2003) and structured the equilibrium between political regimes and economic development (Blondel 1999). More importantly, country case studies have provided powerful, if only preliminary, insights into how political party structures within which politicians and bureaucrats must function shape their incentives and actions in designing and implementing public policy. While still scarce, empirical analyses of this genre have made initial attempts to connect this literature to various policy arenas in major emerging market economies and have followed two distinct approaches.

One approach has focused on the policy impact of party systems and associated policy authority structures in government processes. One prominent study (MacIntyre 2003) has explored how party system concentration and veto authority structure influenced the policy responses of Southeast Asian countries to the Asian financial crisis of the late 1990s. It has clearly shown that both highly concentrated and fragmented party systems impeded swift and effective responses to external economic shocks and that the intermediate configuration of party systems was most effective at tackling financial crises. Following the similar logic of analysis, other studies (Doner et al. 2009; Hicken and Ritchie 2002) have examined the more durable impact of party systemic attributes on innovation systems and policies in randomly selected cases from East Asia, Latin America and the Middle East. Governments operating in concentrated party systems and centralised veto authority structures were more capable of building and maintaining innovation-enhancing institutions than their counterparts operating in fragmented party systems and scattered decision-making structures. While these studies have focused on different issue areas and come to dissimilar conclusions, they have clearly reinforced the central themes of this book—that party systems exert a powerful and, more crucially, predictable, bearing on policy approaches and outcomes.

The other approach has highlighted the causal importance of intra-party organisations in influencing the orientation and patterns of socio-economic policies. Key empirical studies have developed analytical accounts of cross-country differences in the formulation and implementation of administrative reforms (Painter 2004), development policies (Kuhonta 2004) and broader political–economic changes (Kitschelt 2003) across a range of Northeast and Southeast Asian countries, including Japan. The central thesis that has emerged from these studies is that centrally and cohesively organised parties generate stronger incentives for politicians to pursue national-oriented policy objectives through bureaucratic changes, equitable development strategies and socio-economic reforms. Equally importantly, strongly structured political parties are more likely to provide policy-makers with the institutional resources with which to deliver effective and credible public policies. Again, these conclusions have lent robust support to the theoretical argument of this book about the policy effects of intra-party organisational attributes.

It is clear that the explanatory model resting on political party structures developed in this book is applicable across many policy arenas, not just financial and regulatory reforms, in a broad range of East Asian and other emerging market economies. The unique theoretical contribution that sets this book apart from the above-mentioned empirical analyses rests with the interaction of the policy impact of party system structures with that of intra-party organisational attributes. This integrated explanatory model proffers a more powerful perspective on the political dynamics of policy and institutional changes. However, it should not be concluded from the above that different analyses would necessarily be applied to various developing and emerging market countries. It remains for future research to explore the more diverse national milieus within which the external and internal organisational dimensions of political parties combine to shape political incentives and structure policy processes.

Political underpinnings for financial market governance

What does the theoretical argument of this book and the empirical evidence supportive of the argument imply about political underpinnings for financial market reforms and governance, particularly against the backdrop of the global financial crisis of 2008–2009? In the aftermath of the crisis, the view that domestic institutional deficiencies played a crucial role in precipitating the financial meltdown has enjoyed widespread support in academic and policy-making circles. International financial organisations, notably the IMF and the World Bank, have been taking on with great vigour the task of reforming national financial systems in both developed and developing countries. The reform agenda has converged on market regulation, policy transparency, banking supervision and corporate structure. It has emphasised the role of institutions in promoting the discipline of markets and placed great store on getting the right institutional mix for the smooth functioning of financial systems. The agenda has articulated and advocated a set of policy frameworks, rules and standards that govern the behaviour of state and societal actors in the financial sector.[1] The reform programme has amounted to a renewed international effort to enact a new governance paradigm that is most likely to pervade national financial architectures.

Several key elements define this emerging paradigm of financial market governance. In the first place, while the state is expected to play an active role in building strong legal and regulatory systems to ensure financial market stability, it should nourish the financial market as an institution that allows maximum scope for voluntary transactions. Furthermore, there should be a clear and practical scope for self-regulatory organisations and market regulations to become a central institution of financial governance that amplifies supervisory structures, facilitates information flow, allocates resources and manages risks. Finally, good financial governance must be predicated on the building of concomitant institutions—credible legal systems, independent regulatory authorities, robust capital markets and transparent market structures. Institutional reforms are designed to foster market competition, enhance the spontaneous actions of private-sector actors and ultimately improve the Pareto efficiency.

It appears, at first sight, that this governance paradigm is innovative, at least by the standards of the IMF and, to a lesser extent, the World Bank. It has envisaged a more positive and active role for the state than that sanctified in the Washington consensus. As programmes of financial liberalisation and innovations have ended up in regional and global crises, international policy-makers and neo-classical economists have increasingly recognised that market-oriented reforms without strong institutions to facilitate such reforms are most likely to fail. While the new paradigm has provided a novel form of institutional rationality for the existence of efficient financial markets, it has had vital limits. These limits lie in its manifest failure to address the national diversity and political dimensions of financial market governance.

A major plank in the emerging governance paradigm has been the promulgation of a range of global standards in the domains of financial stability, accounting practices and corporate governance. These standards are assumed and argued to be of universal relevance despite national historical differences in financial market structures and regulatory systems. Financial market development and governance, as an integral part of any political economy, are closely linked to the nature of the national economic architecture and the relationships between financial, product and labour markets. In other words, differences in financial systems and governance institutions are central to what makes different models of capitalism divergent. Changes in the configuration of financial markets and governance may unravel these relationships to yield new links between financial and industry, alter the ties between capital and labour and transform development models. The rapid transformation of financial systems risks disturbing the social and political fabric that underpin them (Underhill and Zhang 2010).

The key point here is that the reform and governance of financial markets may differ across countries and that these differences are embedded in the process of patterned conflicts and compromises among a range of domestic political actors. As clearly demonstrated in this book, comparable systemic structural forces did not produce similar market reform approaches and outcomes. Not only did the Southeast Asian countries display divergent reform orientations and trajectories, they also achieved varying degrees of market reform success, in terms of the development of capital markets. Equally importantly, securities market and corporate governance differed across these countries, with regard to both the content of regulation and the relationship of regulators to other government bureaucrats, politicians and regulated firms. These cross-country variations in reform and regulation patterns profoundly shaped the performance of the national economy in the global financial crisis. The empirical findings strongly suggest that the national diversity of capital market reforms and governance is an important function of the political processes of policy and regulatory changes mediated by domestic political institutions. Even in the area of finance, which has become one of the most globally integrated sectors in the world, national differences are likely to remain resilient.

Furthermore, the newly found state-friendly discourse of the emerging governance paradigm has been framed in narrow economic terms as the supply of legal and regulatory rules. It has negated the much broader role of political institutions in market governance in both developed and developing countries. Despite its emphasis on governance, the new paradigm has seldom confronted the issue of state institutions and the politics that underlie them. Market governance appears to be used in place of government in order to sell the reform programmes to increasingly market-oriented developing and emerging market countries. Indeed, the paradigm has treated governance virtually as a managerial tool with which to achieve decision-making rationality and market efficiency. While the building of strong market institutions has occupied the proscenium of the governance agenda, it has paid scant attention to the fact that market reforms are structured within existing political institutions. Designed in its present form, this new paradigm is unlikely to constitute a template for an acceptable and feasible market governance agenda, although it should be welcomed as a key component of policy debates in the aftermath of the global financial crisis.

This book contends that financial market governance is about more than the supply of market-supporting rules and regulations by the state. It is also about more than just achieving institutional efficiency in the maintenance of financial system stability. The effective governance of financial markets requires that close attention be paid to the impor- tance of political institutions in shaping reform policies and regulatory mechanisms. As illustrated in the preceding chapters, domestic political institutions, especially political party structures, mattered significantly to financial market development and governance. The different national configurations of inter-party and intra-party organisations generated the heterogeneous incentives and capabilities of politicians to pursue public-regarding reform policies decisively and resolutely. The resul- tant variations in capital market development and regulation produced the differential national ability to withstand the global financial crisis and to stage a strong recovery from the crisis-induced recession among the three Southeast Asian countries. This book thus establishes a new point of theoretical and policy departure for addressing how politicians operating within different political party structures may shape national financial architectures. It provides prima facie evidence of close linkages between political parties, policy incentives and market outcomes. Only by examining such linkages in broader institutional frameworks would it be possible to develop a stronger basis for understanding political underpinnings for financial market governance.

Notes

1 Politics and Capital Market Reforms

1. Detailed discussions of these models can be found in Hall and Taylor (1998), Keman (1997), Shepsle (2006) and Thelen and Steinmo (1992).
2. Empirical studies are voluminous. For prominent examples, see Haggard and McCubbins (2001), Knack (2003), Przeworski et al. (2000), Stein and Tommasi (2008) and Weaver and Rockman (1993).
3. Cross-country differences in economic policy patterns and policy reforms in developing countries are discussed at length in Bates and Krueger (1993), Haggard and Kaufman (1992a), Krueger (2000) and Stein and Tommasi (2008).
4. See, for instance, Frye and Mansfield (2003), Horowitz and Browne (2008) and Kitschelt et al. (1999) on East Central Europe; Mainwaring and Scully (1995), Mainwaring and Shugart (1997), Nielson (2003) and Stein and Tommasi (2008) on Latin America.
5. Two notable exceptions are Johnson and Crisp (2003) and Nielson (2003). Randall and Svåsand (2002) also make a strong case for considering the two organisational dimensions of political parties in an integrated manner.
6. Some studies (Persson 2002; Persson and Tabellini 2001) find a positive effect of presidentialism while others (Gerring et al. 2009) find a positive effect of parliamentarism and still others (Haggard and Kaufman 1995) find no difference.
7. While recent efforts to re-examine the issue have suggested that democracy generates more public goods provision (Bueno de Mesquita et al 2003; Lake and Baum 2001), they have not ruled out the empirical possibility that some non-democratic regimes may be able to advance public welfare.
8. A non-technical introduction to capital markets and banks is provided in Howells and Bain (1990), especially chapters 1, 3 and 6.
9. For an excellent discussion of how banks and capital markets function differently in different financial systems, see Allen and Gale (2000).
10. Some economists have reversed the causal linkage by arguing that privatisation is more likely to be implemented successfully in deep and liquid stock markets. See, for instance, Bortolotti et al. (2003).
11. See, for instance, Alesina et al. (1995), Chhibber and Nooruddin (2004), Garman et al. (2001), Hallerberg and Basinger (1998), Perotti and Kontopoulos (2002) and Roubini and Sachs (1989) on fiscal policy; Hankla (2006), Nielson (2003) and O'Reilly (2005) on trade liberalisation; Bearce (2003) and Bernhard and Leblang (1999) on monetary and exchange rate policies.
12. Demirgüç-Kunt and Levine (2008) and Levine (2005) provide excellent reviews of recent literature on the positive impact of financial development on economic growth and poverty reduction.

13. While arbitrary, this cut-off point has been widely used in prominent empirical analyses (Angrist 2005; Howard and Roessler 2006: 368; Levitsky and Way 2002: 55; Schedler 2004; Wantchekon 2003: 406) to determine whether elections in authoritarian regimes are competitive.

14. See, for instance, Bellows (1993), Case (1996a: 444–447), Chua (1997, 2005), Ganesan (1996), Mutalib (2002), Sebastian (1997) and Yeo (2002). For a dissenting view, see Rodan (1996a). Mauzy and Milne (2002: 143–153) argue that elections were less competitive in the 1970s and 1980s than in the late 1950s and early 1960s when the opposition was able to secure close to or more than 50 per cent of the total popular vote.

15. Detailed discussions of the constitutional reforms and their impact on the Thai party system and political structures can be found in Hicken (2006), McCargo (2002) and Ockey (2003).

16. Two excellent critical reviews of the literature are Geddes (1995) and Haggard (2000b).

17. The problem of conceptual stretching is discussed at length in Collier and Mahon (1993) and Sartori (1970).

2   Political Parties and Reform Processes

1. For prominent studies that use positive models in the analysis of politicians' interests in economic policy processes, see Alesina (1988) and Persson and Tabellini (2001).

2. The relevant literature is huge; for the most forceful rebuttals of the party decline proposition, see Aldrich (1995), Gunther et al. (2002) and Webb et al. (2002).

3. This has been developed extensively in recent studies on the roles of parties in the new democracies of Africa (Mozaffar et al. 2003; Reynolds and Sisk 1998), Central and Eastern Europe (Kitschelt et al. 1999; McAllister and White 2007), East Asia (Dalton et al. 2008; MacIntyre 2003; Reilly 2006) and Latin America (Carey 2009; Mainwaring 1999; Mainwaring and Scully 1995). For general discussions of party and party system institutionalisation in developing democracies, see Mainwaring and Torcal (2006), Randall and Svåsand (2002) and Webb and White (2007).

4. The electoral and exclusionary varieties of authoritarianism also exhibit significant differences in the legislative, judiciary and media arenas as well as in the electoral arena. It is beyond the scope and purpose of this book to examine these differences. For systematic discussions of electoral authoritarianism and its major dissimilarities from closed authoritarianism, see Diamond (2002), Hadenius and Teorell (2007), Levitsky and Way (2002) and Schedler (2002, 2004, 2006). The following discussion draws on these works.

5. Classical statements of the impact of electoral laws on party systems can be found in Duverger (1954), Lijphart (1994) and Taagepera and Shugart (1989). Prominent works on the consequences of social cleavages are Karvonen and Kuhnle (2001), Lipset and Rokkan (1967) and Meisel (1974). Amorim Neto and Cox (1997) and Boix (2007) have combined electoral institutions and social conflicts in their efforts to explain the number of parties.

6. There are now many theoretical and empirical studies on the electoral and legislative consequences of party system properties, among which the influential and frequently cited are Cox and McCubbins (1993), Jones and McDermott (2004), Laver and Schofield (1991), Mainwaring (1993), Mainwaring and Shugart (1997), Sartori (1997), Warwick (1994) and Webb and White (2007).

7. Duverger (1954), Gibson et al. (1983), Neumann (1956) and Panebianco (1988) are classic statements on the models and typologies of party organisation. Gunther and Diamond (2003), Katz and Mair (1995) and Wolinetz (2002) provide more recent categorising schema. The functions of parties are examined either on the basis of their organisational, electoral, legislative or governmental rationales (Gunther and Diamond 2001; Hershey 2006; Katz and Mair 1995; Keman 2006) or on the basis of their specific goals (Strom 1990a; Wolinetz 2002).

8. The approach that takes the desire of politicians to hold onto power as a given underpins the central arguments of Black (1958) and Downs (1957) in their pioneering research on the policy impact of political institutions and political parties. For recent empirical studies that explicitly employ this approach, see Ames (2001), Bueno de Mesquita et al. (2003), Eaton (2002) and Geddes (1994).

9. This does not necessarily mean that certain social groups and economic interests would not accrue personal benefits from politicians pursuing private-regarding policies. Indeed they may choose to reward those politicians who provide targeted benefits to them, as made clear in this chapter. However, it is more likely that private goods policies, if provided, are confined only to small groups of privileged members within society and are achieved at the expense of public welfare.

10. By emphasising the distinct politics of coalition-building under the two sets of electoral incentives associated with different party systems in the process of capital market reforms, this book finds itself in the company of a growing number of studies that explore the impact of majoritarian versus proportional electoral systems on banking regulation (Rosenbluth and Schaap 2003), corruption (Kunicová and Rose-Ackerman 2005), conflict management (Reynolds and Sisk 1998) and price levels (Rogowski and Kayser 2002). However, while these works examine how electoral rules influence the policy incentives of politicians and policy-making efficiency through their effect on party strategies and structures, this book explores the *direct* impact of political party structures.

11. The party system was not particularly concentrated in India under the Congress Party and in Japan under the Liberal Democratic Party in terms of the effective number of parliamentary parties. However, the party systems were widely described as the one-party dominant systems, primarily because of the electoral and legislative dominance of the two parties. Between 1952 and 1984 (with the exception of 1977), the Congress Party won an average of 45 per cent of the popular vote and 71 per cent of parliamentary seats in the general elections while the Liberal Democratic Party secured an average of 50 per cent of the popular vote and 56 per cent of parliamentary seats in the general elections between 1953 to 1990.

12. This is not the place to discuss the definition, categories and characteristics of veto players and their differences from veto gates. For a detailed analysis of these issues, see Tsebelis (1995, 2002).
13. Most studies have focused on the impact of party system structures and particularly the number of effective parties on government and cabinet stability. For prominent examples, see Grofman and van Roozendaal (1997) and Somer-Topcu and Williams (2008).

3   Variations in Political Party Structures

1. The measure can be defined as 1 divided by the sum of the squared decimal vote or seat shares of each electoral party and is generally presented as follows:

$$N = 1 \Big/ \sum_{i=1}^{n} P_i^2$$

where P_i^2 is the percentage of votes or seats of the ith party squared.

2. Primarily concerned with significant disparities in party sizes, Molinar has proposed a different measure of the number of parties (NP) that weights the winning party more than other parties:

$$NP = 1 + N \left[\sum_{i=1}^{n} (P_i^2 - P_1^2) \Big/ \sum_{i=1}^{n} P_i^2 \right]$$

where N equals $1 \Big/ \sum_{i=1}^{n} P_i^2$ and P_1^2 is the percentage of votes or seats for the winning party squared.

3. For instance, the Parti Islam Se Malaysia (the Islamic Party or PAS) was expelled from the BN in 1977, primarily because its leaders clashed with UMNO leaders over a range of issues and challenged the hegemonic position of the UMNO, particularly in the Malay community. For details, see Jaffar (1979).

4. Comprehensive and detailed analyses of how constitutional reforms generated a more centralised party system in Thailand are provided in Hicken (2006) and Ockey (2003). For a broader and comparative perspective on this issue in Asia-Pacific, see Reilly (2006: 121–145).

5. For further discussion of the early development of the UMNO in comparative perspective, see Funston (1980).

6. Author interview with a former UMNO vice-president, Kuala Lumpur, 3 August 2008.

7. Author interview with a former president of the UMNO Youth Wing, Kuala Lumpur, 20 July 2005.

8. The causes and consequences of these conflicts are discussed at length in Case (1996c: 215–251), Khoo (2003: 71–98), Means (1991: 193–222) and Milne and Mauzy (1999: 39–46).

9. These included the management committees of community centres, citizen's consultative committees, people's associations and residents' committees.

For fuller discussions of the rationale and roles of these institutions, see Chan (1976) and Seah (1985).

10. The process through which the PAP achieved this, particularly in the 1960s and 1970s, is analysed comprehensively in, for example, Bellows (1970), Chan (1976) and Milne and Mauzy (1990: 53–76).

11. Mutalib (2002) and Yeo (2002) provide more detailed examinations of the development and operation of GRCs and their effect on the electoral strength of both the ruling and opposition parties in Singapore.

12. Author interview with a former PAP vice-chairman, Singapore, 15 August 2007. See also Bellows (1970: 123–125).

13. The first-generation PAP leaders—Lee Kuan Yew and the other founding members of the party—had similar educational backgrounds, fought through the battles with the pro-communists in the 1950s and 1960s and established close interactions with each other in the state-building process. These common experiences contributed to the convergence of their world views, value orientations and policy preferences. Important insights into the impact of this socialisation process on PAP organisations can be found in Barr (2000) and Lam and Tan (1999).

14. See, for instance, Anusorn (1998), Murashima et al. (1991), Hicken (2002, 2006, 2009), King (1996), Kramol (1982), McCargo (1997) and Ockey (1994, 2003, 2005).

15. Anusorn (1998), Chai-Anan (1986, 1995), Kramol (1982), Ockey (1994, 2004: 22–55, 2005) and Suchit (1987) have emphasised the causal importance of broad social and political factors while Hicken (2002, 2009) and Chambers (2005, 2008) have focused on electoral institutions as the primary determinants of intra-party organisational configurations.

16. Author interview with a former deputy leader of the Democratic Party, Bangkok, 6 August 2005. See also Anusorn (1998), Chai-Anan (1995) and Suchit (1987).

17. Author interview with a former TRT secretary-general, Bangkok, 17 August 2005. See also McCargo and Ukrist (2005: 236–238).

18. Author interview with a former TRT secretary-general, Bangkok, 17 August 2005.

19. The 1997 constitution required candidates to be members of a political party for at least 90 days to be eligible to compete in parliamentary elections. But it also required elections to be held within 40–50 days once parliament was dissolved. As a result, would-be party switchers did not have enough time to meet the membership requirement and were forced to sit out one election. This enabled the prime minister to prevent individuals and factions from leaving his party by credibly threatening to dissolve parliament and call new elections.

4   Singapore: Market Reform Success

1. While the Singapore Confederation of Industries (SCI) was established in 1996, on the basis of the Singapore Manufacturers' Association, as an umbrella body for all industries, industrialists' responses to government policy initiatives and changes remained fragmented (*EIUCR*-Singapore 4th

Quarter 1995: 11). In 2003, the SCI was renamed the Singapore Manufacturers' Federation to refocus on manufacturing and related industries.

2. More recent empirical analyses conducted along similar lines include Bellows (1995) and Seah (1999).

3. Following the publication of her original article that expounded the administrative state thesis, Chan (1981) modified and refined her argument about the position of bureaucrats vis-à-vis that of politicians. 'I am not arguing that bureaucrats have usurped power from the politicians', Chan conceded, 'Parliament in Singapore is supreme and the cabinet leadership is very much supreme...' (1981: 11).

4. For a brief criticism of this systemic vulnerability argument, see Stubbs (2009: 8) who suggests that it has overstated the importance of security threats, particularly resource constraints, in the development of growth-promoting institutions and policies in East Asia in general and in Singapore in particular.

5. For details of these institutional reforms and policy changes, see Chin (2009), Chua (1993), Mauzy and Milne (2002: 143–168), Mutalib (2002), Tan and Lam (1997), Vasil (2000: 141–174) and Yeo (2002). For critical assessments of these government responses, see Rodan (1996b, 2009), Rodan and Jayasuriya (2007) and Tremewan (1994).

6. These liberalisation measures are discussed at length in MAS (*Annual Report* 1987/88 and 1988/98).

7. Author interview with a former director of the SES, Singapore, 30 July 2007. This was substantiated in local press reports (see *ST* 23 September 1991: 26 and 27 July 1994: 39).

8. The other major objectives were to withdraw from commercial activities in which GLCs were no longer needed and to avoid or reduce competition with private companies.

9. Author interviews with a former deputy managing director of the MAS, Singapore, 19 July 2007 and with a former deputy secretary of the finance ministry, Singapore, 25 July 2007.

10. These economies were Hong Kong, Indonesia, Malaysia, the Philippines, Singapore, South Korea, Taiwan and Thailand.

11. Of course, constraints on participatory spaces and voices remained. It can be argued that the PAP's efforts to energise civil society were designed to enhance its governing legitimacy and efficiency rather than reorient the political system towards a more democratic polity. For relevant discussions, see Chua (2005) and Rodan and Jayasuriya (2007).

12. The six countries were Cambodia, Indonesia, Malaysia, the Philippines and Thailand as well as Singapore.

13. Author calculations, based on data provided in Beck and Al-Hussainy (2010).

14. In early 2004, the Currency Board was abolished and the right to issue currency was invested in the MAS, turning it into a fully functioning central bank.

15. These cases are discussed in detail in *Asiamoney* (December 2000: 28–31), *BT*-Singapore (31 October 2002: 2 and 6 December 2006: 6), *EUICR*-Singapore (March 2006: 24–25), *FT* (22 October 2004: 2), *ST* (18 October 2002: A22) and *WSJ* (10 June 2005: A7).

16. Author calculations, based on data provided in Beck and Al-Hussainy (2010).

5 Thailand: Reform Failures amidst Political Changes

1. Author calculations, based on data provided in Beck and Al-Hussainy (2010).
2. Author interviews with a senior director of the Management Assistance Department of the BOT, Bangkok, 11 August 2005, and with an assistant governor of the BOT, Bangkok, 15 August 2005.
3. These cases were reported in detail in local and foreign presses. For the background, see *BP* (19 April 1993: 18, 32, 15 July 1994: 17), *EIUCR*-Thailand (2nd Quarter 1993: 27–28), *FEER* (3 December 1992: 63–64, 21 January 1993: 57–58, 4 March 1993: 52–53, 6 May 1993: 40–41, 7 July 1994: 63) and *WSJ* (4 June 1993: B5, 28 June 1994: A13).
4. Author calculations, based on data provided in Beck and Al-Hussainy (2010).
5. Detailed discussions of the causes of the financial crisis, which cannot be accommodated here, are provided in, for instance, Pasuk and Baker (2000) and Zhang (2002: 151–193).
6. See, for example, Haggard (2000a) and Warr (2005).
7. MacIntyre (2003), McCargo (2002) and Ockey (2003) provide systematic assessments of the impact of the new constitution on the Thai political system in general and the party structure in particular.
8. Author interview with a former director of the SEC Capital Market Supervision and Development Board, Bangkok, 3 August 2005.
9. Author interviews with a senior research fellow of the Thailand Development Research Institute, Bangkok, 13 July 2007, and with a former head of the SET Market Operation Group, Bangkok, 23 July 2007.
10. These included such poverty-reducing and redistributive policies as the 30-baht health care programme, village development funds and debt cancellation schemes.
11. For instance, the SEC took no legal action against two brokerages that had handled major share transactions made by nominees, transactions that Thaksin's wife had failed to report to regulatory authorities (*BP* 25 October 2001: 19). In July 2005, the SEC accused the managing director of a large gas company (also the brother of a deputy commerce minister) of having submitted fraudulent accounts but failed to press charges against him (*BP* 1 July 2005: 11). In August 2006, the SEC fined but did not indict Thaksin's son for having violated disclosure and tender offer rules in connection with his shareholdings in Shin Corp (*BP* 28 August 2006: 3).
12. Author calculations, based on data provided in Beck and Al-Hussainy (2010).
13. For detailed discussions of the causes and consequences of these conflicts, see Kitti (2010) and Thitinan (2008b).

6 Malaysia: Mixed Record on Reforms

1. More detailed discussions of the evolution of stock exchanges in Malaysia can be found in Aziz (1989) and Gill (2003).
2. Author calculations, based on data provided in Beck and Al-Hussainy (2010).
3. The NEP was enacted in the aftermath of the 1969 inter-racial riots, which the government attributed primarily to growing socio-economic inequalities

between Malays and non-Malays, mainly the Chinese. Under the NEP, economic progress was measured not only in terms of growth but, more importantly, in terms of advances in the economic well-being of Malays. One core component of the NEP was the requirement that firms over a certain size sell 30 per cent of their shares to Malays and that any firm seeking state support undertake to employ at least 30 per cent Malays at all levels. See Bowie (1991) for an excellent discussion of the causes and consequences of the adoption of the NEP.

4. Author interview with a former assistant governor of the NBM, Kuala Lumpur, 3 July 2005. See also the BNM (1999).

5. Many similar cases were reported in local and international presses. See, for example, *AMF* (July/August 1992: 31–33), *EIUCR*-Malaysia (No 3 1992: 29–30), *FEER* (18 July 1991: 66) and *ID* (April 1994: 21).

6. Author calculations based on data provided in the EPU (*Sixth Malaysia Plan 1991–1995* and *Seventh Malaysia Plan 1996–2000*) and the World Bank (2007).

7. There is a vast literature on the impact of the Asian financial crisis on the Malaysian economy, making it unnecessary to rehash debates and discussions here. See, for example, Haggard (2000a) and Jomo (1998).

8. The core elements of capital controls pegged the Malaysian ringgit to the US dollar at a relatively low level, banned the offshore ringgit market and prohibited the repatriation of portfolio funds for 12 months. For debates on the impact of capital controls, see Haggard (2000a: 73–85) and Kaplan and Rodrik (2002).

9. These institutions include Pengurusan Danaharta Nasional Bhd, responsible for acquiring NPL assets, Danamodal Nasional Bhd, designed to recapitalise banks and the Corporate Debt Restructuring Committee. A detailed discussion of the respective roles of these three institutions is provided in Wong et al. (2005).

10. Author calculations, based on data provided in Beck and Al-Hussainy (2010).

11. Author calculations, based on data provided in Beck and Al-Hussainy (2010).

7   Conclusions and Implications

1. The reform agenda is spelt out in minute detail in the IMF (2009, 2010) and the World Bank (2010b). Some of the proposed reform programmes are echoed by neo-classical scholars (see, for example, Avgouleas 2009; Prasad 2010).

References

Adjasi, Charles K.D., and Nicholas B. Biekpe (2008) 'Stock market development and economic growth: The case of selected African countries', *African Development Review* 18 (1): 144–161.

Albritton, Robert B. (2006) 'Thailand in 2005: The struggle for democratic consolidation', *Asian Survey* 46 (1): 140–147.

Aldrich, John H. (1995) *Why Parties? The Origin and Transformation of Party Politics in America*. Chicago: University of Chicago Press.

Alesina, Albert (1988) 'Macro-economics and politics', in Stanley Fisher, ed., *NBER Macro-economics Annual*. Cambridge: MIT Press, pp. 13–52.

Alesina, Albert, Roberto Perotti, Francesco Giavazzi, and Tryphon Kollintzas (1995) 'Fiscal expansions and adjustments in OECD countries', *Economic Policy* 10 (21): 207–248.

Allen, Franklin, and Douglas Gale (2000) *Comparing Financial Systems*. Cambridge: MIT Press.

Ames, Barry (2001) *The Deadlock of Democracy in Brazil*. Ann Arbor: University of Michigan Press.

Ames, Barry, and Timothy J. Power (2007) 'Parties and governability in Brazil', in Paul Webb, and Stephen White, eds, *Political Parties in New Democracies*. Oxford: Oxford University Press, pp. 179–210.

Ammar, Siamwalla, and Andrew MacIntyre (2001) 'The political economy of foodgrain and fertiliser distribution', in Ammar Siamwalla, ed., *The Evolving Roles of the State, Private, and Local Actors in Rural Asia*. Hong Kong: Oxford University Press, pp. 213–270.

Amorim Neto, Octavio, and Gary W. Cox (1997) 'Electoral institutions, cleavage structures, and the number of parties', *American Journal of Political Science* 41 (1): 149–174.

Anderson, Christopher J. (2000) 'Economic voting and political context: A comparative perspective', *Electoral Studies* 19 (2/3): 151–170.

Angrist, Michele Penner (2005) 'Competitive authoritarianism and single-party regimes', Paper presented to the annual convention of the American Political Science Association, Washington, DC, 1–4 September.

Anusorn, Limmanee (1998) 'Thailand', in Wolfgang Sachsenröder and Ulrike E. Frings, eds, *Political Party Systems and Democratic Development in East and Southeast Asia, Volume I: Southeast Asia*. Aldershot: Ashgate, pp. 403–448.

Arestis, Philip, Panicos O. Demetriades, and Kul B. Luintel (2001) 'Financial development and economic growth', *Journal of Money, Credit and Banking* 33 (1): 16–41.

Arghiros, Daniel (1995) 'Political structures and strategies', Occasional Paper No. 31, Centre for Southeast Asian Studies, University of Hull.

Ariff, Mohamed, and Ahmed M. Khalid (2000) *Liberalisation, Growth and the Asian Financial Crisis*. Cheltenham: Edward Elgar.

Aroonsri, Tivakul, and Pongpanu Svetarundra (1993) 'Financial innovation and modernisation of the Thai financial market', *Bank of Thailand Quarterly Bulletin* 33 (4): 21–46.

Arrow, Kenneth (1985) 'Informational structure of firms', *American Economic Review* 75 (2): 303–307.

Ashworth, Scott, and Ethan Bueno de Mesquita (2008) 'Informative party labels with institutional and electoral variation', *Journal of Theoretical Politics* 20 (3): 251–273.

Asiamoney, Hong Kong.

Asia Money and Finance (AMF), Hong Kong.

Asian Finance (AF), Hong Kong.

Avgouleas, Emilios (2009) 'The global financial crisis, the disclosure paradigm, and European financial regulation: The case for reform', unpublished Manuscript, School of Law, University of Manchester.

Aziz, Zeti Akhtar (1989) 'Development of the capital market in Malaysia', in Ng Beoy Kui, ed., *The Development of Capital Markets in the SEACEN Countries*. Kuala Lumpur: The Southeast Asian Central Banks (SEACEN) Research and Training Centre, pp. 89–113.

Bae, Kee-Hong, Warren Bailey, and Connie X. Mao (2006) 'Stock market liberalisation and the information environment', *Journal of International Money and Finance* 25 (3): 404–428.

Bailey, Warren, and Julapa Jagtiani (1994) 'Foreign ownership restrictions and stock prices in the Thai capital market', *Journal of Financial Economics* 36 (1): 57–87.

Bangkok Bank Monthly Review (BBMR), Bangkok.

Bangkok Post (BP), Bangkok.

Bangkok Post Economic Review (BPER), Bangkok.

Bank Negara Malaysia (BNM) (1999) *The Central Bank and the Financial System in Malaysia*. Kuala Lumpur: BNM.

Bank of Thailand (BOT) (various issues) *Annual Economic Report*.

Barr, Michael D. (2000) *Lee Kuan Yew: The Beliefs behind the Man*. Richmond: Curzon.

Barton, Dominic, Paul Coombes and Simon Chiu-Yin Wong (2004) 'Tranparency: Asia's governance challenge', *McKinsey Quarterly* 2 (3): 54–61.

Bates, Robert H., and Anne O. Krueger (eds) (1993) *Political and Economic Interactions in Economic Policy Reform*. Cambridge: Blackwell.

Bawn, Kathleen (1997) 'Choosing strategies to control the bureaucracy: Statutory constraints, oversight, and the committee system', *Journal of Law, Economics and Organisation* 13 (1): 101–126.

Bawn, Kathleen, and Frances Rosenbluth (2006) 'Short versus long coalitions: Electoral accountability and the size of the public sector', *American Journal of Political Science* 50 (2): 251–265.

Bearce, David H. (2003) 'Societal preferences, partisan agents, and monetary policy outcomes', *International Organisation* 57 (4): 373–410.

Beck, Thorsten and Ed Al-Hussainy. (2010) *A New Database on Financial Development and Structure*. Washington, DC: World Bank.

Beck, Thorsten, and Ross Levine (2001) 'Stock markets, banks, and growth: Correlation or causality', Policy Research Working Paper 2670, Washington, DC: World Bank.

Beck, Thorsten, and Ross Levine (2002) 'Industry growth and capital allocation: Does having a market- or bank-based system matter?', *Journal of Financial Economics* 64 (2): 147–180.

Beck, Thorsten, and Ross Levine (2004) 'Stock markets, banks, and growth: Panel evidence', *Journal of Banking and Finance* 28 (3): 423–442.

Beck, Thorsten, Asli Demirgüç-Kunt, and Ross Levine (2007) 'Finance, inequality and the poor', *Journal of Economic Growth* 12 (1): 27–49.

Bekaert, Geert, Campbell R. Harvey, and Christian T. Lundblad (2003) 'Equity market liberalisation in emerging markets', *Journal of Financial Research* 26 (3): 275–299.

Bell, Daniel A., David Brown, Kanishka Jayasuriya, and David Martin Jones (eds) (1995) *Towards Illiberal Democracy in Pacific Asia*. London: Macmillan.

Bellows, Thomas J. (1970) *The People's Action Party in Singapore: Emergence of a Dominant Party System*. New Haven: Yale University Southeast Asian Studies.

Bellows, Thomas J. (1993) 'The Singapore polity: Community, leadership, and institutions', *Asian Journal of Political Science* 1 (1): 113–132.

Bellows, Thomas J. (1995) 'Bureaucracy and development in Singapore', *Asian Journal of Public Administration* 7 (1): 55–69.

Bengtsson, Åsa (2004) 'Economic voting: The effect of political context, volatility and turnout on voters' assignment of responsibility', *European Journal of Political Research* 43 (4): 749–767.

Bernhard, William, and David Leblang (1999) 'Democratic institutions and exchange-rate commitments', *International Organisation* 53 (1): 71–97.

Biglaiser, Glen, and Karl DeRouen (2004) 'The expansion of neo-liberal economic reforms in Latin America', *International Studies Quarterly* 48 (3): 561–578.

Birchfield, Vicki, and Markus M.L. Crepaz (1998) 'The impact of constitutional structures and collective and competitive veto points on income inequality in industrialised democracies', *European Journal of Political Research* 34 (2): 175–200.

Black, Duncan (1958) *The Theory of Committees and Elections*. Cambridge: Cambridge University Press.

Blackburn, Keith, Niloy Bose, and Salvatore Capasso (2005) 'Financial development, financing choice and economic growth', *Review of Development Economics* 9 (2): 135–149.

Blau, Adrian (2008) 'The effective number of parties at four scales', *Party Politics* 14 (2): 167–187.

Blaydes, Lisa (2006) 'Electoral budget cycles under authoritarianism: Economic opportunism in Mubarak's Egypt', Paper presented to the Annual Meeting of the Midwest Political Science Association, Chicago, 20–23 April.

Block, Steven A., Karen E. Ferree, and Smita Singh (2003) 'Multi-party competition, founding elections and political business cycles in Africa', *Journal of African Economies* 12 (3): 444–468.

Blondel, Jean (1999) 'The role of parties and party systems in the democratisation process', in Ian Marsh, Jean Blondel, and Takashi Inoguchi, eds, *Democracy, Governance, and Economic Performance: East and Southeast Asia*. Tokyo: United Nations University Press, pp. 23–46.

Boix, Carles (2007) 'The emergence of parties and party systems', in Carles Boix, and Susan C. Stokes, eds, *Oxford Handbook of Comparative Politics*. Oxford: Oxford University Press, pp. 499–521.

Bortolotti, Bernardo, Marcella Fantini, and Domenico Siniscalco (2003) 'Privatisation around the world: Evidence from panel data', *Journal of Public Economics* 88 (3): 305–332.

Bortolotti, Bernardo, Frank de Jong, Giovanna Nicodano, and Ibolya Schindele (2007) 'Privatisation and stock market liquidity', *Journal of Banking and Finance* 31 (2): 297–316.

Bowie, Alasdair (1991) *Crossing the Industrial Divide*. New York: Columbia University Press.

Bowie, Katherine A. (2008) 'Vote buying and village outrage in an election in Northern Thailand', *Journal of Asian Studies* 67 (2): 469–511.

Bowler, Shaun, David M. Farrell, and Richard S. Katz (eds) (1999) *Party Discipline and Parliamentary Government*. Columbus: Ohio State University Press.

Brambor, Thomas, William Roberts Clark, and Matt Golder (2007) 'Are African party systems different?', *Electoral Studies* 26 (3): 315–323.

Braun, Matias, and Claudio Raddatz (2008) 'The politics of financial development: Evidence from trade liberalisation', *Journal of Finance* 63 (3): 1469–1508.

Brender, Adi, and Allan Drazen (2005) 'Political budget cycles in new versus established democracies', *Journal of Monetary Economics* 52 (4): 1271–1295.

Bresser Pereira, Luiz Carlos, José Maria Maravall, and Adam Przeworski (1993) *Economic Reforms in New Democracies*. Cambridge: Cambridge University Press.

Brooker, Paul (2000) *Non-Democratic Regimes: Theory, Government and Politics*. Basingstoke: Macmillan.

Brown, Robert (1994) *The State and Ethnic Politics in Southeast Asia*. London: Routledge.

Brownlee, Jason (2008) 'Bound to rule: Party institutions and regime trajectories in Malaysia and the Philippines', *Journal of East Asian Studies* 8 (2): 89–118.

Bryant, Ralph C. (1989) 'The evolution of Singapore as a financial centre', in Kernial Singh Sandhu, and Paul Wheatley, eds, *Management of Success: The Moulding of Modern Singapore*. Singapore: Institute of Southeast Asian Studies, pp. 337–372.

Bueno de Mesquita, Bruce, Alastair Smith, Randolph M. Siverson, and James D. Morrow (2003) *The Logic of Political Survival*. Cambridge: MIT Press.

Business Times (BT), Kuala Lumpur.

Business Times (BT), Singapore.

Cain, Bruce E., John A. Ferejohn, and Morris P. Fiorina (1984) 'The constituency service basis of the personal vote for US representatives and British members of parliament', *American Political Science Review* 78 (1): 110–125.

Callahan, William A. (2005) 'The discourse of vote buying and political reform in Thailand', *Pacific Affairs* 78 (1): 95–113.

Callahan, William A., and Duncan McCargo (1996) 'Vote-buying in Thailand's Northeast', *Asian Survey* 36 (4): 376–392.

Carey, John M. (2009) *Legislative Voting and Accountability*. Cambridge: Cambridge University Press.

Carey, John M., and Matthew Soberg Shugart (1995) 'Incentives to cultivate a personal vote', *Electoral Studies* 14 (4): 417–439.

Carlin, Wendy, and Colin Mayer (2003) 'Finance, investment, and growth', *Journal of Financial Economics* 69 (2): 191–226.

Carlson, Matthew, and Mark Turner (2008) 'Public support for democratic governance in Southeast Asia', *Asian Journal of Political Science* 16 (3): 219–239.

Case, William (1994) 'The UMNO party election in Malaysia', *Asian Survey* 34 (10): 916–930.

Case, William (1996a) 'Can the "halfway house" stand? Semi-democracy and elite theory in three Southeast Asian countries', *Comparative Politics* 28 (4): 437–464.

Case, William (1996b) 'UNMO paramountcy', *Party Politics* 2 (1): 115–127.

Case, William (1996c) *Elites and Regimes in Malaysia*. Clayton: Monash Asia Institute.

Case, William (2002) *Politics in Southeast Asia*. London: RoutledgeCurzon.

Case, William (2005) 'Malaysia: New reforms, old continuities, and tense ambiguities', *Journal of Development Studies* 41 (2): 284–309.

Case, William (2006) 'Manipulative skills: How do rulers control the electoral arena?', in Andreas Schedler, ed., *Electoral Authoritarianism: The Dynamics of Unfree Competition*. Boulder: Lynne Rienner, pp. 95–112.

Case, William (2007) 'Democracy's quality and breakdown', Working Paper No. 83, Southeast Asia Research Centre, City University of Hong Kong.

Chai-Anan Samudavanija (1986) 'Political institutionalisation in Thailand', in Robert A. Scalapino, Seizaburo Sato, and Jusuf Wanadi, eds, *Asian Political Institutionalisation*. Berkeley: Institute of East Asian Studies, University of California, pp. 241–260.

Chai-Anan Samudavanija (1995) 'Thailand', in Larry Diamond, Juan J. Linz, and Seymour Martin Lipset, eds, *Politics in Developing Countries*. Boulder: Lynne Rienner, pp. 323–367.

Chalmers, Ian (1992) 'Weakening state controls and ideological change in Singapore', Working Paper No. 13, Asia Research Centre, Murdoch University.

Chalongphob Sussangkarn, and Pakorn Vichyanond (2007) 'Ten years after the financial crisis in Thailand', *Asian Economic Policy Review* 2 (2): 100–118.

Chambers, Paul (2005) 'Evolving toward what? Parties, factions, and coalition behaviour in Thailand today', *Journal of East Asian Studies* 5 (3): 494–520.

Chambers, Paul (2006a) 'Consolidation of Thaksinocracy and crisis of democracy', in Aurel Croissant, and Beate Martin, eds, *Between Consolidation and Crisis*. Berlin: Lit Verlag, pp. 277–328.

Chambers, Paul (2006b) 'Has everything changed in Thai politics under Thaksin?', *Crossroads* 17 (2): 7–33.

Chambers, Paul (2008) 'Factions, parties and the durability of parliaments, coalitions and cabinets: The case of Thailand (1979–2001)', *Party Politics* 14 (3): 299–323.

Chan, Heng Chee (1975) 'Politics in an administrative state', in C.M. Seah, ed., *Trends in Singapore*. Singapore: Institute of Southeast Asian Studies, pp. 51–68.

Chan, Heng Chee (1976) *The Dynamics of One Party Dominance: The PAP at the Grassroots*. Singapore: Singapore University Press.

Chan, Heng Chee (1981) 'The emerging administrative state', in Saw Swee-Hock, and R.S. Bhathal, eds, *Singapore towards the Year 2000*. Singapore: Singapore University Press, pp. 10–14.

Chan, Heng Chee (1985) 'Political parties', in Jon S.T. Quah, Chan Heng Chee, and Seah Chee Meow, eds, *Government and Politics of Singapore*. Singapore: Oxford University Press, pp. 146–172.

Chan, Heng Chee (1989) 'The PAP and the structuring of the political system', in Kernial Singh Sandhu, and Paul Wheatley, eds, *Management of Success: The*

Moulding of Modern Singapore. Singapore: Institute of Southeast Asian Studies, pp. 70–89.

Chan, Heng Chee (2000) 'Internal developments in Singapore', in Verinder Grover, ed., *Singapore Government and Politics*. New Delhi: Deep and Deep Publications, pp. 128–140.

Cheng, Tun-Jen (2003) 'Political institutions and the malaise of East Asian new democracies', *Journal of East Asian Studies* 3 (1): 1–41.

Chhibber, Pradeep (1995) 'Political parties, electoral competition, government expenditures and economic reform in India', *Journal of Development Studies* 32 (1): 74–96.

Chhibber, Pradeep, and Irfan Nooruddin (2004) 'Do party systems count? The number of parties and government performance in the Indian states', *Comparative Political Studies* 37 (2): 152–187.

Chhibber, Pradeep, and Ken Kollman (2004) *The Formation of National Party Systems*. Cambridge: Cambridge University Press.

Chia, Siow Yue (1999) 'Singapore's experience and response', in H.W. Arndt, and Hal Hill, eds, *Southeast Asia's Economic Crisis*. New York: St Martin's Press, pp. 51–66.

Chin, James U.H. (2009) 'Electoral battles and innovations', in Bridget Welsh, James Chin, Arun Mahizhnan, and Tan Tarn How, eds, *Impressions of the Goh Chok Tong Years*. Singapore: Singapore University Press, pp. 71–82.

Chin, Kok Fay, and K.S. Jomo (2000) 'Financial sector rents in Malaysia', in Mushtaq Khan, and Jomo S.K., eds, *Rents, Rent-Seeking and Economic Development*. Cambridge: Cambridge University Press, pp. 304–326.

Chin, Kok Fay, and K.S. Jomo (2001) 'Financial reform and crisis in Malaysia', in Masayoshi Tsurumi, ed., *Financial Big Bang in Asia*. Aldershot: Ashgate, pp. 225–249.

Chong, Alan (2007) 'Singapore's political economy, 1997–2007', *Asian Survey* 47 (6): 952–976.

Chooi, Mun Sou (1991) 'Securities regulation in the region: Malaysia', in Charmain Lye, and Rosalind Lazar, eds, *The Regulation of Financial and Capital Markets*. Singapore: SNP Publishers, pp. 14–29.

Chua, Beng-Huat (1993) 'Beyond formal structures: Democratisation in Singapore', *Asian Studies Review* 17 (1): 99–106.

Chua, Beng-Huat (1997) 'Still awaiting new initiatives: Democratisation in Singapore', *Asian Studies Review* 21 (2): 120–133.

Chua, Beng-Huat (2005) 'Liberalisation without democratisation: Singapore in the next decade', in Francis Loh Kok Wah, and Joakim Öjendal, eds, *Southeast Asian Responses to Globalisation*. Copenhagen: Nordic Institute of Asian Studies, pp. 57–82.

CLSA (various issues) *CG Watch*. Hong Kong: CLSA.

Collier, David, and James E. Mahon (1993) 'Conceptual "stretching" revisited: Adapting categories in comparative analysis', *American Political Science Review* 87 (4): 845–855.

Collier, David, and Steven Levitsky (1997) 'Democracy with adjectives: Conceptual innovation in comparative research', *World Politics* 49 (3): 430–451.

Coppedge, Michael (1998) 'The dynamic diversity of Latin American party systems', *Party Politics* 4 (4): 547–568.

Cox, Gary W. (1990) 'Centripetal and centrifugal incentives in electoral systems', *American Journal of Political Science* 34 (4): 903–935.

Cox, Gary W. (2007) 'Authoritarian elections and leadership succession, 1975–2000', Manuscript, Department of Political Science, University of California, San Diego.

Cox, Gary W., and Mathew D. McCubbins (1993) *Legislative Leviathan: Party Government in the House*. Berkeley: University of California Press.

Cox, Gary W., and Michael F. Thies (1998) 'The cost of intra-party competition: The single, non-transferable vote and money politics in Japan', *Comparative Political Studies* 31 (3): 267–291.

Cox, Gary W., and Mathew D. McCubbins (2001) 'The institutional determinants of economic policy outcomes', in Stephan Haggard, and Mathew D. McCubbins, eds, *Presidents, Parliaments, and Policy*. Cambridge: Cambridge University Press, pp. 21–63.

Crepaz, Markus M.L. (1996) 'Constitutional structures and regime performance in 18 industrialised democracies: A test of Olson's hypothesis', *European Journal of Political Research* 29 (1): 87–104.

Croissant, Aurel (2006) 'Conclusion', in Aurel Croissant, and Beate Martin, eds, *Between Consolidation and Crisis*. Berlin: Lit Verlag, pp. 331–362.

Croissant, Aurel, and Jörn Dosch (2003) 'Parliamentary elections in Thailand, March 2000 and January 2001', *Electoral Studies* 22 (2): 153–193.

Croissant, Aurel, and Daniel J. Pojar (2006) 'The parliamentary election in Thailand, February 2005', *Electoral Studies* 25 (2): 184–191.

Crone, Donald K. (1988) 'State, social elites, and government capacity in Southeast Asia', *World Politics* 40 (2): 252–268.

Crotty, William (1971) 'Party effort and its impact on the vote', *American Political Science Review* 65 (2): 439–450.

Crouch, Harold (1992) 'Authoritarian trends, the UMNO split and the limits to state power', in Joel S. Khan, and Francis Loh Kok Wah, eds, *Fragmented Vision*. Honolulu: University of Hawaii Press, pp. 21–43.

Crouch, Harold (1996a) *Government and Society in Malaysia*. Ithaca: Cornell University Press.

Crouch, Harold (1996b) 'Malaysia: Do elections make a difference?', in R.H. Taylor, ed., *The Politics of Elections in Southeast Asia*. Cambridge: Cambridge University Press, pp. 114–135.

Dahl, Robert A. (1971) *Polyarchy: Participation and Opposition*. New Haven: Yale University Press.

Dalton, Russell, Doh Chull Shin, and Yun-han Chu (eds) (2008) *Party Politics in East Asia*. Boulder: Lynne Reinner.

De Haan, Jakob, and Clemens L.J. Siermann (1995) 'New evidence on the relationship between democracy and economic growth', *Public Choice* 86 (1–2): 175–198.

de la Torre, Augusto, Juan Carlos Gozzi, and Sergio L. Schmukler (2007) 'Stock market development under globalisation: Wither the gains from reforms?', *Journal of Banking and Finance* 31 (4): 1731–1754.

Demirgüç-Kunt, Asli, and Vojislav Maksimovic (2002) 'Funding growth in bank-based and market-based financial systems: Evidence from firm-level data', *Journal of Financial Economics* 65 (3): 337–363.

Demirgüç-Kunt, Asli, and Ross Levine (2008) 'Finance, financial sector policies, and long-run growth', Policy research Working Paper No. 4469, Washington, DC: World Bank.

Deunden Nikomborirak (2005) 'Building good corporate governance after the crisis', in Ho Khai Leong, ed., *Reforming Corporate Governance in Southeast Asia.* Singapore: Institute of Southeast Asian Studies, pp. 200–222.

Diamond, Larry (2002) 'Elections without democracy: Thinking about hybrid regimes', *Journal of Democracy* 13 (2): 21–35.

Dixon, Chris (2004) 'Post-crisis restructuring: Foreign ownership, corporate resistance and economic nationalism in Thailand', *Contemporary Southeast Asia* 26 (1): 45–72.

Dollar, David, and Mary Hallward-Driemeier (2000) 'Crisis, adjustment, and reform in Thailand's industrial firms', *World Bank Research Observer* 15 (1): 1–22.

Dominguez, Jorge I. (ed.) (1997) *Technopols: Freeing Politics and Markets in Latin America in the 1990s.* Pennsylvania: Pennsylvania State University Press.

Doner, Richard F., Bryan K. Ritchie, and Dan Slater (2005) 'Systemic vulnerability and the origins of developmental states', *International Organisation* 59 (2): 327–361.

Doner, Richard F., Allen Hicken, and Bryan K. Ritchie (2009) 'Political challenges of innovation in the developing world', *Review of Policy Research* 26 (1–2): 151–171.

Dornbusch, Rudiger, and Sebastian Edwards (eds) (1995) *Reform, Recovery and Growth: Latin America and the Middle East.* Chicago: University of Chicago Press.

Downs, Anthony (1957) *An Economic Theory of Democracy.* New York: Harper.

Druckman, James N. (1996) 'Party factionalism and cabinet durability', *Party Politics* 2 (3): 397–407.

Dumont, Patrick, and Jean-François Caulier (2005) 'The effective number of relevant parties', Manuscript, Department of Political and Science Sciences, University of Luxembourg.

Duncan, Ronald C. (1995) 'Insulating the technopols: The politics of economic reform', *Agenda* 2 (1): 93–98.

Dunleavy, Patrick, and François Boucek (2003) 'Constructing the number of parties', *Party Politics* 9 (3): 291–315.

Duverger, Maurice (1954) *Political Parties.* London: Methuen.

East Asia Analytical Unit (EAAU) (2000) *Transforming Thailand.* Barton: EAAU, Department of Foreign Affairs and Trade.

Eaton, Kent (2002) *Politicians and Economic Reform in New Democracies.* Pennsylvania: Pennsylvania State University Press.

Economic Planning Unit (EPU, Prime Minister's Department, Malaysia) (various issues). *Malaysia Plan.* Kuala Lumpur: EPU.

The Economist, London.

Economist Intelligence Unit Country Report (EIUCR), London.

Ekamol Kiriwat (1993) 'Financial sector reforms: Thailand', in Shakil Faruqi, ed., *Financial Sector Reforms in Asian and Latin American Countries.* Washington, DC: World Bank, pp. 115–126.

Far Eastern Economic Review (FEER), Hong Kong.

Financial Times (FT), London.

Fisman, Raymond, and Inessa Love (2004) 'Financial development and growth in the short- and long-run', Policy Research Working Paper No. 3319, Washington, DC: World Bank.

Fock, Siew Tong, and Ann Chai Wong (2001) 'Post-East Asian financial crisis', *Review of Pacific Basin Financial Markets and Policies* 4 (4): 495–521.

Fraser, Donald R., Hao Zhang, and Chek Derashid (2006) 'Capital structure and political patronage: The case of Malaysia', *Journal of Banking and Finance* 30 (4): 1291–1308.

Fry, Maxwell J. (1995) *Money, Interest, and Banking in Economic Development.* Baltimore: Johns Hopkins University Press.

Frye, Timothy, and Edward D. Mansfield (2003) 'Fragmenting protection: The political economy of trade policy in the post-communist world', *British Journal of Political Science* 33 (4): 635–657.

Fuchs-Schündeln, Nicola, and Norbert Funke (2004) 'Stock market liberalisation: Financial and macro-economic implications', *Review of World Economics* 140 (3): 730–761.

Funston, N.J. (1980) *Malay Politics in Malaysia.* Selangor: Heinemann Educational Books.

Gandhi, Jennifer, and Adam Przeworski (2007) 'Authoritarian institutions and the survival of autocrats', *Comparative Political Studies* 40 (11): 1279–1301.

Ganesan, N. (1996) 'Democracy in Singapore', *Asian Journal of Political Science* 4 (2): 63–79.

Garman, Christopher, Stephan Haggard, and Eliza Willis (2001) 'Fiscal decentralisation: A political theory with Latin American cases', *World Politics* 53 (2): 205–236.

Geddes, Barbara (1994) *Politicians' Dilemma: Building State Capacity in Latin America.* Berkeley: University of California Press.

Geddes, Barbara (1995) 'The politics of economic liberalisation', *Latin American Research Review* 30 (2): 195–214.

Geddes, Barbara (1999) 'What do we know about democratisation after twenty years?', *Annual Review of Political Science* 2: 115–144.

Geddes, Barbara (2003) *Paradigms and Sand Castles: Theory Building and Research Design in Comparative Politics.* Ann Arbor: University of Michigan Press.

Geddes, Barbara (2005) 'Why parties and elections in authoritarian regimes?', Paper presented to the annual convention of the American Political Science Association, Washington, DC, 1–4 September.

George, Alexander L., and Andrew Bennett (2005) *Case Studies and Theory Development in the Social Sciences.* Cambridge: MIT Press.

Gerring, John, Strom C. Thacker, and Carola Moreno (2005) 'Centripetal democratic governance: A theory and global inquiry', *American Political Science Review* 99 (4): 567–581.

Gerring, John, and Strom C. Thacker (2008) *A Centripetal Theory of Democratic Governance.* Cambridge: Cambridge University Press.

Gerring, John, Strom C. Thacker, and Carola Moreno (2009) 'Are parliamentary systems better?', *Comparative Political Studies* 42 (3): 327–359.

Ghazali, Nazli A. Mohd, and Pauline Weetman (2006) 'Perpetuating traditional influences: Voluntary disclosure in Malaysia following the economic crisis', *Journal of International Accounting, Auditing and Taxation* 15 (2): 226–248.

Ghesquiere, Henry (2007) *Singapore's Success.* Singapore: Thomson.

234 *References*

Ghosh, Rama (2000) 'Privatisation in Singapore', in B.N. Ghosh, ed., *Privatisation: The ASEAN Connection*. Huntington: Nova Science, pp. 207–231.

Ghosh, Swati R. (2006) *East Asian Finance: The Road to Robust Markets*. Washington, DC: World Bank.

Giannetti, Daniela, and Michael Laver (2008) 'Party cohesion, party discipline and party factions in Italy', in Daniela Giannetti, and Kenneth Benoit, eds, *Intra-Party Politics and Coalition Governments*. London: Routledge, pp. 146–168.

Giap, Tan Khee, and Chen Kang (1999) 'Singapore's dichotomised financial system', in *Rising to the Challenge in Asia: A Study of Financial Markets*. Manila: Asian Development Bank, pp. 81–140.

Gibson, Jaems L., Cornelius P. Cotter, and John F. Bibby (1983) 'Assessing party organisational strength', *American Journal of Political Science* 27 (2): 193–222.

Gill, Ranjit (2003) *The Making of Malaysia Inc.* London: ASEAN Academic Press.

Gilligan, Thomas W., and Keith Krehbiel (1989) 'Asymmetric information and legislative rules with a heterogeneous committee', *American Journal of Political Science* 33 (2): 459–490.

Golden, Miriam A., and Eric C.C. Chang (2001) 'Competitive corruption: Factional conflict and political malfeasance in post-war Italian Christian democracy', *World Politics* 53 (4): 588–622.

Golden, Miriam A., and Lucio Picci (2008) 'Pork-barrel politics in post-war Italy, 1953–94', *American Journal of Political Science* 52 (2): 268–289.

Gomez, Edmund Terence (1990) *Politics in Business: UMNO's Corporate Investments*. Kuala Lumpur: Forum.

Gomez, Edmund Terence (1991) *Money Politics in the Barisan Nasional*. Kuala Lumpur: Forum.

Gomez, Edmund Terence (1994) *Political Business: Corporate Involvement of Malaysian Political Parties*. Townsville: Centre for Southeast Asian Studies, James Cook University of North Queensland.

Gomez, Edmund Terence (1996a) *The 1995 Malaysian General Election*. Singapore: Institute of Southeast Asian Studies.

Gomez, Edmund Terence (1996b) 'Electoral funding of general, state, and party elections in Malaysia', *Journal of Contemporary Asia* 26 (1): 81–99.

Gomez, Edmund Terence (1998) 'Malaysia', in Wolfgang Sachsenröder, and Ulrike E. Frings, eds, *Political Party Systems and Democratic Development in East and Southeast Asia, Volume I: Southeast Asia*. Aldershot: Ashgate, pp. 226–288.

Gomez, Edmund Terence (2002) 'Political business in Malaysia', in Edmund Terence Gomez, ed., *Political Business in East Asia*. London: Routledge, pp. 82–114.

Gomez, Edmund Terence, and Jomo Kwame Sundaram (1997) *Malaysia's Political Economy*. Cambridge: Cambridge University Press.

Gomez, Edmund Terence, and Jomo Kwame Sundaram (1999) 'Malaysia', in Ian Marsh, Jean Blondel, and Takashi Inoguchi, eds, *Democracy, Governance, and Economic Performance: East and Southeast Asia*. Tokyo: United Nations University Press, pp. 230–260.

Gonzalez, Maria de los Angeles (2002) 'Do changes in democracy affect the political budget cycle? Evidence from Mexico', *Review of Development Economics* 6 (2): 204–224.

Gourevitch, Peter, and James Shinn (2005) *Political Power and Political Control*. Princeton: Princeton University Press.

Grofman, Bernard, and Peter van Roozendaal (1997) 'Modelling cabinet durability and termination', *British Journal of Political Science* 27 (4): 419–451.

Grossman, Gene M., and Elhanan Helpman (2006) 'Party discipline and pork-barrel politics', Working paper No. 2006-11, Institute of Governmental Studies, University of California, Berkeley.

Gunther, Richard, and Larry Diamond (2001) 'Types and functions of parties', in Larry Diamond, and Richard Gunther, eds, *Political Parties and Democracy*. Baltimore: Johns Hopkins University, pp. 3–39.

Gunther, Richard, José Ramón-Montero, and Juan J. Linz (eds) (2002) *Political Parties: Old Concepts and New Challenges*. Oxford: Oxford University Press.

Gunther, Richard, and Larry Diamond (2003) 'Species of political parties: A new typology', *Party Politics* 9 (2): 167–199.

Gupta, Nandini, and Kathy Yuan (2009) 'On the growth effect of stock market liberalisation', *Review of Financial Studies* 22 (11): 4715–4752.

Guriev, Sergei, and William L. Megginson (2007) 'Privatisation: What have we learned?', in François Bourguignon, and Boris Pleskovic, eds, *Beyond Transition*. Washington, DC: World Bank, pp. 249–296.

Gwartney, James, and Robert Lawson (various issues) *Economic Freedom of the World*. Washington, DC: CATO Institute.

Hadenius, Axel, and Jan Teorell (2007) 'Pathways from authoritarianism', *Journal of Democracy* 18 (1): 143–156.

Hager, Gregory L., and Jeffrey C. Talbert (2000) 'Look for the party label: Party influences on voting in the US House', *Legislative Studies Quarterly* 25 (1): 75–99.

Haggard, Stephan (1997) 'Democratic institutions, economic policy, and development', in Christopher Clague, ed., *Institutions and Economic Development*. Baltimore: Johns Hopkins University, pp. 121–149.

Haggard, Stephan (1999a) 'Governance and growth', *Asian-Pacific Economic Literature* 13 (2): 30–42.

Haggard, Stephan (1999b) 'An external view of Singapore's developed status', in Linda Low, ed., *Singapore: Towards a Developed Status*. Singapore: Oxford University Press, pp. 345–375.

Haggard, Stephan (2000a) *The Political Economy of the Asian Financial Crisis*. Washington, DC: Institute for International Economics.

Haggard, Stephan (2000b) 'Interest, institutions, and policy reform', in Anne O. Krueger, ed., *Economic Policy Reform: The Second Stage*. Chicago: University of Chicago Press, pp. 21–57.

Haggard, Stephan, and Robert E. Kaufman (eds) (1992a) *The Politics of Economic Adjustment*. Princeton: Princeton University Press.

Haggard, Stephan, and Robert E. Kaufman (1992b) 'Introduction', in Stephan Haggard, and Robert E. Kaufman, eds, *The Politics of Economic Adjustment*. Princeton: Princeton University Press, pp. 3–40.

Haggard, Stephan, and Sylvia Maxfield (1993) 'Political explanations of financial policy in developing countries', in Stephan Haggard, Chung H. Lee, and Sylvia Maxfield, eds, *The Politics of Finance in Developing Countries*. Ithaca: Cornell University Press, pp. 293–325.

Haggard, Stephan, and Steven B. Webb (1994) 'Introduction', in Stephan Haggard and Steven B. Webb, eds, *Voting for Reform*. New York: Oxford University Press, pp. 1–36.

Haggard, Stephan, and Robert E. Kaufman (1995) *The Political Economy of Democratic Transitions*. Princeton: Princeton University Press.

Haggard, Stephan, and Mathew D. McCubbins (eds) (2001) *Presidents, Parliaments, and Policy*. Cambridge: Cambridge University Press.

Haggard, Stephan, and Linda Low (2002) 'State, politics, and business in Singapore', in Edmund Terence Gomez, ed., *Political Business in East Asia*. London: Routledge, pp. 301–323.

Hall, Peter A., and Rosemary C.R. Taylor (1998) 'Political science and the three new institutionalisms', in Karol Soltan, Eric M. Uslaner, and Virginia Haufler, eds, *Institutions and Social Order*. Ann Arbor: University of Michigan Press, pp. 15–44.

Hallerberg, Mark, and Scott Basinger (1998) 'Internationalisation and changes in tax policy in OECD countries', *Comparative Political Studies* 31 (3): 321–352.

Hamilton-Hart, Natasha (2002) *Asian States, Asian Bankers: Central Banking in Southeast Asia*. Ithaca: Cornell University Press.

Hamilton-Hart, Natasha, and Jomo Kwame Sundaram (2003) 'Financial policy and governance in Southeast Asia', in Jomo Kwame Sundaram, ed., *Southeast Asia's Paper Tigers*. London: Routledge, pp. 220–279.

Handley, Paul (1997) 'More of the same: Politics and business, 1987–96', in Kevin Hewison, ed., *Political Change in Thailand*. London: Routledge, pp. 94–113.

Hankla, Charles R. (2006) 'Party strength and international trade', *Comparative Political Studies* 39 (9): 1133–1156.

Hanson, James A., Patrick Honohan, and Giovanni Majnoni (eds) (2003) *Globalisation and National Financial Systems*. Oxford: Oxford University Press.

Harwood, Alison. 1996. 'Financing capital market intermediaries in Malaysia', in Hal S. Scott, and Philip A. Wellons, eds, *Financing Capital Market Intermediaries in East and Southeast Asia*. The Hague: Kluwer, pp. 159–200.

Häusler, Gerd, Donald J. Mathieson, and Jorge Roldos (2003) 'Trends in developing-country capital markets around the world', in Robert E. Litan, Michael Pomerleano and V. Sundararajan, eds, *The Future of Domestic Capital Markets in Developing Countries*. Washington, DC: Brookings Institution Press, pp. 21–44.

Helliwell, John F. (1994) 'Empirical linkages between democracy and economic growth', *British Journal of Political Science* 24 (2): 225–248.

Heng, Swee Keat (2009) 'A review of Singapore's economic and financial system', opening remarks at the MAS's *Annual Report 2008/2009* News Conference, Singapore, 16 July.

Henry, Peter Blair (2000) 'Do stock market liberalisations cause investment boom?', *Journal of Financial Economics* 58 (3): 301–334.

Henry, Peter Blair, and Peter Lombard Lorentzen (2003) 'Domestic capital market reform and access to global finance: Making markets work', Working Paper No. 10064, Cambridge: National Bureau of Economic Research.

Heracleous, Loizos (1999) 'Privatisation', *International Journal of Public Sector Management* 12 (5): 432–444.

Hershey, Marjorie Randon (2006) 'Political parties as mechanisms of social choice', in Richard S. Katz, and William Crotty, eds, *Handbook of Party Politics*. London: Sage Publications, pp. 75–88.

Hew, Denis (2005) 'Singapore as a regional financial centre', in Donna Vandenbrink, and Denis Hew, eds, *Capital Markets in Asia*. Singapore: Institute of Southeast Asian Studies, pp. 139–168.

Hewison, Kevin (2005) 'Neo-liberalism and domestic capital: The political outcomes of the economic crisis in Thailand', *Journal of Development Studies* 41 (2): 310–330.

Hicken, Allen D. (2002) *Parties, Pork and Policy: Policymaking in Developing Democracies*. PhD dissertation, University of California, San Diego.

Hicken, Allen (2006) 'Party fabrication: Constitutional reform and the rise of Thai Rak Thai', *Journal of East Asian Studies* 6 (3): 381–407.

Hicken, Allen (2009) *Building Party Systems in Developing Democracies*. Cambridge: Cambridge University Press.

Hicken Allen, and Bryan K. Ritchie (2002) 'The origin of credibility: Enhancing institutions in Southeast Asia', Paper presented to the annual convention of the American Political Science Association, Boston, 28 August–1 September.

Ho, Khai Leong (2003) *Shared Responsibilities, Unshared Power: The Politics of Policy-Making in Singapore*. Singapore: Eastern Universities Press.

Ho, Khai Leong (2005) 'Corporate governance reform and the management of the GLCs', in Ho Khai Leong, ed., *Reforming Corporate Governance in Southeast Asia*. Singapore: Institute of Southeast Asian Studies, pp. 269–313.

Holmes, Phil, and Mei Wa Wong (2001) 'Foreign investment, regulation and price volatility in Southeast Asian stock markets', *Emerging Markets Review* 2 (2): 371–386.

Honohan, Patrick (2004) 'Financial development, growth and poverty: How close are the links?', in C.A.E. Goodhart, ed., *Money, Finance and Growth*. London: Macmillan, pp. 1–37.

Horowitz, Shale, and Uk Heo (eds) (2001) *The Political Economy of International Financial Crises*. Lanham: Rowman and Littlefield.

Horowitz, Shale, and Eric C. Browne (2008) 'Party systems and economic policy change in post-communist democracies', *Comparative Politics* 41 (1): 21–40.

Howard, Marc Morjé, and Philip G. Roessler (2006) 'Liberalising electoral outcomes in competitive authoritarian regimes', *American Journal of Political Science* 50 (2): 365–381.

Howells, Peter, and Keith Bain (1990) *Financial Markets and Institutions*. London: Longman.

Huber, John D. (1998) 'How does cabinet instability affect political performance? Portfolio volatility and health care cost containment in parliamentary democracies', *American Political Science Review* 92 (3): 577–591.

Huneeus, Carlos (2000) 'Technocrats and politicians in an authoritarian regime', *Journal of Latin American Studies* 32 (3): 461–501.

Imai, Masami (2006) 'Mixing family business with politics in Thailand', *Asian Economic Journal* 20 (3): 241–256.

Inman, Robert P., and Daniel L. Rubinfeld (1997) 'Rethinking federalism', *Journal of Economic Perspectives* 11 (4): 43–64.

International Monetary Fund (IMF) (2005) *Global Financial Stability Report*. Washington, DC: IMF.

International Monetary Fund (IMF) (2009) *Lessons of the Financial Crisis for Future Regulation of Financial Institutions and Markets and for Liquidity Management*. Washington, DC: IMF.

International Monetary Fund (IMF) (2010) *Global Financial Stability Report.* Washington, DC: IMF.

Investors Digest (ID), Kuala Lumpur.

Isa, Mansor (1997) 'The Malaysian capital market', in Ahmad Mahdzen, ed., *Southeast Asia on the Growth Path.* Selangor Darul Ehsan: University Pertanian Malaysia Press, pp. 183–193.

Ito, Hiro, Juthathip Jongwanich, and Akiko Terada-Hagiwara (2009) 'What makes developing Asia resilient in a financially globalised world', Working Paper No. 181, Manila: Asian Development Bank.

Jacobson, Gary C. (1985) 'Party organisation and distribution of campaign resources: Republicans and Democrats in 1982', *Political Science Quarterly* 100 (4): 603–625.

Jaffar, Kamarudin (1979) 'Malay political parties: An interpretative essay', *Southeast Asian Affairs 1979*, Singapore: Institute of Southeast Asian Studies, pp. 211–220.

Jalilian, Hossein, and Colin Kirkpatrick (2005) 'Does financial development contribute to poverty reduction?', *Journal of Development Studies* 41 (4): 636–656.

Janda, Kenneth (1980) *Political Parties: A Cross-National Survey.* New York: Free Press.

Janda, Kenneth, and Tyler Colman (1998) 'Effects of party organisation on performance during the "gold age" of parties', *Political Studies* 46 (3): 611–632.

Johnson, Gregg B., and Brian F. Crisp (2003) 'Mandates, power and policies', *American Journal of Political Science* 47 (1): 128–142.

Johnson, Simon, and Todd Mitton (2003) 'Cronyism and capital controls: Evidence from Malaysia', *Journal of Financial Economics* 67 (3): 351–382.

Johnston, R. Barry (1989) 'Distressed financial institutions in Thailand', Working Paper No. 89/4, Washington, DC: IMF.

Jomo, Kwame Sundaram (1987) 'Economic crisis and policy response in Malaysia', in Richard Robison, Kevin Hewison, and Richard Higgott, eds, *Southeast Asia in the 1980s.* North Sydney: Allen and Unwin, pp. 113–148.

Jomo, Kwame Sundaram (ed.) (1995) *Privatising Malaysia.* Boulder: Westview Press.

Jomo, Kwame Sundaram (1998) 'Malaysia's debacle: Whose fault?', *Cambridge Journal of Economics* 22 (6): 707–722.

Jomo, Kwame Sundaram (2003) *M Way: Mahathir's Economic Legacy.* Kuala Lumpur: Forum.

Jones, David R., and Monika L. McDermott (2004) 'The responsible party government model in House and Senate elections', *American Journal of Political Science* 48 (1): 1–12.

Jones, David Seth (2003) 'Budgetary policy in Singapore', in Linda Low, and Douglas M. Johnston, eds, *Singapore Inc.* Singapore: Eastern Universities Press, pp. 131–156.

Jones, Steven L., William L. Megginson, Robert C. Nash, and Jeffrey M. Netter (1999) 'Share issue privatisations as financial means to political and economic ends', *Journal of Financial Economics* 53 (2): 217–253.

June Charoenseang, and Pornkamol Manakit (2002) 'Financial crisis and restructuring in Thailand', *Journal of Asian Economics* 13 (5): 597–613.

Kaplan, Ethan, and Dani Rodrik (2002) 'Did the Malaysian capital controls work?', in Sebastian Edwards and Jeffrey Frankel, eds, *Preventing*

Currency Crises in Emerging Markets. Chicago: Chicago University Press, pp. 393–440.

Karl, Terry Lynn (1995) 'The hybrid regimes of central America', *Journal of Democracy* 6 (3): 72–86.

Karuntarat Boonyawat, Seksak Jumreornvong and Piman Limpaphayom (2005) 'Insider trading: Evidence from Thailand', *Thammasat Review* 10 (1): 49–92.

Karvonen, Lauri, and Stein Kuhnle (eds) (2001) *Party Systems and Voter Alignments Revisited.* London: Routledge.

Kasian Tejapira (2006) 'Toppling Thaksin', *New Left Review* 39: 5–37.

Kastner, Scott L., and Chad Rector (2003) 'International regimes, domestic veto-players, and capital controls policy stability', *International Studies Quarterly* 47 (1): 1–22.

Katz, Richard S., and Peter Mair (1995) 'Changing models of party organisation and party democracy: The emergence of the cartel party', *Party Politics* 1 (4): 5–28.

Kawai, Masahiro, and Ken-ichi Takayasu (1999) 'The economic crisis and financial sector restructuring in Thailand', in *Rising to the Challenge in Asia, Volume 11 Thailand.* Manila: Asian Development Bank.

Keman, Hans (1997) 'Approaches to the analysis of institutions', in Bernard Steunenberg, and Frans van Vught, eds, *Political Institutions and Public Policy.* Dordrecht: Kluwer Academic Publishers, pp. 1–28.

Keman, Hans (2006) 'Parties and government: Features of governing in representative democracies', in Richard S. Katz, and William Crotty, eds, *Handbook of Party Politics.* London: Sage Publications, pp. 160–174.

Kesselman, Mark (1966) 'French local politics: A statistical examination of grass roots consensus', *American Political Science Review* 60 (4): 963–973.

Khong, Cho-Oon (1995) 'Singapore: Political legitimacy through managing conformity', in Muthiah Alagappa, ed., *Political Legitimacy in Southeast Asia.* Stanford: Stanford University Press, pp. 108–135.

Khoo, Boo Teik (2003) *Beyond Mahathir: Malaysian Politics and Its Discontents.* London: Zed Books.

Kim, Byung-Kook (2002) 'The politics of financial reform in Korea, Malaysia, and Thailand', *Journal of East Asian Studies* 2 (1): 185–240.

Kim, E. Han, and Vijay Singal (2000) 'Stock market openings: Experience of emerging economies', *Journal of Business* 73 (1): 25–66.

King, Daniel E. (1997) 'Thailand in 1996', *Asian Survey* 37 (2): 160–166.

King, Dan (1999) 'Thailand', in Ian March, Jean Blondel, and Takashi Inoguchi, eds, *Democracy, Governance, and Economic Performance: East and Southeast Asia.* Tokyo: United Nations University Press, pp. 203–229.

King, Daniel, and Jim LoGerfo (1996) 'Thailand: Toward democratic stability', *Journal of Democracy* 7 (1): 102–117.

Kitti Prasirtsuk (2007) 'From political reform and economic crisis to coup d'etat in Thailand', *Asian Survey* 47 (6): 872–893.

Kitti Prasirtsuk (2010) 'Thailand in 2009', *Asian Survey* 50 (1): 203–210.

Kitschelt, Herbert (2003) 'Competitive party democracy and political-economic reform in Germany and Japan', in Kozo Yamamura, and Wolfgang Streeck, eds, *The End of Diversity?* Ithaca: Cornell University Press, pp. 334–363.

Kitschelt, Herbert, Zdenka Mansfeldova, Radoslaw Markowski, and Gabor Toka (1999) *Post-Communist Party Systems: Competition, Representation, and Inter-Party Co-operation*. Cambridge: Cambridge University Press.

Knack, Stephen (ed.) (2003) *Democracy, Governance and Growth*. Ann Arbor: University of Michigan Press.

Koh, At Tee, and Koh How Eng (2002) 'National technology policy: The Singapore experience', in Mukul G. Asher, David Newman, and Thomas P. Snyder, eds, *Public Policy in Asia*. Westport: Quorum Books, pp. 265–282.

Koh, Gillian (1997) 'Bureaucratic rationality in an evolving developmental state', *Asian Journal of Political Science* 5 (2): 114–141.

Kraiyudht Dhiratayakinant (1992) 'The political economy of decision-making', in David G. Timberman, ed., *The Politics of Economic Reform in Southeast Asia*. Manila: Asian Institute of Management, pp. 31–48.

Kramol Tongdhamachart (1982) *Toward a Political Party Theory in Thai Perspective*. Singapore: Maruzen Asia.

Krueger, Anne O. (ed.) (2000) *Economic Policy Reform: The Second Stage*. Chicago: University of Chicago Press.

Krugman, Paul (1999) *The Accidental Theorist*. London: Penguin Books.

Kuhonta, Erik Martinez (2004) 'The political economy of equitable development', Paper presented to the Workshop on Comparative and Historical Analysis, Stanford University, 19 April.

Kuhonta, Erik Martinez (2008) 'The paradox of Thailand's 1997 "people's constitution" ', *Asian Survey* 48 (3): 373–392.

Kuhonta, Erik Martinez, and Alex M. Mutebi (2006) 'Thaksin triumphant: The implications of one-party dominance in Thailand', *Asian Affairs: An American Review* 33 (1): 39–51.

Kuhonta, Erik Martinez, Dan Slater, and Tuong Vu (2008) 'Introduction: The contributions of Southeast Asian political studies', in Erik Martinez Kuhonta, Dan Slater, and Tuong Vu, eds, *Southeast Asia in Political Science*. Stanford: Stanford University Press, pp. 1–29.

Kunicová, Jana, and Susan Rose-Ackerman (2005) 'Electoral rules and constitutional structures as constraints on corruption', *British Journal of Political Science* 35 (3): 573–606.

Kuster, Stephan, and Felipe Botero (2008) 'How many is too many? Assessment of party system fragmentation measures with data from Latin America', Paper presented to the annual convention of the American Political Science Association, Boston, 28–31 August.

La Porta, Rafael, Florencio Lopez-de Silanes, and Andrei Shleifer (2006) 'What works in securities laws?', *Journal of Finance* 61 (1): 1–32.

Laakso, Markku, and Rein Taagepera (1979) 'Effective number of parties: A measure with application to West Europe', *Comparative Political Studies* 12 (1): 3–27.

Lake, David A., and Matthew A. Baum (2001) 'The invisible hand of democracy: Political control and the provision of public services', *Comparative Political Studies* 34 (6): 587–621.

Lall, Ashish, and Ming-Hua Liu (1997) 'Liberalisation of financial and capital markets: Singapore is almost there', *Law and Policy in International Business* 28 (3): 619–647.

Lam, Peng Er, and Kevin Y.L. Tan (1999) *Lee's Lieutenants: Singapore's Old Guard*. St Leonards: Allen and Unwin.

Laver, Michael, and Norman Schofield (1991) *Multi-party Government: The Politics of Coalition in Europe*. Oxford: Oxford University Press.

Lawson, Key, and Peter Merkl (1988) *When Parties Fail: Emerging Alternative Organisations*. Princeton: Princeton University Press.

Lee, Chung H., and Stephan Haggard (1995) 'Introduction: Issues and Findings', in Stephan Haggard, and Chung H. Lee, eds, *Financial Systems and Economic Policy in Developing Countries*. Ithaca: Cornell University Press, pp. 1–27.

Lee, Eliza W.Y., and M. Shamsul Haque (2006) 'The new public management reform and governance in Asian NICs', *Governance* 19 (4): 605–626.

Lee, Kuan Yew (2000) *From Third World to First, The Singapore Story: 1965–2000*. New York: HarperCollins.

Lee, Lo Yen (1995) *Privatisation in Singapore*. Singapore: Singapore Institute of Labour Studies.

Lee, Sheng-Yi (1984a) 'Financial institutions and markets in Singapore', in Michael T. Skully, ed., *Financial Institutions and Markets in Southeast Asia*. London: Macmillan, pp. 226–295.

Lee, Sheng-Yi (1984b) 'Issues in banking and finance in Singapore', *Southeast Asian Affairs 1984*. Singapore: Institute of Southeast Asian Studies, pp. 294–307.

Lee, Soo Ann (2009) 'The economist prime minister', in Bridget Welsh, James Chin, Arun Mahizhnan, and Tan Tarn How, eds, *Impressions of the Goh Chok Tong Years in Singapore*. Singapore: Singapore University Press, pp. 220–229.

Levine, Ross (2001) 'International financial liberalisation and economic growth', *Review of International Economics* 9 (4): 688–702.

Levine, Ross (2002) 'Bank-based or market-based financial systems: Which is better?', *Journal of Financial Intermediation* 11 (4): 398–428.

Levine, Ross (2005) 'Finance and growth: Theory and evidence', in Philippe Aghion, and Steven N. Durlauf, eds, *Handbook of Economic Growth, Volume 1A*. The Hague: Elsevier, pp. 865–934.

Levine, Ross, and Sara Zervos (1996) 'Stock market development and long-run growth', Policy Research Working Paper No. 1582, Washington, DC: World Bank.

Levine, Ross, and Sara Zervos (1998) 'Capital control liberalisation and stock market development', *World Development* 26 (7): 1169–1183.

Levitsky, Steven, and Lucan A. Way (2002) 'The rise of competitive authoritarianism', *Journal of Democracy* 13 (2): 51–65.

Lewis, Peter, and Howard Stein (1997) 'Shifting fortunes: The political economy of financial liberalisation in Nigeria', *World Development* 25 (1): 5–22.

Lijphart, Arend (1994) *Electoral Systems and Party Systems: A Study of Twenty-Seven Democracies, 1945–1990*. Oxford: Oxford University Press.

Lijphart, Arend (1999) *Patterns of Democracy*. New Haven: Yale University Press.

Lim, Chong Yah et al. (1991) *Policy Options for the Singapore Economy*. Singapore: McGraw-Hill.

Lim, Guan Hua (1998) 'Strategies for financial sector development', in Toh Mun Heng, and Tan Kong Yam, eds, *Competitiveness of the Singapore Economy*. Singapore: Singapore University Press, pp. 195–245.

Lim, Hong Hai (2002) 'Public administration: The effects of executive dominance', in Francis Loh Kok Wah, and Khoo Boo Teik, eds, *Democracy in Malaysia*. Richmond: Curzon, pp. 165–197.

Lim, Hong Hai, and Kian Ming Ong (2006) 'Electoral campaigning in Malaysia', in Christian Schafferer, ed., *Election Campaigning in East and Southeast Asia*. Aldershot: Ashgate, pp. 55–77.

Lim, Linda Y.C. (1999) 'Free market fancies: Hong Kong, Singapore and the Asian financial crisis', in T.J. Pempel, ed., *The Politics of the Asian Economic Crisis*. Ithaca: Cornell University Press, pp. 101–115.

Lim, Linda Y.C., and Pang Eng Fong (1991) *Foreign Direct Investment and Industrialisation in Malaysia, Singapore, Taiwan and Thailand*. Paris: Development Centre of the OECD.

Lin, See-Yan (1994) 'The current state of the Malaysian financial system', *Pacific-Basin Finance Journal* 2 (1): 113–138.

Lindberg, Staffan I. (2006) *Democracy and Elections in Africa*. Baltimore: Johns Hopkins University Press.

Linz, Juan J. (1994) 'Presidential or parliamentary democracy: Does it make a difference?', in Juan J. Linz, and Arturo Valenzuela, eds, *The Future of Presidential Democracy*. Baltimore: Johns Hopkins University Press, pp. 3–87.

Lipset, Seymour M., and Stein Rokkan (1967) *Party Systems and Voter Alignments: Cross-National Perspectives*. New York: Free Press.

Litan, Robert E., Michael Pomerleano, and V. Sundararajan (eds) (2003) *The Future of Domestic Capital Markets in Developing Countries*. Washington, DC: Brookings Institution Press.

Lizzeri, Alessandro, and Nicola Persico (2005) 'A drawback of electoral competition', *Journal of the European Economic Association* 3 (6): 1318–1348.

Lohmann, Susanne (1998) 'An information rationale for the power of special interests', *American Political Science Review* 92 (4): 809–827.

Loriaux, Michael, Meredith Woo-Cumings, Kent E. Calder, Sylvia Maxfield, and Sofía Pérez (1997) *Capital Ungoverned: Liberalising Finance in Interventionist States*. Ithaca: Cornell University Press.

Low, Linda (2006) *The Political Economy of a City-State Revisited*. Singapore: Marshall Cavendish.

Lupia, Arthur, and Mathew D. McCubbins (2000) 'Representation or abdication? How citizens use institutions to help delegation succeed', *European Journal of Political Research* 37 (2): 291–307.

MacIntyre, Andrew (2003) *The Power of Institutions: Political Architecture and Governance*. Ithaca: Cornell University Press.

Magaloni, Beatriz (2006) *Voting for Autocracy: Hegemonic Party Survival and Its Demise in Mexico*. Cambridge: Cambridge University Press.

Mahizhnan, Arun (1994) 'Developing Singapore's external economy', in *Southeast Asian Affairs*, Singapore: Institute of Southeast Asian Studies, pp. 285–299.

Mainwaring, Scott (1993) 'Presidentialism, multi-partism, and democracy: The difficult combination', *Comparative Political Studies* 26 (2): 198–228.

Mainwaring, Scott P. (1999) *Rethinking Party Systems in the Third Wave of Democratisation*. Stanford: Stanford University Press.

Mainwaring, Scott, and Timothy R. Scully (eds) (1995) *Building Democratic Institutions: Party Systems in Latin America*. Stanford: Stanford University Press.

Mainwaring, Scott, and Matthew Soberg Shugart (eds) (1997) *Presidentialism and Democracy in Latin America*. Cambridge: Cambridge University Press.

Mainwaring, Scott, and Mariano Torcal (2006) 'Party system institutionalisation and party system theory after the third wave of democratisation', in Richard S. Katz, and William Crotty, eds, *Handbook of Party Politics*. London: Sage Publications, pp. 204–227.

Mair, Peter (1996) 'Party systems and structures of competition', in Lawrence LeDuc, Richard G. Niemi, and Pippa Norris, eds, *Comparing Democracies: Elections and Voting in Global Perspective*. London: Sage Publications, pp. 83–106.

Malaysian Business (MB), Kuala Lumpur.

Mansfield, Edward D., Helen V. Milner, and Jon C. Pevehouse (2007) 'Vetoing co-operation: The impact of veto players on preferential trading arrangements', *British Journal of Political Science* 37 (3): 403–432.

Maravall, José María (1997) *Regimes and Markets: Democratisation and Economic Change in Latin America*. Oxford: Oxford University Press.

Marsh, Ian, Jean Blondel, and Takashi Inoguchi (1999) *Democracy, Governance, and Economic Performance*. Tokyo: United Nations University Press.

Martell, Rodolfo, and René M. Stulz (2003) 'Equity-market liberalisation as country IPO's', *American Economic Review* 93 (2): 97–101.

Mauzy, Diane K., and R.S. Milne (2002) *Singapore Politics under the People's Action Party*. London: Routledge.

Mauzy, Diane K., and Shane J. Barter (2008) 'Learning to lose? Not if UMNO can help it', in Edward Friedman, and Joseph Wong, eds, *Political Transitions in Dominant Party Systems*. London: Routledge, pp. 211–230.

Mayhew, David R. (1974) *Congress: The Electoral Connection*. New Haven: Yale University Press.

Mayhew, David R. (1986) *Placing Parties in American Politics*. Princeton: Princeton University Press.

McAllister, Ian, and Stephan White (2007) 'Political parties and democratic consolidation in post-communist societies', *Party Politics* 13 (2): 197–216.

McCargo, Duncan (1997) 'Thailand's political parties: Real, authentic and actual', in Kevin Hewison, ed., *Political Change in Thailand*. London: Routledge, pp. 114–131.

McCargo, Duncan (2000) *Politics and the Press in Thailand*. London: Routlege.

McCargo, Duncan (2002) 'Thailand's January 2001 general elections: Vindicating Reform', in Duncan McCargo, ed., *Reforming Thai Politics*. Copenhagen: Nordic Institute of Asian Studies, pp. 247–260.

McCargo, Duncan, and Ukrist Pathmanand (2005) *The Thaksinisation of Thailand*. Copenhagen: Nordic Institute of Asian Studies.

McCubbins, Mathew D., and Michael F. Thies (1997) 'As a matter of factions: The budgetary implications of shifting factional control in Japan's LDP', *Legislative Studies Quarterly* 22 (3): 293–328.

McGillivray, Fiona (2004) *Privileging Industry: The Comparative Politics of Trade and Industrial Policy*. Princeton: Princeton University Press.

Means, Gordon (1991) *Malaysian Politics: The Second Generation*. Singapore: Oxford University Press.

Means, Gordon P. (1998) 'Soft authoritarianism in Malaysia and Singapore', in Larry Diamond, and Marc F. Plattner, eds, *Democracy in East Asia*. Baltimore: Johns Hopkins University Press, pp. 96–110.

Megginson, William L. (2005) *The Financial Economics of Privatisation*. Oxford: Oxford University Press.

Megginson, William L., and Jeffrey M. Netter (2001) 'From state to market: A survey of empirical studies on privatisation', *Journal of Economic Literature* 39 (2): 321–389.

Meisel, John (1974) *Cleavages, Parties and Values in Canada*. London: Sage Publications.

Miller, Gary J. (2005) 'The political evolution of principal-agent models', *Annual Review of Political Science* 8: 203–225.

Milne, R.S. (1991) 'The politics of privatisation in the ASEAN states', *ASEAN Economic Bulletin* 7 (3): 322–334.

Milne, R.S., and Diane K. Mauzy (1990) *Singapore: The Legacy of Lee Kuan Yew*. Boulder: Westview Press.

Milne, R.S., and Diane K. Mauzy (1999) *Malaysian Politics under Mahathir*. London: Routledge.

Mithani, Dawood M., and Pairat Watcharaphun (2000) 'Privatisation in Thailand', in B.N. Ghosh, ed., *Privatisation: An ASEAN Connection*. Huntington: Nova Science.

Mitton, Todd (2006) 'Stock market liberalisation and operating performance at the firm level', *Journal of Financial Economics* 81 (4): 625–647.

Mohamad, Mahathir et al. (1991) *Malaysia's Capital Market*. Selangor Darul Ehsan: Pelanduk Publications.

Molinar, Juan (1991) 'Counting the number of parties: An alternative index', *American Political Science Review* 85 (4): 1383–1391.

Monetary Authority of Singapore (MAS) (various issues) *Annual Report*.

Monetary Authority of Singapore (MAS) (2009) *Financial Stability Review*. Singapore: MAS.

Montes, Manuel F., and Tan Khee Giap (1999) 'Developing the financial services industry in Singapore', in Seiichi Masuyama, Donna Vandenbrink, and Chia Siow Yue, eds, *East Asia's Financial Systems*. Singapore: Institute of Southeast Asian Studies, pp. 231–259.

Mooi, Susan Tho Lai, and Jooky Lim (2006) 'Insider trading', in M. Fazilah Abdul Samad, ed., *The Malaysian Financial System*. Kuala Lumpur: University Malaya Press, pp. 127–142.

Mori, Nobuhiro, and Yoshiro Tsutsui (1993) 'The industrial organisation of financial markets in Thailand', *Asian Economic Journal* 7 (1): 71–88.

Morley, James W. (ed.) (1993) *Driven by Growth: Political Change in the Asia-Pacific Region*. Armonk: M.E. Sharpe.

Mozaffar, Shaheen, James Scarritt, and Glen Galaich (2003) 'Electoral institutions, ethnopolitical cleavages, and party systems in Africa's emerging democracies', *American Political Science Review* 97 (3): 379–390.

Mulligan, Casey B., Ricard Gil, and Xavier Sala-i-Martin (2004) 'Do democracies have different public policies than non-democracies?', *Journal of Economic Perspectives* 18 (1): 51–74.

Murashima, Eiji, Nakharin Mektrairat, and Somkiat Wanthana (1991) *The Making of Modern Thai Political Parties*. Tokyo: Institute of Developing Economies.

Murray, David (1996) 'The 1995 national elections in Thailand', *Asian Survey* 36 (4): 361–375.

Murray, David (1997) 'The Thai parliamentary elections of 1995 and 1996', *Electoral Studies* 16 (3): 379–386.

Muscat, Robert J. (1994) *The Fifth Tiger: A Study of Thai Development Policy*. Armonk: M.E. Sharpe.

Musolf, Lloyd D., and J. Frederick Springer (1979) *Malaysia's Parliamentary System: Representative Politics and Policy-Making in a Divided Society*. Boulder: Westview Press.

Mutalib, Hussin (2002) 'Constitutional-electoral reforms and politics in Singapore', *Legislative Studies Quarterly* 27 (4): 659–672.

Mutalib, Hussin (2004) *Parties and Politics: A Study of Opposition Parties and the PAP in Singapore*. Singapore: Marshall Cavendish Academic.

Mutebi, Alex M. (2008) 'Explaining the failure of Thailand's anti-corruption regime', *Development and Change* 39 (1): 147–171.

Muzaffar, Chandra (1989) *Challenges and Choices in Malaysian Politics and Society*. Penang: Aliran Kesedaran Negara.

Myerson, Roger B. (1993) 'Incentives to cultivate favoured minorities under alternative electoral systems', *American Political Science Review* 87 (4): 856–869.

Nadeau, Richard, Richard G. Niemi, and Antoine Yoshinaka (2002) 'A cross-national analysis of economic voting: Taking account of the political context across time and nations', *Electoral Studies* 21 (3): 403–423.

Nambiar, Shankaran (2009) 'Malaysia and the global crisis', Working Paper No. 148, Tokyo: Asian Development Bank Institute.

Nation, Bangkok.

Neher, Clark D. (1988) 'Thailand in 1987: Semi-successful semi-democracy', *Asian Survey* 28 (2): 192–201.

Nelson, Michael H. (2001) 'Thailand', in Dieter Nohlen, Florian Grotz, and Christof Hartmann, eds, *Elections in Asia and the Pacific*. Oxford: Oxford University Press, pp. 261–320.

Nelson, Michael H. (2005) 'Analysing provincial political structures in Thailand', Working Paper No. 79, Southeast Asia Research Centre, City University of Hong Kong.

Nelson, Michael H. (2007) 'Institutional incentives and informal local political groups (phuak) in Thailand: Comments on Allen Hicken and Paul Chambers', *Journal of East Asian Studies* 7 (1): 125–147.

Neumann, Sigmund (ed.) (1956) *Modern Political Parties: Approaches to Comparative Politics*. Chicago: Chicago University Press.

New Straits Times (NST), Kuala Lumpur.

Ng, Chee Yuen (1987) 'The Singapore economy in 1986', *Southeast Asian Affairs*. Singapore: Institute of Southeast Asian Studies, pp. 290–303.

Ng, Chee Yuen (1989) 'Privatisation in Singapore', *ASEAN Economic Bulletin* 5 (3): 290–318.

Ngiam, Kee Jin (1996) 'Singapore as a financial centre', in Takatoshi Ito, and Anne O. Krueger, eds, *Financial Deregulation and Integration in East Asia*. Chicago: University of Chicago Press, pp. 359–386.

Nielson, Daniel L. (2003) 'Supplying trade reform: Political institutions and liberalisation in middle-income presidential democracies', *American Journal of Political Science* 47 (3): 470–491.

Nielson, Daniel L., and Matthew Soberg Shugart (1999) 'Constitutional change in Colombia', *Comparative Political Studies* 32 (3): 313–341.

Noble, Gregory W. (1998) *Collective Action in East Asia: How Ruling Parties Shape Industrial Policy*. Ithaca: Cornell University Press.

Nunberg, Barbara (2002) 'Civil service quality after the crisis: A view of five Asian cases', *Asian Journal of Political Science* 10 (2): 1–21.

Nyblade, Benjamin, and Steven R. Reed (2008) 'Who cheats? Who loots? Political competition and corruption in Japan, 1947–1993', *American Journal of Political Science* 52 (4): 926–941.

Ockey, James (1994) 'Political parties, factions, and corruption in Thailand', *Modern Asian Studies* 28 (2): 251–277.

Ockey, James (2003) 'Change and continuity in the Thai political party system', *Asian Survey* 43 (4): 663–680.

Ockey, James (2004) *Making Democracy: Leadership, Class, Gender, and Political Participation in Thailand*. Honolulu: University of Hawai'i Press.

Ockey, James (2005) 'Variations on a theme: Societal cleavages and party orientations through multiple transitions in Thailand', *Party Politics* 11 (6): 728–747.

Olcott, Martha Brill, and Marina Ottaway (1999) 'The challenge of semi-authoritarianism', Working Paper No. 7, Washington, DC: Carnegie Endowment for International Peace.

Ooi, Can Seng (1998) 'Singapore', in Wolfgang Sachsenröder, and Ulrike E. Frings, eds, *Political Party Systems and Democratic Development in East and Southeast Asia, Volume I: Southeast Asia*. Aldershot: Ashgate, pp. 343–402.

Opper, Sonja (2004) 'The political economy of privatisation: Empirical evidence from transition economies', *Kyklos* 57 (4): 559–586.

Orathai Kokpol (2002) 'Electoral politics in Thailand', in Aurel Croissant, Gabriele Bruns, and Marei John, eds, *Electoral Politics in Southeast and East Asia*. Singapore: Friedrich Ebert Stiftung, pp. 277–320.

O'Reilly, Robert F. (2005) 'Veto points, veto players, and international trade policy', *Comparative Political Studies* 38 (6): 652–675.

Ottaway, Marina (2003) *Democracy Challenged: The Rise of Semi-Authoritarianism*. Washington, DC: Carnegie Endowment for International Peace.

Painter, Martin (2004) 'The politics of administrative reform in East and Southeast Asia', *Governance* 17 (3): 361–386.

Pakorn Vichyanond (1994) *Thailand's Financial System*. Bangkok: Thailand Development Research Institute.

Panebianco, Angelo (1988) *Political Parties: Organisation and Power*. Cambridge: Cambridge University Press.

Pang, Cheng Lian (1971) *Singapore's People's Action Party*. Singapore: Oxford University Press.

Pasuk Phongpaichit (2004) 'Thailand under Thaksin: Another Malaysia?', Working Paper No. 109, Asia Research Centre, Murdoch University.

Pasuk Phongpaichit, and Chris Baker (2000) *Thailand's Crisis*. Singapore: Institute of Southeast Asian Studies.

Pasuk Phongpaichit, and Chris Baker (2002) *Thailand: Economy and Politics*. Selangor Darul Ehsan: Oxford University Press.

Pasuk Phongpaichit, and Chris Baker (2004) *Thaksin: The Business of Politics in Thailand*. Chiang Mai: Silkworm Books.

Pasuk Phongpaichit, and Chris Baker (2008) 'Thaksin's populism', *Journal of Contemporary Asia* 38 (1): 62–83.

Patro, Dilip K. (2005) 'Stock market liberalisation and emerging market country fund premiums', *Journal of Business* 78 (1): 135–168.

Pepinsky, Thomas (2007) 'Autocracy, elections, and fiscal policy: Evidence from Malaysia', *Studies in Comparative International Development* 42 (1): 136–163.

Perotti, Enrico C., and Pieter van Oijen (2001) 'Privatisation, political risk and stock market development in emerging economies', *Journal of International Money and Finance* 20 (1): 43–69.

Perotti, Enrico C., and Ernst-Ludwig von Thadden (2006) 'The political economy of corporate control and labour rents', *Journal of Political Economy* 114 (1): 145–174.

Perotti, Roberto, and Yianos Kontopoulos (2002) 'Fragmented fiscal policy', *Journal of Public Economics* 86 (2): 191–222.

Persico, Nicola, José Carlos Rodríguez-Pueblita, and Dan Silverman (2007) 'Factions and political competition', Working Paper No. 13008, National Bureau of Economic Research.

Persson, Torsten (2002) 'Do political institutions shape economic policy?', *Econometrica* 70 (3): 883–905.

Persson, Torsten, and Guido Tabellini (2001) 'Political institutions and policy outcomes: What are the stylised facts?', Discussion Paper No. 2827, London: Centre for Economic Policy Research.

Pomerleano, Michael (2009) 'What is the impact of the global financial crisis on the banking system in East Asia?', Working Paper No. 146, Tokyo: Asian Development Bank Institute.

Posusney, Marsha Pripstein (2002) 'Multi-party elections in the Arab world', *Studies in Comparative International Development* 36 (4): 34–62.

Powell, G. Bingham (2000) *Elections as Instruments of Democracy*. New Haven: Yale University Press.

Praipol Koomsup (2003) 'State enterprise and privatisation in Thailand', *Chulalongkorn Journal of Economics* 15 (1): 1–33.

Prasad, Eswar S. (2010) 'Financial sector regulation and reforms in emerging markets', Working Paper No. 16428, Cambridge, MA: National Bureau of Economic Research.

Primo, David M., and James M. Snyder (2008) 'Party strength, the personal vote, and government spending', Manuscript, Department of Political Science, University of Rochester.

Przeworski, Adam, and Henry Teune (1970) *The Logic of Comparative Social Inquiry*. Malabar: Krieger.

Przeworski, Adam, and Fernando Limongi (1993) 'Political regimes and economic growth', *Journal of Economic Perspectives* 7 (3): 51–69.

Przeworski, Adam, Michael E. Alvarez, José Antonio Cheibub, and Fernando Limongi (2000) *Democracy and Development: Political Institutions and Well-Being in the World*. Cambridge: Cambridge University Press.

Public Sector Divestment Committee (PSDC) (1987) *Report of the Public Sector Divestment Committee*. Singapore: PSDC.

Puthucheary, Mavis, and Norani Othman (eds) (2005) *Elections and Democracy in Malaysia*. Bangi: Penerbit Universiti Kebangsaan Malaysia.

Rajan, Raghuram G., and Luigi Zingales (2003) 'The great reversals: The politics of financial development in the twentieth century', *Journal of Financial Economics* 69 (1): 5–50.

Ramseyer, J. Mark, and Frances McCall Rosenbluth (1993) *Japan's Political Market*. Cambridge: Harvard University Press.

Randall, Vicky, and Lars Svåsand (2002) 'Party institutionalisation in new democracies', *Party Politics* 8 (1): 5–29.

Reilly, Benjamin (2006) *Democracy and Diversity: Political Engineering in the Asia-Pacific*. Oxford: Oxford University Press.

Reynolds, Andrew, and Timothy D. Sisk (1998) 'Elections and electoral systems: Implications for conflict management', in Timothy D. Sisk, and Andrew Reynolds, eds, *Elections and Conflict Management in Africa*. Washington, DC: United States Institute of Peace Press, pp. 11–36.

Rice, Stuart A. (1925) 'The behaviour of legislative groups: A method of measurement', *American Political Science Review* 40 (1): 60–72.

Rieger, Hans Christof (2001) 'Singapore', in Dieter Nohlen, Florian Grotz, and Christof Hartmann, eds, *Elections in Asia and the Pacific*. Oxford: Oxford University Press, pp. 239–260.

Robison, Richard (1989) 'Structures of power and the industrialisation process in Southeast Asia', *Journal of Contemporary Asia* 19 (4): 371–397.

Rodan, Garry (1993) 'Preserving the one-party state in contemporary Singapore', in Kevin Hewison, Richard Robison, and Garry Rodan, eds, *Southeast Asia in the 1990s*. St Leonards: Allen and Unwin, pp. 75–108.

Rodan, Garry (1996a) 'Elections without representation: The Singapore experience under the PAP', in R.H. Taylor, ed., *The Politics of Elections in Southeast Asia*. Cambridge: Cambridge University Press, pp. 61–89.

Rodan, Garry (1996b) 'State-society relations and political opposition in Singapore', in Garry Rodan, ed., *Political Oppositions in Industrialising Asia*. London: Routledge, pp. 95–127.

Rodan, Garry (1997) 'Singapore', in Garry Rodan, Kevin Hewison, and Richard Robison, eds. *The Political Economy of Southeast Asia*. Melbourne: Oxford University Press, pp. 148–178.

Rodan, Gary (2004a) 'International capital, Singapore's state companies and security', *Critical Asian Studies* 36 (3): 479–499.

Rodan, Gary (2004b) *Transparency and Authoritarian Rule in Southeast Asia*. London: RoutledgeCurzon.

Rodan, Garry (2009) 'Goh's consensus politics of authoritarian rule', in Bridget Welsh, James Chin, Arun Mahizhnan, and Tan Tarn How, eds, *Impressions of the Goh Chok Tong Years*. Singapore: Singapore University Press, pp. 61–70.

Rodan, Garry, and Kanishka Jayasuriya (2007) 'The technocratic politics of administrative participation', *Democratisation* 14 (5): 795–815.

Rodrik, Dani (2000) 'Participatory politics, social co-operation, and economic stability', *American Economic Review* 90 (2): 140–144.

Rogowski, Ronald, and Mark Andreas Kayser (2002) 'Majoritarian electoral systems and consumer power: Price-level evidence from the OECD countries', *American Journal of Political Science* 46 (3): 526–539.

Roland, Gérard (ed.) (2008) *Privatisation: Successes and Failures*. New York: Columbia University Press.

Rosenbluth, Frances, and Ross Schaap (2003) 'The domestic politics of banking regulation', *International Organisation* 57 (2): 307–336.

Roubini, Nouriel, and Jeffrey D. Sachs (1989) 'Political and economic determinants of budget deficits in the industrial democracies', *European Economic Review* 33 (4): 903–938.

Rousseau, P.L., and P. Wachtel (2000) 'Equity markets and growth: Cross-country evidence on timing and outcomes, 1980–1995', *Journal of Banking and Finance* 24 (4): 1933–1957.

Saalfeld, Thomas (2008) 'Intra-party conflict and cabinet survival in 17 West European democracies', in Daniela Giannetti, and Kenneth Benoit, eds, *Intra-Party Politics and Coalition Governments*. London: Routledge, pp. 169–186.

Samuels, David J. (1999) 'Incentives to cultivate a party vote in candidate-centric electoral systems: Evidence from Brazil', *Comparative Political Studies* 32 (4): 487–518.

Samuels, David (2004) 'Presidentialism and accountability for the economy in comparative perspective', *American Political Science Review* 98 (3): 425–436.

Sartori, Giovanni (1970) 'Concept misformation in comparative politics', *American Political Science Review* 64 (4): 1033–1053.

Sartori, Giovanni (1976) *Parties and Party Systems: A Framework for Analysis*. Cambridge: Cambridge University Press.

Sartori, Giovanni (1997) *Comparative Constitutional Engineering*. Basingstoke: Palgrave Macmillan.

Schedler, Andreas (2002) 'The menu of manipulation', *Journal of Democracy* 13 (2): 36–50.

Schedler, Andreas (2004) 'Degrees and patterns of party competition in electoral autocracies', Paper presented to the annual convention of the American Political Science Association, Chicago, 2–5 September.

Schedler, Andreas (2006) 'The logic of electoral authoritarianism', in Andreas Schedler, ed., *Electoral Authoritarianism: The Dynamics of Unfree Competition*. Boulder: Lynne Rienner, pp. 1–23.

Seah, Chee Meow (1985) 'Para-political institutions', in Jon S.T. Quah, Chan Heng Chee, and Seah Chee Meow, eds, *Government and Politics of Singapore*. Singapore: Oxford University Press, pp. 173–194.

Seah, David Chee-Meow (1999) 'The administrative state: Quo vadis?', in Linda Low, ed., *Singapore: Towards a Developed Status*. Singapore: Oxford University Press, pp. 250–270.

Sebastian, Leonard C. (1997) 'The logic of the guardian state: Governance in Singapore's development experience', *Southeast Asian Affairs 1997*. Singapore: Institute of Southeast Asian Studies, pp. 278–298.

Securities and Exchange Commission (SEC) (2002) *Develop and Supervise the Thai Capital Market*. Bangkok: SEC.

Sferza, Serenella (2002) 'Party organisation and party performance: The case of the French Socialist Party', in Richard Gunther, José Ramón Montero, and Juan J. Linz, eds, *Political Parties: Old Concepts and New Challenges*. Oxford: Oxford University Press, pp. 166–190.

Shepsle, Kenneth A. (2006) 'Rational choice institutionalism', in R.A.W. Rhodes, Sarah A. Binder, and Bert A. Rockman, eds, *Oxford Handbook of Political Institutions*. Oxford: Oxford University Press, pp. 23–38.

Shi, Min, and Jakob Svensson (2006) 'Political budget cycles: Do they differ across countries and why?', *Journal of Public Economics* 90 (4): 1367–1389.

Shleifer, Andrei (1998) 'State versus private ownership', *Journal of Economic Perspectives* 12 (4): 133–150.

Shugart, Matthew S., Melody Ellis Valdini, and Kati Suominen (2005) 'Looking for locals: Voter information demands and personal vote-earning attributes of legislators under proportional representation', *American Journal of Political Science* 49 (2): 437–449.

Silva, Eduardo Bonilla (1998) *The State and Capital in Chile: Business Elites, Technocrats, and Market Economics*. Boulder: Westview Press.

Sinclair, Barbara (2006) 'Legislative cohesion and presidential policy success', in Reuven Y. Hazan, ed., *Cohesion and Discipline in Legislatures*. London: Routledge, pp. 41–56.

Singh, Bilveer (2007) *Politics and Governance in Singapore*. Singapore: McGraw-Hill.

Singh, Ranjit Ajit, and Zainal Aznam Yusof (2005) 'Development of the capital market in Malaysia', in Donna Vanderbrink, and Denis Hew, eds, *Capital Markets in Asia*. Tokyo: Club Foundation for Global Studies, pp. 206–231.

Skully, Michael T. (1984) 'Financial institutions and markets in Thailand', in Michael T. Skully, ed., *Financial Institutions and Markets in Southeast Asia*. London: Macmillan, pp. 296–378.

Skully, Michael T., and George J. Viksnins (1987) *Financing East Asia's Success*. London: Macmillan.

Slater, Dan (2003) 'Iron cage in an iron fist: Authoritarian institutions and the personalisation of power in Malaysia', *Comparative Politics* 36 (1): 81–102.

Smith, Peter H., and Melissa R. Ziegler (2008) 'Liberal and illiberal democracy in Latin America', *Latin American Politics and Society* 50 (1): 31–57.

Snyder, James M., and Michael M. Ting (2002) 'An informational rationale for political parties', *American Journal of Political Science* 46 (1): 90–110.

Sombat Chantornvong (2000) 'Local godfathers in Thai politics', in Ruth McVey, ed., *Money and Power in Provincial Thailand*. Singapore: Institute of Southeast Asian Studies, pp. 53–73.

Somchai Phatharathananunth (2008) 'The Thai Rak Thai Party and elections in North-eastern Thailand', *Journal of Contemporary Asia* 38 (1): 106–123.

Somer-Topcu, Zeynep, and Laron K. Williams (2008) 'Survival of the fittest: Cabinet duration in post-communist Europe', *Comparative Politics* 40 (3): 313–329.

Somjai Phagaphasvivat (1988) *Thai Capital Market*. Bangkok: S.S. Consultant & Research.

Son, Hyun H., and Emmanuel A. San Andres (2009) 'How has Asia fared in the global crisis', Working Paper No. 174, Manila: Asian Development Bank.

Soon, Teck-Wong, and C. Suan Tan (1993) *Singapore: Public Policy and Economic Development*. Washington, DC: World Bank.

Spiller, Pablo T., and Mariano Tommasi (2003) 'The institutional foundations of public policy: A transactions approach with application to Argentina', *Journal of Law, Economics and Organisation* 19 (2): 281–306.

Spolaore, Enrico (2004) 'Adjustments in different government systems', *Economics and Politics* 16 (2): 117–146.

Stasavage, David (2005) 'Democracy and education spending in Africa', *American Journal of Political Science* 49 (2): 343–358.

Stein, Ernesto, and Mariano Tommasi (eds) (2008) *Policymaking in Latin America*. Washington, DC: Inter-American Development Bank.

Stokes, Susan C. (2007) 'Is vote buying undemocratic?', in Frederic Charles Schaffer, ed., *Elections for Sale: The Causes and Consequences of Vote Buying*. Boulder: Lynne Rienner, pp. 81–99.

Straits Times (ST), Singapore.

Strom, Kaare (1990a) 'A behavioural theory of competitive political parties', *American Political Science Review* 34 (2): 565–598.

Strom, Kaare (1990b) *Minority Government and Majority Rule*. Cambridge: Cambridge University Press.

Stubbs, Richard (2009) 'Whatever happened to the East Asian developmental state?', *Pacific Review* 22 (1): 1–22.

Suchit Bunbongkarn (1987) 'Political institutions and processes', in Somsakdi Xuto, ed., *Government and Politics of Thailand*. Singapore: Oxford University Press, pp. 41–74.

Suchit Bunbongkarn (1990) 'The role of major political forces in the Thai political process', in Clark D. Neher, and Wiwat Mungkandi, eds, *U.S.-Thailand Relations in a New International Era*. Berkeley: Institute of East Asian Studies, University of California.

Sunday Times, Singapore.

Surin Maisrikrod (2008) 'Civil society, accountability and governance in Thailand', in Terence Chong, ed., *Globalisation and Its Counter-Forces in South-East Asia*. Singapore: Institute of Southeast Asian Studies, pp. 97–116.

Sylla, Richard (1999) 'Shaping the US financial system, 1690–1913: The dominant role of public finance', in Richard Sally, Richard Tilly, and Gabriel Tortella, eds, *The State, the Financial System, and Economic Modernisation*. Cambridge: Cambridge University Press, pp. 249–270.

Taagepera, Rein (1999) 'Supplanting the effective number of parties', *Electoral Studies* 18 (4): 497–504.

Taagepera, Rein, and Matthew Soberg Shugart (1989) *Seats and Votes: Effects and Determinants of Electoral Systems*. New Haven: Yale University Press.

Taagepera, Rein, and Matthew Soberg Shugart (1993) 'Predicting the number of parties: A quantitative model of Duverger's mechanical effect', *American Political Science Review* 87 (3): 455–464.

Tam, On Kit, and Monica Guo-Sze Tan (2007) 'Ownership, governance and firm performance in Malaysia', *Corporate Governance* 15 (2): 208–222.

Tan, Chwee Huat (2005) *Financial Markets and Institutions in Singapore*. Singapore: Singapore University Press.

Tan, Ee Khoon, Sharon Tan, and Irene Tang (1989) 'Development of the capital market in Singapore', in Beoy Kui Ng, ed., *The Development of Capital Markets in the SEACEN Countries*. Kuala Lumpur: The SEACEN Research and Training Centre, pp. 201–250.

Tan, Jeff (2008) *Privatisation in Malaysia*. London: Routledge.

Tan, Kenneth Paul (2003) 'Crisis, self-reflection, and rebirth in Singapore's national life cycle', *Southeast Asian Affairs*, Singapore: Institute of Southeast Asian Studies, pp. 241–258.

Tan, Kevin L.Y. (2001) 'Malaysia', in Dieter Nohlen, Florian Grotz, and Christof Hartmann, eds, *Elections in Asia and the Pacific*. Oxford: Oxford University Press, pp. 143–184.

Tan, Kevin L.Y., and Peng Er Lam (1997) *Managing Political Change in Singapore*. London: Routledge.

Tara Siam Business Information (TSBI) (1994) *Thai Financial Company Sectoral Study*. Bangkok: TSBI.

Tavits, Margit (2007) 'Clarity of responsibility and corruption', *American Journal of Political Science* 51 (1): 218–229.

Tay, Simon S.C. (2001) 'Island in the world', *Southeast Asian Affairs*, Singapore: Institute of Southeast Asian Studies, pp. 270–309.

Taylor, R.H. (1996) *The Politics of Elections in Southeast Asia*. Cambridge: Cambridge University Press.

Teh, Yik Koon (2002) 'Money politics in Malaysia', *Journal of Contemporary Asia* 32 (3): 338–345.

Teo, George (1991) 'Regulation of the securities market in Singapore', in Charmain Lye, and Rosalind Lazar, eds, *The Regulation of Financial and Capital Markets*. Singapore: SNP Publishers, pp. 9–13.

Thanee Chaiwat, and Pasuk Phongpaichit (2008) 'Rents and rent-seeking in the Thaksin era', in Pasuk Phongpaichit and Chris Baker, eds, *Thai Capital after the 1997 Crisis*. Singapore: Institute of Southeast Asian Studies, pp. 249–266.

Thangavelu, Shandre Mugan (2009) 'Spreading the benefits of growth and managing inequality', in Bridget Welsh, James Chin, Arun Mahizhnan and Tan Tarn How, eds, *Impressions of the Goh Chok Tong Years*. Singapore: Singapore University Press, pp. 230–239.

Thelen, Kathleen, and Sven Steinmo (1992) 'Historical institutionalism in comparative politics', in Sven Steinmo, Kathleen Thelen, and Frank Longstreth, eds, *Structuring Politics: Historical Institutionalism in Comparative Politics*. Cambridge: Cambridge University Press, pp. 1–32.

Thitinan Pongsudhirak (2003) 'Thailand: Democratic authoritarianism', *Southeast Asian Affairs*. Singapore: Institute of Southeast Asian Studies.

Thitinan Pongsudhirak (2008a) 'Thaksin: Competitive authoritarian and flawed dissident', in John Kane, Haig Patapan, and Benjamin Wong, eds, *Dissident Democrats: The Challenge of Democratic Leadership in Asia*. London: Palgrave Macmillan, pp. 67–84.

Thitinan Pongsudhirak (2008b) 'Thailand since the coup', *Journal of Democracy* 19 (4): 140–153.

Traisorat, Tull (2000) *Thailand: Financial Sector Reform and the East Asian Crises*. The Hague: Kluwer.

Tremewan, Christopher (1994) *The Political Economy of Social Control in Singapore*. London: Macmillan.

Tsebelis, George (1995) 'Decision making in political systems: Veto players in presidentialism, parliamentarism, multicameralism and multipartyism', *British Journal of Political Science* 25 (3): 289–325.

Tsebelis, George (1999) 'Veto players and law production in parliamentary democracies: An empirical analysis', *American Political Science Review* 93 (3): 591–608.

Tsebelis, George (2002) *Veto Players: How Political Institutions Work*. Princeton: Princeton University Press.

Underhill, Geoffrey R.D., and Xiaoke Zhang (2010) 'Public interest, national diversity and global financial governance', in Geoffrey R.D. Underhill, Jasper Blom, and Daniel Mügge, eds, *Global Financial Integration Thirty Years On*. Cambridge: Cambridge University Press, pp. 287–303.

Unger, Daniel (1998) *Building Social Capital in Thailand*. Cambridge: Cambridge University Press.

van de Walle, Nicolas, and Kimberly Smiddy Butler (1999) 'Political parties and party systems in Africa's illiberal democracies', *Cambridge Review of International Affairs* 13 (1): 14–27.

Van Rijckeghem, Caroline, and Beatrice Weder (2009) 'Political institutions and debt crises', *Public Choice* 138 (3/4): 387–408.

Vasil, Raj (2000) *Governing Singapore*. St Leonards: Allen and Unwin.

Wahab, Effiezal A. Abdul, Janice C.Y. How, and Peter Verhoeven (2007) 'The impact of the Malaysian code on corporate governance', *Journal of Contemporary Accounting and Economics* 3 (2): 106–129.

Wall Street Journal (*WSJ*, eastern edition), New York.

Walter, Andrew (2008) *Governing Finance*. Ithaca: Cornell University Press.

Walter, Ingo (1993) *High Performance Financial Systems*. Singapore: Institute of Southeast Asian Studies.

Wantchekon, Leonard (2003) 'Clientelism and voting behaviour: Evidence form a field experiment in Benin', *World Politics* 55 (3): 399–422.

Ware, Alan (1996) *Political Parties and Party Systems*. Oxford: Oxford University Press.

Warr, Peter (ed.) (2005) *Thailand beyond the Crisis*. London: Routledge.

Warwick, Paul V. (1994) *Government Survival in Parliamentary Democracies*. Cambridge: Cambridge University Press.

Wattenberg, Martin P. (1986) *The Decline of American Political Parties*. Cambridge: Harvard University Press.

Way, Lucan A. (2004) 'The sources and dynamics of competitive authoritarianism in Ukraine', *Journal of Communist Studies and Transition Politics* 20 (1): 143–161.

Weaver, R. Kent, and Bert A. Rockman (eds) (1993) *Do Institutions Matter? Government Capabilities in the United States and Abroad*. Washington, DC: Brookings Institution.

Webb, Paul (2002a) 'Introduction: Political parties in advanced industrial democracies', in Paul Webb, David M. Farrell, and Ian Holliday, eds, *Political Parties in Advanced Industrial Democracies*. Oxford: Oxford University Press, pp. 1–15.

Webb, Paul (2002b) 'Conclusion: Political parties and democratic control in advanced industrial societies', in Paul Webb, David M. Farrell, and Ian Holliday, eds, *Political Parties in Advanced Industrial Democracies*. Oxford: Oxford University Press, pp. 438–460.

Webb, Paul, David M. Farrell, and Ian Holliday (eds) (2002) *Political Parties in Advanced Industrial Democracies*. Oxford: Oxford University Press.

Webb, Paul, and Stephen White (eds) (2007) *Party Politics in New Democracies*. Oxford: Oxford University Press.

Weingast, Barry R. (1995) 'The economic role of political institutions', *Journal of Law, Economics and Organisation* 11 (1): 1–31.

Wellhofer, E. Spencer (1979) 'The effectiveness of party organisation: A cross-national, time series analysis', *European Journal of Political Research* 7 (2): 205–224.

Wellons, Philip, Dimitri Germidis, and Bianca Glavanis (1986) *Banks and Specialised Financial Intermediaries in Development*. Paris: Development Centre of the Organisation for Economic Co-operation and Development.

Wellons, Philip A., and Takuo Horikoshi (1996) 'Financing capital market intermediaries in Thailand', in Hal S. Scott, and Philip A. Wellons, eds, *Financing Capital Market Intermediaries in East and Southeast Asia*. The Hague: Kluwer, pp. 269–298.

Weyland, Kurt (2002) *The Politics of Market Reform in Fragile Democracies*. Princeton: Princeton University Press.

White, Steven (2004) 'Stakeholders, structure and the failure of corporate governance reform initiatives in post-crisis Thailand', *Asia Pacific Journal of Management* 21 (1): 103–122.

Wildgen, John (1971) 'The measurement of hyper-fractionalisation', *Comparative Political Studies* 4 (2): 233–243.

Wilson, Rodney (1999) 'The political economy of financing development in Malaysia', in B.N. Ghosh, and Muhammad Syukri Salleh, eds, *Political Economy of Development in Malaysia*. Kuala Lumpur: Utusan Publications, pp. 124–143.

Wolinetz, Steven B. (2002) 'Beyond the catch-all party: Approaches to the study of parties and party organisation in contemporary democracies', in Gunther Richard, José Ramón-Montero, and Juan J. Linz, eds, *Political Parties: Old Concepts and New Challenges*. Oxford: Oxford University Press, pp. 136–165.

Wong, Sook Ching, Jomo K.S., and Chin Kok Fay (2005) *Malaysian 'Bail Outs'?* Singapore: Singapore University Press.

World Bank (2007) *Privatisation Transaction Data*. Washington, DC: World Bank.

World Bank (2010a) *Transforming the Rebound into Recovery*. Washington, DC: World Bank.

World Bank (2010b) *Global Economic Prospects*. Washington, DC: World Bank.

Worthington, Ross (2003) *Governance in Singapore*. London: RoutledgeCurzon.

Yap, O. Fiona (2003) 'Non-electoral responsiveness mechanisms: Evidence from the Asian less democratic newly industrialising countries', *British Journal of Political Science* 33 (3): 491–514.

Yeo, Lay Hwee (2002) 'Electoral politics in Singapore', in Aurel Croissant, Gabriele Bruns, and Marei John, eds, *Electoral Politics in Southeast and East Asia*. Singapore: Friedrich Ebert Stiftung, pp. 203–232.

Zahid, Shahid N. (ed.) (1995) *Financial Sector Development in Asia*. Hong Kong: Oxford University Press.

Zhang, Xiaoke (2002) *The Changing Politics of Finance in Korea and Thailand*. London: Routledge.

Zhang, Xiaoke (2003) 'Political structures and financial liberalisation in pre-crisis East Asia', *Studies in Comparative International Development* 38 (1): 64–92.

Zhang, Xiaoke (2005) 'The changing politics of central banking in Taiwan and Thailand', *Pacific Affairs* 78 (3): 377–401.

Zhang, Xiaoke (2007) 'Political parties and financial development: Evidence from Malaysia and Thailand', *Journal of Public Policy* 27 (3): 341–374.

Zhang, Xiaoke (2009a) 'From banks to markets: Malaysian and Taiwanese finance in transition', *Review of International Political Economy* 16 (3): 382–408.

Zhang, Xiaoke (2009b) 'Between decisiveness and credibility: Transforming the securities industry in Singapore and Thailand', *Journal of Development Studies* 45 (9): 1381–1402.

Zhang, Xiaoke, and Geoffrey R.D. Underhill (2003) 'Private capture, policy failures and financial crisis', in Geoffrey R.D. Underhill, and Xiaoke Zhang, eds, *International Financial Governance under Stress*. Cambridge: Cambridge University Press, pp. 243–262.

Index